Culture and Power in South Asian Islam

This book explores the myriad diversities of South Asian Islam from a historical perspective attuned to the lived practices of Muslims in various portions of South Asia, outside of Urdu, Persian, or Arabic language perspectives. These perspectives are, in some cases, taken both from literal regions rarely noticed within discussions of South Asian Islam, such as Sri Lanka, Bengal, and Tamil Nadu. In other contributions the perspectives draw on historiographic interventions about the role of fakīrs in South Asian history, qasbahs in South Asian history, and the role of Aligarh students within the Pakistan movement. As a collection of voices aimed at stimulating debate about the range and diversity of South Asian Islam, the book probes meanings and markers of categories such as "Indic," "Islamicate," and "local" or "global" Islam within the context of South Asia. Relevant to debates in the history of South Asia as well as Islamic studies, this collection will serve as a reference point for discussions about South Asian Islam as well as the nature and role of vernacularization as a cultural process. This book was originally published as a special issue of *South Asian History and Culture*.

Neilesh Bose is Assistant Professor of History at St. John's University, New York City, USA. A scholar of South Asian history, decolonization, cultural history and intellectual history, his research examines the history of religion, culture, and language in nineteenth and twentieth century South Asia. He also holds active research interests in imperial history and the history of migrations and diaspora.

SOUTH ASIAN HISTORY AND CULTURE

David Washbrook - *University of Cambridge, UK*
Boria Majumdar - *University of Central Lancashire, UK*
Sharmistha Gooptu - *South Asia Research Foundation, India*
Nalin Mehta - *La Trobe University, Melbourne*

This series offers a forum that will provide an integrated perspective on the field at large. It brings together research on South Asia in the humanities and social sciences, and provides scholars with a platform covering, but not restricted to, their particular fields of interest and specialization. Such an approach is critical to any expanding field of study, for the development of more informed and broader perspectives, and of more overarching theoretical conceptions.

The series achieves a multidisciplinary forum for the study of South Asia under the aegis of established disciplines (e.g. history, politics, gender studies) combined with more recent fields (e.g. sport studies, sexuality studies). A focus is also to make available to a broader readership new research on film, media, photography, medicine and the environment, which have to date remained more specialized fields within South Asian studies.

A significant concern for the series is to focus across the whole of the region known as South Asia, and not simply on India, as most 'South Asia' forums inevitably tend to do. We are most conscious of this gap in South Asian studies and work to bring into focus more scholarship on and from Pakistan, Bangladesh, Sri Lanka, Nepal and other parts of South Asia.

Health, Culture and Religion in South Asia
Critical Perspectives
Edited by Assa Doron and Alex Broom

Minority Nationalisms in South Asia
Edited by Tanweer Fazal

Gujarat Beyond Gandhi
Identity, Society and Conflict
Edited by Nalin Mehta and Mona Mehta

South Asian Transnationalisms
Cultural Exchange in the Twentieth Century
Edited by Babli Sinha

Religious Cultures in Early Modern India
New Perspectives
Edited by Rosalind O'Hanlon and David Washbrook

Gender and Masculinities
Histories, Texts and Practices in India and Sri Lanka
Edited by Assa Doron and Alex Broom

Television At Large in South Asia
Edited by Aswin Punathambekar and Shanti Kumar

Mapping South Asian Masculinities
Men and Political Crises
Edited by Chandrima Chakraborty

Culture and Power in South Asian Islam
Defying the Perpetual Exception
Edited by Neilesh Bose

Culture and Power in South Asian Islam

Defying the perpetual exception

Edited by
Neilesh Bose

Routledge
Taylor & Francis Group
LONDON AND NEW YORK

First published 2015
by Routledge
2 Park Square, Milton Park, Abingdon, Oxfordshire OX14 4RN

and by Routledge
711 Third Avenue, New York, NY 10017, USA

First issued in paperback 2017

Routledge is an imprint of the Taylor & Francis Group, an informa business

British Library Cataloguing in Publication Data
A catalogue record for this book is available from the British Library

ISBN 13: 978-1-138-05926-9 (pbk)
ISBN 13: 978-1-138-88571-4 (hbk)

Typeset in Times
by RefineCatch Limited, Bungay, Suffolk

Publisher's Note
The publisher accepts responsibility for any inconsistencies that may have arisen during the conversion of this book from journal articles to book chapters, namely the possible inclusion of journal terminology.

Disclaimer
Every effort has been made to contact copyright holders for their permission to reprint material in this book. The publishers would be grateful to hear from any copyright holder who is not here acknowledged and will undertake to rectify any errors or omissions in future editions of this book.

Contents

Citation Information

The chapters in this book were originally published in *South Asian History and Culture*, volume 5, issue 2 (April 2014). When citing this material, please use the original page numbering for each article, as follows:

Chapter 1: Introduction
Defying the perpetual exception: culture and power in South Asian Islam
Neilesh Bose
South Asian History and Culture, volume 5, issue 2 (April 2014) pp. 141–146

Chapter 2
The solidarity agenda: Aligarh students and the demand for Pakistan
Amber H. Abbas
South Asian History and Culture, volume 5, issue 2 (April 2014) pp. 147–162

Chapter 3
Beyond centre-periphery: qasbahs and Muslim life in South Asia
M. Raisur Rahman
South Asian History and Culture, volume 5, issue 2 (April 2014) pp. 163–178

Chapter 4
Asian and Islamic crossings: Malay writing in nineteenth-century Sri Lanka
Ronit Ricci
South Asian History and Culture, volume 5, issue 2 (April 2014) pp. 179–194

Chapter 5
Can 'Om' be an Islamic term? Translations, encounters, and Islamic discourse in vernacular South Asia
Torsten Tschacher
South Asian History and Culture, volume 5, issue 2 (April 2014) pp. 195–211

Chapter 6
Remapping Muslim literary culture: folklore, Bulbul, and world-making in late colonial Bengal
Neilesh Bose
South Asian History and Culture, volume 5, issue 2 (April 2014) pp. 212–225

Chapter 7

Breaking the begging bowl: morals, drugs, and madness in the fate of the Muslim faqīr
Nile Green
South Asian History and Culture, volume 5, issue 2 (April 2014) pp. 226–245

Chapter 8

A matrilineal Sufi shaykh in Sri Lanka
Dennis B. McGilvray
South Asian History and Culture, volume 5, issue 2 (April 2014) pp. 246–261

Chapter 9: Epilogue

Margins of anxiety and centres of confidence
A. Azfar Moin
South Asian History and Culture, volume 5, issue 2 (April 2014) pp. 262–265

Please direct any queries you may have about the citations to clsuk.permissions@cengage.com

Notes on Contributors

Amber H. Abbas is Assistant Professor of History and Asian Studies at St. Joseph's University, Philadelphia, USA. Her research focuses on the period of transition associated with the 1947 Independence and Partition of India, and its particular impact on South Asian Muslims.

Neilesh Bose is Assistant Professor of History at St. John's University, New York City, USA. A scholar of South Asian history, decolonization, cultural history and intellectual history, his research examines the history of religion, culture, and language in nineteenth and twentieth century South Asia. He also holds active research interests in imperial history and the history of migrations and diaspora.

Nile Green is Professor of History at UCLA, Los Angeles, USA. His research interests include positioning Islam and Muslims in global history through such topics as intellectual and technological interchange between Asia and Europe; Muslim global travel writings; the transnational genealogy of Afghan modernism; and the world history of 'Islamic' printing.

Dennis McGilvray is Professor in the Department of Anthropology at the University of Colorado, Boulder, CO, USA. He is currently exploring transnational Sufism and Muslim saints' shrines in Sri Lanka and southern India, as well as conducting fieldwork on matrilocal marriage and dowry patterns among Tamils and Muslims in post-conflict Sri Lanka.

A. Azfar Moin is Assistant Professor of Religious Studies at the University of Texas, Austin, TX, USA. His current research focuses on ritual violence and kingship in late medieval and early modern Iran, Central Asia, and South Asia.

M. Raisur Rahman is Assistant Professor of South Asian History at Wake Forest University, Winston-Salem, North Carolina, USA. His research interests include modern South Asia, Indo-Muslim history and culture, colonialism, nationalism, Urdu literature, history of ideas, local history, and Islam and modernity.

Ronit Ricci is a Researcher in the School of Culture, History and Language at the Australian National University, Canberra, Australia. Her research interests include language study, translation, the roles stories play in human lives and comparative literary studies.

Torsten Tschacher is Lecturer in Tamil Language and Culture at the Centre for Modern Indian Studies, University of Göttingen, Germany. His main interests are the history of religion in South India and Tamil literature with a focus on Islam and Muslim communities, as well as historical and contemporary links between South India and Southeast Asia.

INTRODUCTION

Defying the perpetual exception: culture and power in South Asian Islam

Neilesh Bose

Department of History, University of North Texas, Philadelphia, PA, USA

In a recent anthology of writings on Muslim South Asian culture and history,[1] Barbara Metcalf discusses South Asia's frequent casting as 'marginal' to the historical and cultural centres of the Islamic world. According to her, as opposed to being slotted as an appendage to the heartland of Arabia and Arabic-speaking Islam, South Asia

> should be thought of not as a periphery of Islam and Muslim life, but as a center...relationships of trade, political regimes, colonial and neocolonial interventions, and Muslim networks of scholarship, pilgrimage, and patronage, have sustained flows of people, goods, ideas, back and forth from South Asia for centuries.[2]

Though this reflection is doubtlessly essential for understanding South Asia in the context of Islamic and global history, it begs the question of power, marginalization and hegemony within South Asian Islam itself. The history of Islam in South Asia is not only contemporaneous with the broader historical development of Islam but also deeply tied to the historical development of modern regional, linguistic and political change in South Asia. Just as the history of Islam in South Asia is not a mere outlier to the history of Islam in its birthplace, expressions of and practices within South Asian Islamic traditions are not separate from, but rather are embedded within the various regional, linguistic and political histories of South Asia. With this perspective, research uncovering intra-South Asian practices of hegemony, cultural confidence and diffidence, and marginalization vis-à-vis the classical traditions in Persian, Arabic and Urdu languages assumes the utmost importance. In addition to accumulating a more precise empirical vision of the Islamic world in languages such as Tamil, Bengali and Malay, the articles in this volume ask whether methodological innovations may be found by looking outside the 'canons' of Islamic South Asia. How does the vast archive of lived experience in non-canonical languages and traditions of Muslim South Asia complicate the concept of an 'Islamicate' South Asia?

Any complications of the term 'Islamicate' must then revisit the very context of interactions and encounters within South Asia and allow for a critical revision of 'Indic' and 'Islamicate' as fluid markers of sameness and identity, freed from rigid links between religion and culture. The historical literature of modern Muslim South Asia is still plagued with the ghosts of interpretive ambivalence regarding the icon of Muslim politics, Mohammed Ali Jinnah. Current research rejects the notion that Jinnah represented a 'separatist' impulse that directly led to the creation of Pakistan, but the substantive options, open to scholars if this rejection is accepted, have not been fully pursued.

What this rejection offers scholars the opportunity to do is to reexamine the so-called 'vernacular' traditions, literary and otherwise, without the baggage of colonial/modern blinders associated with such binaries as 'classical' and 'vernacular' in the study of languages, traditions and cultures. If Jinnah's ideological stance and Muslim politics in colonial India were not so narrowly constituted, as is understood in the current scholarship,[3] then the entire history of Muslim India in the colonial period may begin to take a new shape. The precise meanings and markers of workers in the All-India Muslim League, and the diverse groups of Muslims who creatively engaged with different meanings of Pakistan, would find a place in history outside of a simplistic 'separatism' but embedded within the complexities of the impending end of British imperial India and broader global changes in modern politics. Additionally, Muslims writing in languages like Tamil, Telugu and Bengali (often not studied through the lens of Muslim perspectives) would fit into histories not reducible to narrowly defined poles of 'classical' and 'vernacular' languages of religion and culture.

The present collection sets out to empirically chart diversities of the Muslim South Asian experience across time, space and language. Just as we would fail to properly understand the range of the Muslim world by following the dictates of iconoclasts and conquerors, we would also to fail to properly understand Muslim South Asia if we only studied prominent politicians and intellectuals, writing in languages like Urdu and English, associated with the Pakistan movement at its heights, or heads of state, or the *ulema* writing in Arabic, Urdu or Persian. Akin to how subaltern studies and various critiques of nationalist Indian historiography sought to decentre the official historical archive and narrative of the 'nation', this collection decentres the oft-unquestioned role of Urdu, Persian and Arabic in historical conversations about South Asian Muslims and Islam. Organized by three themes – spatial reorderings, literary culture and the imagination, and a re-evaluation of reform in Muslim South Asia – this set of essays examines Muslims in South Asia outside of a narrow binary of high and low cultures or 'official' Muslim languages (Arabic, Persian, Urdu) and allegedly non-Muslim vernaculars, such as Bengali, Tamil and Malay.

Studies of South Asian Islam include a diverse set of questions that have been pursued in a variety of ways. One could state that the study of South Asian Islam itself must be perceived in terms of some version of marginality or centrality, as the entirety of the Muslim traditions in texts, practices and politics are, at some level, removed from the centre of Islam in the Arabian heartland and in the Arabic language. This has presented, in nearly every strand of scholarship, a concerted effort to grapple with locality and distance from centres, however understood, in South Asian experiences.

A variety of debates have energized the more recent study of South Asian Muslim texts and practices. One such set of debates includes scholarship emanating from India, which focuses on anthropological and sociological research on precolonial Islamic culture and practice, in order to situate Islam in local contexts. From Aziz Ahmed's 1964 *Studies in Islamic Culture in the Indian Environment*, a constant push from scholars to maintain particular standards of objectivity over and above ongoing contemporary politics has resulted in research about Islam in the precolonial and pre-modern world. In the mid-1970s, Imtiaz Ahmad began a tradition of reversing the empirical abyss regarding Indian Muslims through the editing of collected essays about caste, family, kinship, ritual and modernization regarding Muslim India. The most recent book in this tradition was the 2004 volume, *Lived Islam in South Asia: Adaptation, Accommodation and Conflict* (co-edited with Helmut Reifeld), which published the findings of a 2002 conference on correcting the imbalance of a perceived overemphasis on West Asia and negative stereotypes about Islam.

Another vivid strand of South Asian Muslim historiography includes debates about Muslim politics in colonial India. A long tradition of scholarship has investigated the political history of Muslims in colonial and postcolonial India, with an emphasis on the nineteenth and pre-1947 twentieth century experience from north India and the Punjab. As an enlargement of the vision of these studies, this volume considers the political itineraries of Muslims outside of the north Indian colonial 'centre', including the icon of M.A. Jinnah, the politics of Urdu and the grappling with representation at the power centres of colonial India. As a complement to such historiography, this collection approaches literary-cum-political discourse in other contexts, such as Muslim literary culture in Bengal of the 1930s, north Indian *qasbahs* of the late nineteenth century, the recollections of 1940s Aligarh graduates and the criminalization of Muslim *faqīrs* in colonial India. All of these examples probe a world influenced by – but not wholly determined by – north Indian, Urdu-centric Sunni Muslim figures of power and cultural capital.

Articles in this collection that explore this liminal Muslim world emerge out of the March 2011 conference entitled 'Margins and Centers in South Asian Islam: An Interdisciplinary Inquiry', held at the University of North Texas. A few articles delivered are not published here, such as articles on Nepali Muslim culture and the politics of colonial-era activists Zafrullah Khan and Syed Amir Ali. Three new articles, about *faqīrs* and the criminalization of begging in colonial India, *qasbahs* in the late nineteenth century and Malay manuscripts traversing various points in the Indian Ocean, are included. The conference discussed a range of issues central to the contemporary scholarship on South Asian Islam, understood through the above-mentioned themes of spatial reorderings, literary culture and reform in South Asian Islam.

Section I, 'Spatial Re-Orderings', underscores new approaches to space in modern Muslim South Asia by looking anew at both the oral history of the iconic Aligarh school and its graduates over time as well as the unit of the *qasbah* in South Asian history and culture. M. Raisur Rahman discusses one particular *qasbati* intellectual, Chaudhary Muhammad Ali of Rudauli, active from the late nineteenth century through and beyond the 1947 partition of British India. Rudauli, surveyed by Rahman in this article, functioned as a quintessential *qasbah* locale, in between the size of a city and a small town, also serving as a hub for religious, literary and medical training and cultivation in the colonial period, just like other *qasbahs* such as Amroha, Badaun and Bilgram. Through an analysis of the life and writings of Ali, Rahman shows how *qasbati* intellectual life and the multicultural and multi-religious nature of *qasbahs* compares favourably with the *adda*-based culture of colonial Calcutta and deserves serious attention within the study of South Asian Islam. Amber Abbas utilizes interviews with graduates of Aligarh Muslim University, alive and active during the Pakistan movement (1940–1947), in order to explore the meanings of Pakistan in oral history. Abbas argues that rather than displaying a nationalism or Muslim identity politics, the history of Aligarh graduates shows a 'solidarity agenda', or a commitment to social and economic uplift, animating the movement for Pakistan. Rather than the striving for a territorial space separate from India, Abbas shows how, for Aligarh students of the 1940s, Pakistan referred to an obligation to educate, uplift and better the lot of Indian Muslims. Both Abbas and Rahman explore entry points into Muslim South Asia beyond urban, national and state-directed frames of reference.

Section II, 'Literary Culture and the Imagination', continues the theme of disrupting traditional frames of reference for South Asian Islam through examinations of literary culture in Bengali, Tamil and Malay. From Ronit Ricci and Torsten Tschacher's articles, we find a query about the nature of 'marginalization' itself. A portion of the title of the entire volume, regarding the 'perpetual exception', is derived from Tschacher's work. In his critique of the existing historiography, literature in Tamil Muslim contexts has, until this point, been treated as either the 'perpetual exception' to developments elsewhere or wholly derivative of 'classical traditions'. Through an investigation of issues in early modern and modern Tamil Muslim literary criticism, Tschacher, however, opens a new approach to the study of Muslim literary cultures in South Asia, suspending the usage of 'classical' and 'vernacular'.

Ricci, also, in her study of Malay manuscripts in Sri Lanka of the late eighteenth and early nineteenth centuries, demonstrates how Sri Lankan Malays, in their crossroads between Malay and Arabic literary and religious cultures, in effect, challenge assumptions about local cultures of South Asian and South-east Asian Islam. Born out of the complex history of the Dutch and British Empires in Southern Asia and evidenced by multilingual familiarity with the Arab-centric world of Western Asia as well as diverse references in South Asia, the world of Sri Lankan Malays complicates any simplistic notion of 'margin and centre' and rather, points to crossroads, connections and movement within South Asian Islam.

Finally, Neilesh Bose's examination of interwar literary culture in Bengal shows a vibrant world of folklore collection and theorization, literary criticism and critical discussions of the pan-Indian Islamic landscape. Bengali Muslim literary critics of this time period were no mere imitators, but rather sought to critically engage and integrate themselves into pre-existing Muslim Indian Urdu culture as well as Bengali Hindu literary culture. Rather than the lens of nationalism, Bose views these writers through a series of 'world-making' practices, in which critics and writers sought to integrate Islam and Islamic reference points with Bengali Hindu literature and into a new 'world literature' through a Bengali Muslim vantage point. Tschacher, Ricci and Bose, all capture the particular quality of Muslim South Asian literary production that reflects local aspirations tied to a broader Islamic world in languages like Tamil, Malay and Bengali. Writers in these languages, across time and space, have consistently interpreted their own as belonging within the world of Islam and equally shaped by the local worlds within which they were embedded.

Section III, 'Reform and Modern South Asian Islam', critically examines the history of *faqīr* in colonial India and political strategies of Muslims in Sri Lanka, both within the broader context of the history and anthropology of reformist Islam in South Asia. Nile Green's historical examination of morals, mendicancy and drug usage in colonial India analyses the central figure of the *faqīr*, which held a glorious precolonial history in the broader Islamic world as well as in India. The meaning and importance of the *faqīr* transformed in the colonial period from a position of piety to one of marginalization, and began to represent insanity, backwardness and poverty by the late nineteenth century. Through a study of diverse sources, Green shows how Muslim reformers, Indian nationalists and Christian missionaries alike rendered obsolete older, pious conceptions of the *faqīr* in service of a reformed and 'modern' sensibility. As a complement to Green's understanding of the world of reform in colonial India, Mcgilvray presents an anthropological view into the life and work of a Sri Lankan Sufi *shaykh*, A.S.A. Abdul Majeed Makkattar, a charismatic leader who has drawn opposition from reformist organizations in Sri Lanka, of Salafist, Wahabi and Touheed varieties. What is remarkable about Makkattar, who currently heads a global Sufi *tāriqā*, is his claim of belonging within the family of the Prophet Muhammad. At one level, Makkattar is connected via the

Yemeni *sayyid* merchant Shaykh Ismail, who migrated to the then Dutch Ceylon in the eighteenth century. Ismail's son Shayk Abdussamat Maulana, Makkatar's grandfather, settled in Akkaraipattu in Lanka, the grandfather of Makkatar. McGilvray, however, also demonstrates, through careful analysis, how he also claims this lineage back to the Prophet through locally understood Dravidian matrilineal kinship recognition, thereby demonstrating the both durability of Dravidian kinship practices and their inclusion into a broader Islamic world. Green and McGilvray both tackle elements of the familiar story of reformist Islamic South Asian history, but from the perspective of changes to South Asian culture and politics that a precise history of reformist Islam brings to light.

All articles assembled here point to a distinct focus on the idea of 'cultural confidence and diffidence', which emerged in the conference discussions. Norbert Elias' *The Civilizing Process* and its relationship with Muslim modernity in South Asia arose at different points in the discussion, noting how perhaps the ideas of cultural confidence and diffidence may be used to explain the varieties of South Asian Islam found over time and across spaces in different practical and intellectual contexts. Just as Elias' signal contribution to European historiography demonstrates the historical creation of a 'civilizing process', as opposed to a settled fact of 'civilization', through the recognition of alterity and diversity within the very nature of European modern experiences (French and English contrasted with German, for example), these articles brings out the diversity within approaches to Islamic civilization in South Asia: not defined wholly by the 'centres' vis-à-vis Arabic, Persian and Urdu, and yet mindful of the encounter between centre and non-centre. In his epilogue, A. Azfar Moin discusses the relationship between centre and non-centre with reference to the most iconic of Muslim empires in Asia, the Mughal Empire.

This approach brings together discussions inherent in South Asian historiography, with a focus on subaltern perspectives and practices in conversation with a method cited traditionally in European medieval history, that of the 'civilizing' process. Lest readers mistake that 'civilizing' as a trope replicates the '*ashraf-ajlaf*' divide that has long characterized political, cultural and social relations within Muslim South Asia, it may be noted that the emphasis on practice and processes that point to both subalternity and civilizing impulses may actually yield historiographic returns on the study of Muslim South Asia across temporal and spatial thresholds. Confidence and diffidence both wax and wane in every formation of community and in this context, and given that South Asian Islam has touched most forms of political organization and mobilization (nation, community, minority, ruling elites of empires, etc.), it behooves scholars to specify when, how and where margins and centres appear and wane in South Asian Islam.

This collection expands our empirical knowledge of South Asian Islam by including previously neglected regions and linguistic archives (southern India and Sri Lanka, original research in Bengali, Tamil and Malay). It also offers newer methodological lenses, such as oral history, urban history and literary history, for the reconsideration of existing issues in South Asian studies. It examines, for instance, the ability to transcend the 1947 temporal divider by means of the recording of oral history as well as how Muslim political actors in colonial India, outside of the centres of political power, made choices that energized local milieus. Furthermore, it shows that Islam in South Asia crosses and has always crossed not only the internal boundaries of South Asian nation states but has also been connected with South-east Asian cultures and linguistic flows. It is hoped that the essays provoke rethinking of the nature and extent of Muslim South Asian histories in the overlapping contexts of nation, religion and empire without being overtaken or crippled by any one of them.

Notes

1. Metcalf, *Islam in South Asia in Practice.*
2. Ibid., xvii.
3. Jalal, *Sole Spokesman*; Roy, "High Politics of India's Partition"; and Singh, *Jinnah, Partition, Independence* for a recent appraisal.

Bibliography

Ahmad, Imtiaz, and Helmut Reinfeld, eds. *Lived Islam in South Asia: Adaptation, Accommodation and Conflict*. Delhi: Social Science Press, 2004.

Ahmed, Aziz. *Studies in Islamic Culture in the Indian Environment*. Delhi: Oxford University Press, 1964.

Elias, Norbert. *The Civilizing Process: Sociogenetic and Psychogenetic Investigations*. Oxford: Basil Blackwell, 1978.

Jalal, Ayesha. *Sole Spokesman: Jinnah, the Muslim League and the Demand for Pakistan*. Cambridge: Cambridge University Press, 1985.

Metcalf, Barbara, ed. *Islam in South Asia in Practice*. Princeton, NJ: Princeton University Press, 2009.

Roy, Asim. "The High Politics of India's Partition: The Revisionist Perspective." *Modern Asian Studies* 24, no. 2 (1990): 385–408.

Singh, Jaswant. *Jinnah, Partition, Independence*. New York: Oxford University Press, 2010.

Section I:
Spatial Re-Orderings

The solidarity agenda: Aligarh students and the demand for Pakistan

Amber H. Abbas

Department of History, St. Joseph's University, Philadelphia, PA, USA

Since its founding by Sir Sayyid Ahmad Khan, the educational institution at Aligarh functioned as an incubator of Muslim aspirations. During its early years, future leaders of the Indian National Congress, the Khilafat Movement, and the Pakistan Movement emerged from its classrooms and playing fields. Aligarh students participated in all of these movements, and from 1937 to 1947 it was a key site of pro-Pakistan activism. Student activity during this later period, and especially election work, at Aligarh Muslim University (AMU) has been interpreted as part of a state-centred history of Muslim nationalism that culminates in Pakistan. However, by separating Aligarh students' activism in the period 1930s–1940s from the creation of Pakistan, it actually becomes possible to discern their motivations and to differentiate them from post-1947 statist narratives. This framework exposes the central priority of Muslim uplift as a separate objective from that of independent statehood. Interviews of former Aligarh students, in both India and Pakistan, reveal the complexity of their allegiance to politics, the university and the community. What drew students to political movements in Aligarh? Why did the Pakistan movement attract so many students in this elite institution? I argue that the Pakistan movement was substantively similar to earlier political movements of Muslim empowerment at AMU and that the solidarity agenda driving student activity was not tied directly to the creation of a separate state of Pakistan. This examination moves away from the 1947 borders to investigate the objectives that drew students to the movement for Pakistan long before a notion of Pakistan as a territorially sovereign state actually existed.

Introduction

In an undated letter, probably from December 1945, Fayazuddin Tariq, a student at the Aligarh Muslim University (AMU) wrote a letter to Mohammad Ali Jinnah seeking Muslim League support for the foundation of a Medical College at the University. He noted his return address as Maris Road, Aligarh, Pakistan.[1] The return address suggests a conundrum, for in 1945, there was no territory yet defined as Pakistan, and its later definition did not include the city of Aligarh, 90 miles southeast of New Delhi.[2] The return address should ensure the successful delivery of a reply, so why did Fayazuddin Tariq so confidently refer to this imaginary geography?

The answer is embedded in the complex history of the AMU and its relationship with Muslim politics and the Muslim community more broadly. The students of AMU are frequently invoked as the foot soldiers of the political movement, led by the All-India Muslim League that culminated in the foundation of the independent state of Pakistan in 1947. Their electioneering work has been credited as a difference-maker for the Muslim League in the 1945 and 1946 Indian national and provincial assembly elections that revealed, for the first time, widespread support for the League's agenda. The tight connection between student electioneering and Muslim League success suggests that the students at the university supported the League and its stated goal of Pakistan. Thus, Muslim nationalism at Aligarh takes on comprehensive significance with respect to the project of state making – the creation of both India and Pakistan – and the place of Muslims in both states. However, by de-linking Aligarh students' activism in the 1930s and 1940s from its outcome – the creation of Pakistan – it becomes possible clearly to discern multiple visions for the future of Indian Muslims among the students and to reassess the meaning of the Pakistan demand at Aligarh University.

An interpretive shift that re-centres the interests of the students who drove the Pakistan movement at AMU exposes other political objectives and moves away from questions of loyalty and separatism that have cast a shadow over the institution, which has remained in India, since independence. To view AMU through the static lens of 1947 is to freeze it in time, to disregard the environment of active debate at the university and to imprison the institution's reputation within the anxieties born of only one of its important political moments. Many students at Aligarh supported the Muslim League and spoke enthusiastically in favour of Pakistan. However, this imagined Pakistan was one rooted in the local, shared experience of Aligarh students, not one located in a distant place. In this environment, Pakistan was the symbol of the political empowerment for Muslims that the university valued at its core. It was not, several former students report, until Pakistan was actually created that they even considered relocating there. Examining the movement historically and through the lived experiences of its former students makes it possible to separate the values of the Pakistan movement at the university from the statist narratives that seek to appropriate it, exposing both change and continuity over time.

Re-historicizing the movement clarifies the experience of students who had to navigate the shifting politics of the institution that was not only their school but also their home. Student support for the Muslim League and its agenda represents continuity with earlier political movements on the campus, and their attachment to politics was deeply rooted in Aligarh's institutional history and values. Investigation of these earlier movements reveals the centrality of a solidarity agenda at the heart of student commitment to them. This solidarity agenda may be defined in terms of student commitment to raising the status of Indian Muslims. Though AMU students in no way represented average Indian Muslims, the discussion below shows that they maintained an attachment to Muslim uplift exemplified by their institution, and the same was evident in their political work. In the context of the university's other major political moments – that of its founding after the crisis of 1857 and its conversion from college to university in the midst of the non-cooperation movement in 1920 – the Muslim League movement of the late 1930s and 1940s appears anomalous only in its outcome.

Sir Sayyid Ahmad Khan and the future of Muslim India

Political ideas gained currency at the university during periods of difficulty, when the students perceived an external threat to their very existence. Student activists at Aligarh were drawn to politics out of an enduring concern for the status of their community: its integrity, safety and, above all, its advancement. This was not simply a selfless and idyllic concern. Aligarh boys fully expected that they would be the leaders of an empowered Muslim community. Since its founding, the students had been exalted as representing the future of Muslim India. Their own welfare was tied to the community's fortunes; although their experience did not represent that of the majority of India's Muslims, Aligarh students embodied a unique liminal space between the leadership of the Muslim community and the masses of Indian Muslims whose lives bore little relation to their own.[3]

Sir Sayyid Ahmad Khan, the founder of the Mohammadan Anglo-Oriental College (MAO), the institution that became AMU, raised the spectre of Muslim decline relative to Hindus under the British colonial system in the wake of the 1857 Revolt. The uprising of 1857 highlighted for him the vulnerability of the Muslim position – as the deposed rulers of India – and he set about trying to rehabilitate Muslims who, as a whole, he felt were in a state of decline. This perception of decay, of 'relative deprivation'[4] is key to the politics of rejuvenation engendered at AMU and provided the original motivation for Sir Sayyid Ahmad Khan to argue for an institution to serve Muslim boys.[5]

The perception of deprivation spurred a shoring up of elite Muslim values in the period after 1857 and helped Sir Sayyid to generate support for his controversial ideas. Lack of education, and especially English education, he argued, would exclude Muslims from consideration for many lucrative posts, commerce and social interactions with 'European fellow subjects'.[6] Despite this negative narrative, the period after 1857 was actually one of the consolidations of the ideals of the middle classes in Northern India. As Anil Seal has revealed, the Muslims in the North-west Provinces and Awadh (today Uttar Pradesh, where Aligarh is located) did not suffer the extreme alienation of Muslims in other regions, especially Bengal. The Muslim population in these northern regions was urban, many were landholders or professionals; as late as the 1880s, 'Muslims continued to hold more than 45 percent of all of the uncovenanted and judicial posts in the provinces'.[7] Still, to the Muslim elite – the *ashraf* – it is remembered as a period of relative deprivation during which their community fell under the suspicion and shadow of disloyalty.

Sir Sayyid's efforts to rejuvenate Muslims grew from a strong foundation of British loyalism; his attachment to power shaped the environment he sought to create in his educational institution, where the sons of the Muslim elite would be prepared for colonial service. He recruited English administrators and faculty, classes were taught in English, and though he always sought to maintain a strong tie to traditional Muslim and religious education, he believed that British technology, science, and civilization would benefit Muslims and better serve them to participate in the existing colonial system.

The environment that Sir Sayyid and other early leaders in Aligarh sought to cultivate prioritized the brotherhood of students residing within its walls. Sir Sayyid articulated a version of his vision in 1871 when he argued that 'the children of the noble, and well-to-do Muhammadans should be kept at a distance from their homes... they should be brought up and educated in a particular manner, and under special care'; all of the boys should be compelled to learn and say their prayers and 'all of them should be made to wear one and the same dress'.[8] This model privileged the *ashraf*, and so it is surprising that the university simultaneously cultivated an attachment to diversity. Non-Muslim students were always welcome, and though special arrangements were made for their dietary and residential needs, they looked and dressed just like the Muslim students.[9] However, though unity at Aligarh was represented by conformity to the values of *ashraf* Muslims, vibrant debate on a range of political and social matters had all along been a part of the institution's intellectual life.

The Aligarh Union, where these debates often took place, was founded by its first principal, Theodore Beck, but it was not long after Beck's departure and subsequent death in 1899 (which followed closely on Sir Sayyid's own) that the atmosphere at Aligarh turned against the British staff. These tensions echoed growing anti-British, anti-imperial sentiments in India and abroad but were equally defined by local, institutional concerns.

In an unpublished pamphlet, Hameed-ud-Din Khan, who began his education at the MAO College in 1909, remembers that as a student he 'gradually realized that the general atmosphere [in Aligarh] was definitely anti-British… I cannot say how far we were influenced by the political tempo, steadily rising in the country, but we had sufficient sources of irritation of our own'.[10] Students were embittered at seeing Indian staff and officials treated as inferior to the British on formal occasions and found the British hostile to Indian national aspirations and even what Khan calls 'the world of Islam'. The conflict with the English staff over institutional governance was emblematic of the students' discontent with imperialism, and 'created a highly favorable atmosphere… for the reception of Mahatma Gandhi's non-cooperation Movement' when nationalist leaders, including Aligarh Old Boys Mohamad and Shaukat Ali, recruited Aligarh students in 1920.[11] This pattern of engagement was repeated in later movements; Aligarh boys engaged in broader movements when those movements provided an outlet for more localized concerns. As Hameed-ud-din Khan reports, student enthusiasm for non-cooperation fit with the impulse to wrest control of the institution from the English guides into whose hands Sir Sayyid had entrusted it. The decision of some students to participate in non-cooperation by walking out of the MAO College, because it received state funding, dramatically joined the national and the local as it coincided with the campaign to establish Aligarh as a full-fledged university.[12]

The campaign for the Muslim University was a cause dear to the hearts of many associated with Aligarh – Sir Sayyid had hoped the MAO College would ultimately become a university – but the visions for the form and leadership of the new university varied widely. The Ali Brothers resisted government affiliation, but other leaders, including the MAO Principal Ziauddin Ahmad, clung to it. Ziauddin shied away from the nationalist call to abandon government funding, took shelter in the conservatism of British loyalism (consistent with his mentor Sir Sayyid's position) and looked to the government for Aligarh's future stability. The Ali Brothers continued their movement to resist government affiliation, and in October 1920, Mohamad Ali founded the Jamia Millia Islamia, the 'Muslim National University' in the Aligarh Mosque.[13] The British Parliament accelerated the incorporation of AMU in the face of the nationalist challenge presented by non-cooperation. Still the Jamia Millia Islamia, that 'lusty child of non-cooperation', overshadowed the founding of AMU on December 1st.[14] The temporal and spatial coincidence of two new institutions of learning that laid claim to the same intellectual history (but held sacred opposing philosophies: one of British loyalism, and one of anti-imperialism) links their histories through this period. The leaders of both the conservative and the progressive factions of Aligarh Old Boys, Ziauddin Ahmed, the principal of the MAO College, and Mohamad Ali, famed Khilafat leader, were erstwhile contemporaries at Aligarh. This shared history reveals the diversity of beliefs that emerged from that enclosed and protected environment.

As the influence of the nationalist movement grew, many students abandoned the loyalism of the university's founding father in favour of participation in the larger domain of anti-imperial politics. The Khilafat Movement invoked a rhetoric of pan-Islamism that drew India's Muslims into a broader field of resistance. As Gail Minault has argued, however, the purpose of this rhetoric was really to draw India's Muslims together around a set of shared values, to develop a broader Muslim constituency. These values found purchase among those associated with Aligarh because they were based on powerful symbols in the Muslim imagination: the Muslim caliphate and Muslim solidarity. Minault's study concludes, 'Islam as a religion and social order contains within itself certain symbols and networks of influence which allow for the development of alternative structures of mobilization'.[15] The university provided the framework for mobilization in support of an apparently foundational institution of the Muslim faith and the authority. The students expressed solidarity with the idea that by suppressing the differences between and among them, Muslims could present a challenge to international imperialism, in service not only of their own community but also of India.

Student engagement in both Gandhian non-cooperation and the Khilafat Movement has sometimes been highlighted as Aligarh's true legacy, as a way to downplay the significance of the Muslim League period of the late 1930s and 1940s and its connection to Pakistan. However, considering that neither the nationalist nor the Muslim League movement attracted all of Aligarh's students, they both expose the multiplicity of opinion and allegiance that could survive in this environment – Aligarh never represented a unified way of thinking about India or the role of Muslims in it. Retired Aligarh Professor of Arabic Riazur Rahman Sherwani was the son of a prominent League leader, but himself held nationalist views. He emphasized the importance of this ethos of toleration when I first interviewed him on the terrace of his home in Aligarh in 2008.

> I want to tell you one thing… even from an earlier period when there was no Muslim League, even from that time, there has always been a section of teachers and students in this institution, when it was MAO College as well as when it became the University, who thought on different lines from the administration of the university, or from the majority of the students… Through all the phases, there have been students here and teachers also, whose line of action was different from that of the majority. I also belonged to that minority.[16]

The university's forte was its attachment to 'the gospel of free enquiry, or large-hearted toleration, and of a pure morality', the values etched in stone at the entrance to the College Hall.[17]

Continuity and change at AMU

By examining the transition between the enthusiastic moment around the founding of both the Jamia Millia Islamia and the AMU in 1920 and the wild popularity of the League fewer than 20 years later, the continuity of the values undergirding both becomes clear. The 1920s were moribund at Aligarh; the university was plagued by financial difficulties,[18] internal political strife[19] and the effects of the departure of some staff and students for the Jamia Millia Islamia.[20] Throughout the 1930s, however, Indian nationalist sentiment remains evident in student publications, including *The Aligarh Magazine*. In 1930, an appeal to the Muslim public that appeared in the *Magazine* was couched in nationalist rhetoric though driven by an appeal to the shared heritage of Muslims, and Aligarh's record in drawing them together. The appeal called on donors to support Aligarh with funds on the basis that

> …in the annals of Hindustan no other scheme has ever been launched on such lofty ideals and such sure basis to unite the peoples of this vast country, divided into so many provinces varying in climate, language, race, religions and color… Though some may be included to look upon [it] as a purely Muslim affair, in fact it was the first step taken by the great founder of the MAO College towards the nationalization of India… An India of the 26 provinces but united by one common bond of 'a brotherhood' called the 'Aligarian Brotherhood'.[21]

The appeal goes on to suggest that in Aligarh both regional and religious identities dissolved into that of the 'typical man' defined as 'the future citizen of India'. It is discernibly anti-imperialist; the very possibility of an Indian citizen, without reference to the Imperial State, was aspirational, formed on the basis of Indian unity, and endowed with the priorities of the Aligarh University.

In the late 1930s, by contrast, Marxist historian and former Aligarh student, Irfan Habib, clearly remembers, 'there was a Congress flag always flying on the room adjoining the road of MacDonnell Hostel'[22] and he firmly maintains that Aligarh remained largely nationalist then. This anecdote is telling, for while it serves in his memory as evidence of the presence of Congress supporters/nationalists, it also stands out in its singularity. The flag is remarkable in part because there was only one. Habib was young and could not have remembered the days in the 1920s when the nationalist non-cooperators were so persuasive at Aligarh that they were able to found a new institution on its campus. By 1942, when Congress announced the Quit India Resolution, Habib further recalls that 'nothing stirred' in AMU. Congress had become so weak there in the wake of the Lahore Resolution of 1940 – that outlined the demand for Muslim sovereignty in the form of Pakistan – that they did not even hold any meetings or processions in support of Quit India at the Aligarh University.[23] In the course of a decade, the campus had undergone a political transformation that left its permanent mark.

This transformation was linked to trends in politics beyond the university, and especially the increasingly public competition between the Indian National Congress and the Muslim League for the allegiance of Indian Muslims. In 1937, the Indian National Congress' election success allowed them to form provincial ministries under the Government of Indian Act 1935. In March, Jawaharlal Nehru had issued a call to Congress to 'make a special effort to enroll Muslim Congress members' and to engage them in practical politics while protecting the 'religious, linguistic and cultural rights of minorities'.[24] Muslims felt threatened by Congress' Mass Contacts Campaign; it appeared to them to be an effort to drive a wedge between the Muslim masses and its traditional leadership.[25] This was a politically polarizing time as Muslims came to grips with the reality of parliamentary democracy. The League had not fared well in the 1937 elections, winning only a few of the designated Muslim seats and League–Congress alliances broke down.[26] In response, at the October 1937 League Session, Mohammad Ali Jinnah re-articulated the League's commitment to the 'social and economic uplift' of 'Mussalmans all over India [that] are numerically in a minority and weak, educationally backward, and economically nowhere'.[27] With this statement, the League launched a campaign to challenge the Indian National Congress in recruitment, and it began growing its membership rolls dramatically.[28]

The constitution of the All India Muslim Students' Federation, founded at Aligarh,[29] which Mohammad Ali Jinnah himself helped to draft, specifically articulates its aim to 'arouse political consciousness among the Muslim students and to prepare them to take their proper share in the struggle for the freedom of the country'.[30] This rhetoric both engages the solidarity agenda – the commitment to the broader Muslim community – and suggests that Muslim students had a critical role to play in an existing struggle.

The publication in 1938 of the Pirpur Report by the Muslim League finally undermined Congress' claims to communal representation in the eyes of the Muslim community. The Pirpur Report was a litany of Muslim Grievances collected from Congress governed provinces alleging anti-Muslim sentiment on the part of regular citizens and the authorities.[31] Though some former Aligarh students suspect that the episodes it described were at best exaggerated, or at worst, 'imaginary', the Pirpur Report served to foment Muslim mistrust of the Congress Ministries.[32] As a minority, the report seems to suggest, Muslims could not have instigated communal unrest or be held accountable for its perpetuation, for as a group they simply did not have that kind of social power. The report was received in Muslim India with terrific anxiety, exposing weakness in the community at a time when Muslims had just begun to turn their attention to the League and its mission of empowerment. Former student Masood ul Hasan remembers that it was the 'widely publicized' Pirpur Report that finally turned the tide at Aligarh; the League began formally to establish itself there.[33] Late in 1938 The Pro-Vice Chancellor, A.B.A. Haleem, went so far as to estimate that 'about 90% of the students of the University have strong Muslim League sympathies and it is no exaggeration to say that out of 114 members of the staff about 100 at least are Muslim Leaguers'.[34] Even at AMU, the beating heart of the movement to reinvigorate Muslim nationalism, it was a sense of Muslim marginalization especially under Congress rule in UP, and fomented by the League's anti-Congress propaganda, that drew indignant Aligarh students into the centre of the demand for Pakistan. This sense of marginalization, the 'relative deprivation' of the elite, was a construction of the Aligarh environment, but it linked the university students to the Muslim community outside. The Pirpur Report created the sense of crisis that motivated the students to move beyond the borders of their institution and to engage actively in political work.

During a March 1940 visit to Aligarh, Jinnah spoke about the difference between Minority and Nation. Since the advent of separate electorates, he noted, most people assumed that the Muslims were a minority requiring safeguards and governmental or legislative protection of their rights. In fact, this was the rhetorical strategy Jinnah himself had used throughout the 1930s. Now he pushed the idea that when 'we used this term... what we meant was that the Muslims were a political entity and that must be preserved at all costs'.[35] The difference here was between the helpless minority and an empowered political force. Jinnah turned away from the earlier rhetoric of decline, deployed by reforming Muslim leaders before him, notably Sir Sayyid Ahmad Khan, and turned a sense of exclusion into a call for action. Whereas the concept of Minority had given Muslims a relative sense of protection, and Hindus a sense of power, the concept of nationhood made possible a demand for political equality. To fortify this demand, the masses would have to be drawn to the movement based on the only identity they shared with League leaders and the *ashraf:* that of being Muslim. Former student and retired Pakistani General Ghulam Umar recalled this message clearly when observed:

> [Quaid-e-Azam] visited Aligarh and I was a student there. He addressed the students and during his address he used the word 'Muslim India'. One of the students got up and asked him, 'Where is Muslim India? There are some provinces where Muslims are in the majority, four or five provinces, but otherwise, Muslims are in Bengal, in Madras, everywhere. What is this Muslim India?' And [Jinnah] said, 'There is not a corner of India from which a Muslim student is not present here. This is Muslim India. In other words, that was his concept of Muslim community.[36]

Jinnah defined Aligarh as the centre of Muslim India and convinced the students that they represented it; hence, India's Muslims were like them, regardless of their regional or linguistic origin. These young Urdu-speaking elites subscribed wholeheartedly to the idea that Jinnah had inherited from the university's founder Sir Sayyid Ahmad Khan that the Muslims were a united 'moral community', with a shared heritage and future. Jinnah and other Muslim politicians had urged the students to focus on their studies, to support their community, and prepare themselves for the 'future responsibility' that would fall on their shoulders as leaders of the Muslim community,[37] for, as he told them, 'What Aligarh thinks today, Muslim India will think tomorrow'.[38] With this kind of encouragement, the students came to see themselves as critical players in the future of their community, determined to draw Muslims to the League for the purpose of developing its, and their, political power.

This political entity demanded more than just acknowledgement, however. A territorial demand was key to the League's agenda.[39] In an address to the Punjab Muslim Students' Federation in March 1941, Jinnah unambiguously declared, 'We are a nation and a nation must have a territory', a nation 'must have a territorial state and that is what you want to get'.[40] Throughout the 1940s, student correspondence with Jinnah and others referred to Pakistan as the objective of the Muslim League. However, as Ayesha Jalal and others have argued earlier, this notion was poorly defined.[41] There is ample evidence to suggest that the question of completely separate statehood remained unresolved until very late in the negotiations for Pakistan.

There was already a precedent for semi-autonomous statehood with which the students of Aligarh were intimately familiar. In addition to the support of local landholders and nawabs,[42] the leaders of the Aligarh University and of the Hyderabad State had been serving in one another's institutions since Aligarh's foundation; the Nizam of Hyderabad was the Chancellor of the University[43]; the Nawab of Rampur its Pro-Chancellor and a significant financial patron[44]; and Nawab Ali Hasan Khan of Bhopal 'was a great admirer of Sir Sayed and... helped Aligarh college with money and support'.[45] The Nawab of Chatttari, a local *zamindar* (landlord) and Aligarh patron, was the Prime Minister of Hyderabad State from 1941 to 1943 and again in 1947; he also served as Chancellor of Osmania University in Hyderabad. It was not inconceivable therefore that a Muslim state could exist within a larger Indian polity, and Aligarh's links to Hyderabad, Rampur, Bhopal and other Muslim princely states supported it. Again, the conditions of the local environment conditioned the student response to a broader political movement. The environment in which they lived represented the possibility of Muslim self-government and semi-autonomy marked by solidarity within and among Muslims. There was, therefore, no conflict between a Pakistan demand that was both territorial and part of India.

The solidarity agenda

By emphasizing self-rule and solidarity, Jinnah drew the students away from a narrative of decline and rejuvenation, and into one of self-reliance. A critical part of this was an appeal for solidarity within and among Muslims themselves. Jinnah recognized, and it was clearly apparent to him from his political work in the provinces, that Muslims, though unified at least nominally by their shared faith, were divided by a variety of factional loyalties. His claim to political equality could never stand without at least apparent solidarity among Muslims. The students were key to ensuring this outcome. He repeatedly told them, 'Muslims must remain in complete unity and solidarity amongst yourselves. Nobody can help you if you quarrel among yourselves'.[46]

This narrative resonated at Aligarh, an institution built on an ethos of Muslim unity that even now jealously protects its legacy as a place free from communal or factional strife. This is a fiction of sorts, and while the Aligarh environment may not have been marked by communal strife, there remained a good deal of factionalism in the student body.[47] Even during the 1940s, the high era of the League's influence, their supporters were divided into academic, regional and sectarian affiliates: the Students of the Engineering College, the Assam Students Association, the Frontier Students of the Aligarh Muslim University (among others) communicated directly with Jinnah and other League leaders. A study of student letters revealed requests for personal and political guidance,[48] for political influence over local personnel decisions within the university,[49] and affirmations of their faith and confidence in the League leadership and support for Pakistan alongside requests for funds to support electioneering work.[50] The student correspondence reflects a distinct sense of intimacy with Jinnah that indicates the belief that his message was designed specifically for them. They request his input as a patron and guide, not just as a political leader. The students who supported the League treated Jinnah, in their correspondence, as if he were one of their teachers, deeply engaged in the details of their daily lives.

Despite this intimacy, other political groups including Congress and the Leftists functioned, at least nominally, on the campus, though occasionally under threat from the League's supporters. Nasim Ansari, a Leftist graduate, describes a university where among the students were 'representatives of every province in India and followers of every party' where 'whether the differences between them were based upon class or upon theories, they were not concealed in any way'.[51] However, as one former student put it, the majority of students 'were pro- university… [and] conscious that if they do something wrong that will bring a bad name, not to themselves, but to their alma mater'.[52] This perspective suggests a kind of harmony based on shared affection for the institution, though others suggested that the growing Muslim League monopoly during this period extended to personal insecurities. Riazur Rahman Sherwani, then a Congress supporter, noted in an interview, 'My father was always anxious that I may be harmed physically due to my views. Because the majority of the students were of a different point of view, so his main anxiety was my safety'.[53] Sherwani's is only one of many accounts that confirm the League's influence; the effort to consolidate a united front was perpetuated through all manner of persuasion, not all of it peaceful.[54]

After the League's approval of the Lahore Resolution in 1940, the students focused their 'moral and intellectual support' on propaganda for the Pakistan Movement.[55] As early as 1941 Jinnah invited the students to become League workers during their vacations. He told them to 'devote [them]selves more and more to the constructive programme… the spread of literacy, social uplift, economic betterment, and greater political consciousness and discipline among our people'. Then, he promised, when 'the time comes, and when you are ready, I will tell you what do to'.[56] The time came in 1945 when, in preparation for the elections, Muslim League politicians impressed upon the students that the situation was 'life or death' for the League and the Muslim Nation; the results of the elections would determine the viability and influence of the Muslim political community.[57] One former student described Jinnah's appeals to students as being the result of the fact that 'he knew what revolution [a student can] bring in the masses. That is what actually happened'.[58] Students participated in fundraising, propaganda and pamphlet distribution, voter canvassing, and the establishment of polling stations.[59]

Aligarh became a key site for the League's recruitment, and Liaqat Ali Khan, Chairman of the Muslim League Central Parliamentary Board, was instrumental in organizing the students for election work. Retired Pakistani General and former student Iqbal Shafi recalled that Liaqat personally interviewed the groups who wanted to go electioneering. Shafi's group of six or seven boys encountered political opponents in both Punjab and the Northwest Frontier Province, two Muslim majority provinces that were officially opposed to the League, but he argued, 'That was the thing. Government against you, but the masses with Quaid-e-Azam. That was the atmosphere! We were in between'.[60] The liminality that Shafi describes here captures the nature of the students' position. They were neither leaders nor representatives, but they provided a key link between: carrying their enthusiasm for Pakistan beyond the walls of their institution into the hinterlands to build solidarity and to facilitate the uplift of their fellow Muslims. Several interviewees reported that, while on these electioneering visits, they spoke to gatherings of people, particularly after the nighttime prayers.[61] Abdul Rashid Khan, now teaching at Karachi's Sir Syed University of Engineering and Technology, recalled, 'We went to towns and villages to convince the people to vote for Pakistan. In those days we were very staunch supporters'.[62] The students' election work, in their minds, made a significant difference in the outcome of the elections, even in minority provinces. Abdul Rashid Khan, who had worked in the Hindu estate of Balrampur in UP,[63] argued, 'My feeling is that Pakistan could not be formed without their vote. They voted 100% [for Pakistan]'.[64] Mukhtar Zaman writes that the Aligarh boys, in particular, 'looked impressive' in their black sherwanis and Turkish caps and 'left a mark on the imagination of the masses'.[65] Through this work, students redirected their energy away from a narrative of marginalization and towards one of empowerment through action.

It is in the reflections of the former students on their decision to leave for Pakistan or to stay in India that their motives emerge most clearly. Without exception, it was a decision made quickly. The young people who had supported the League, even those who had worked for the elections, made no preparations to leave India. Though many of them were from minority provinces, it was not obvious that they would be required to shift to Pakistan to receive the benefits of autonomy. Abdul Rashid Khan remembered, 'The aim was that the Muslims living in India – it was not to be that all the population should shift here – that was the aim that Pakistan will look after the interests of Muslims in the minority in India'.[66] This testimonial, and the position it represents, perhaps, is the surest sign that Pakistan meant something different to Aligarh's student activists than it means today. When migration to Pakistan became an option that required physical dislocation, departure from established homes, these young people had to choose, sometimes between family and future.

Those former students who remained in India generally reflect on the League period with bitterness, with the feeling that as a result of its involvement with the League, 'Aligarh had to pay heavily later on, we still have to pay for it'.[67] Few are willing to admit to even a fleeting desire to migrate to Pakistan. Retired Aligarh Zoology Professor Ather Siddiqi, however, frankly confessed, 'I wanted to go. I also wanted to go! But my father would not allow me to go'.[68] In contrast, Ghulam Umar of the Pakistan Army remarked, 'My decision was in favor of Pakistan. Look at my associations with Quaid-e-Azam, look at my presence in that [Muslim League] session [of 1940]. For me, there was no two thoughts about it'.[69] And Wajahat Husain, who had left Aligarh in 1944 and gone into training at the Indian Military Academy, noted that when he had the opportunity to choose between India and Pakistan, the choice was clear, 'The fact is that I had made up my mind when Pakistan was established… I have never regretted it'.[70] In none of these cases is there evidence of a deeply rooted separatist sentiment. Pakistan's opportunities called students there, or the roots of home held them back. In retrospect, for those who settled in Pakistan, its establishment was the fulfilment of the dream of Muslim solidarity they had pursued at Aligarh and in support of the League. For those remaining in India, Pakistan appeared not as the logical outcome of their actions but as its opposite. It disrupted the continuity of the solidarity agenda at Aligarh and left the institution on the margins of the Muslim society for which its students had fought.

Students were drawn to election work by a desire to fit in, to be involved, and to be a part of something important. Former student and retired Aligarh University Professor of English Masood ul-Hasan described the allure of the League; he remembered, 'The Congress volunteers had their Young Men's Corps. Even the Khaksars, they had theirs.

The ordinary young student, the ordinary young man, he was left out'. The League seemed to present an opportunity to fulfil the students' desire for 'self-manifestation'.[71] In their actions as young men, they wanted to contribute to the sustenance of the 'moral community' centred in Aligarh, but the creation of Pakistan severely damaged the cohesiveness and status of that same 'moral community'. Ather Siddiqi described his realization that he would be better off in India as an experience of 'coming to his senses'. He told me, 'Our sentiments and emotions were pro-Muslim League, but when rational thinking increased...I realized that Pakistan was the wrong thing'.[72]

Conclusion

The history of political activity at Aligarh has shown that the students were always eager to distinguish themselves, to establish their political credentials, though the movements to which they were attracted changed with the times. The thread that runs through all three major political moments at Aligarh prior to 1947 is that of solidarity – Muslims came together to support one another for the advancement of the community as a whole. By separating the outcome of the Pakistan demand from the political mobilization that made it possible, we can see why the students were attracted to the League's rhetoric. There was no suggestion that the students would be required to migrate elsewhere to enjoy Pakistan's fruits. Rather, the Pakistan Movement, driven by Muslims bound together by common interest, and led by Aligarh students, would give 'expression to the hidden feelings of Muslim nation (sic)'.[73] In his speeches before the Aligarh Union, Jinnah frequently emphasized the rapid growth of the Muslim League since 1938. In November 1942, he told them that in 1939 the League had become big enough, influential enough, that it was no longer possible for the British to ignore it – but now, in 1942, the League was strong enough 'to make as big a hell, if not bigger, as Congress can'.[74] This is a significant declaration considering the impact of the League's political losses in the 1937 election, and it primed the students to keep working for the League; the outcome of political action was strength, and it was measurable, and it was growing. In case the students had not fully grasped the implication of the rhetorical shift from minority to nation, Jinnah clarified: 'It is not a question of concession or compromise, protection or safeguards. It is a question of the inherent birthright of Mussalmans to self-determination as a national group inhabiting this sub-continent to establish their own states in those zones where they are in a majority'.[75]

The students were mobilized by the terms of the demand for Pakistan, drawn to the empowering ideal of representing themselves as a Nation to be reckoned with, rather than as a Minority to be protected. This critical shift in the Muslim League rhetoric drew the students in, even before the formal passing of the Lahore Resolution in 1940. They were spurred towards this choice by the criticisms of the Congress Ministries in the late 1930s that made it appear that Hindus were abusing Muslims in every corner of India. The election campaign, organized through the University, appeared to be the modern way of responding to this oppression, and the students enthusiastically travelled, sometimes very far afield, to educate Muslims in towns and villages about the new force to be reckoned with. Pakistan, for them, was very real, even if they didn't understand it to mean that they would have to move to a specific territory. Pakistan, for them, was an obligation to educate and uplift other Muslims, to draw in and protect their own and to attain a measure of political power and influence. The students understood Pakistan to mean Muslim India, and Jinnah had told them that they represented Muslim India. There was no other significant question of territoriality. Thus, in 1945, a student wrote his address as

Aligarh, Pakistan. This student understood the priorities of Pakistan such that Aligarh and Pakistan were contiguous, even if not territorially coincident.

Notes

1. Fayazuddin Tariq to M.A. Jinnah (Urdu). N.d. FMA, F 962/81, PNA.
2. Some have claimed that Jinnah envisioned a corridor connecting Pakistan's East and West wings which might have included the city of Aligarh. Verma, "Present Pakistan Plan." In 1940, the Nawab of Mamdot had indeed fronted a plan including corridors. Talbot, *An American Witness*, 63–7.
3. David Lelyveld's study best establishes the objectives of an Aligarh education. Lelyveld, *Aligarh's First Generation.*
4. Minault, *The Khilafat Movement*, 50.
5. For more on Sir Sayyid Ahmad Khan, see Lelyveld, *Aligarh's First Generation*; Minault, *Secluded Scholars*; and Graham, *The Life and Works.*
6. Sayyid Ahmad Khan et al., "To His Excellency the Viceroy, August 1, 1867," in Malik, *Sir Sayyid Ahmad Khan's Educational Philosophy*, 39–40.
7. Seal, *Emergence of Indian Nationalism*, 304–5.
8. Syed Ahmed Khan, "Translation of the Report," in Malik, *Sir Sayyid Ahmad Khan's Educational Philosophy*, 170.
9. Zakir Ali Khan, Interview with the author, August 10, 2006. Hindu students, were, for some time, 'accommodated either in the thatched bungalows, or in hired Railway bungalows outside the University compound.' Khan, *Note by Aftab*, 90.
10. Khan, *Attitudes and Trends*, 1.
11. Ibid.
12. For a recently revised examination of the campaign for the Muslim University, see Minault and Lelyveld, "The Campaign for a Muslim University, 1898–1920," in Minault, *Gender, Language and Learning*, 220–73.
13. Ibid., 270.
14. The phrase first appeared in a report by a special correspondent in the *Independent* on 7 November 1920. In 1946, Jawaharlal Nehru admitted to having been the correspondent. See Tonki, *Aligarh and Jamia*, 94–5.
15. Minault, *The Khilafat Movement*, 211.
16. Sherwani, Interview with the author, July 6, 2008.
17. Nizami, *History of the Aligarh Muslim University*, 255.
18. Upon his retirement from the position of Vice Chancellor in 1926, Aftab Ahmad Khan noted that the Geography department suffered from lack of globes, and the hostels were overcrowded and in want of furniture. Khan, *Note by Aftab*, 17–8, 27, 29, 71.
19. Ibid. Ahmad, *Reply to the Vice Chancellor*; and Khan, *Brief Comment on Dr. Ziauddin's Reply.* In 1926, a conflict between Aftab Ahmad Khan, Vice Chancellor and Ziauddin Ahmad, then Pro-Vice Chancellor, came to a head in a series of heated public exchanges.
20. Ahmad, *Reply to the Vice Chancellor*, 31. Ziauddin mentions this in his exchange with Aftab. Minault and Lelyveld have shown that some of the students who were drawn to the new Jamia Millia Islamia returned to Aligarh when it became clear that Jamia had few resources for actually providing the students with a well-rounded education. Minault and Lelyveld, "Campaign for a Muslim University," 271.
21. Alavi, "A Plea for Sahibzada Memorial Fund," 44.
22. Habib, Interview with the author, Aligarh, June 28, 2009.
23. Ibid. The British attributed the quiet at Aligarh to Ziauddin Ahmad's influence and his cooperation with the authorities. "Revolutionary Activities by Congress in Punjab and UP, August 13, 1942." Cited in Chopra, *Quit India Movement*, 59. Mukhtar Zaman recalls the non-Muslim students at Allahabad University taking out a procession in response to the arrest of the Congress Working Committee, but the Muslim students remained aloof. Zaman, *Students' Role*, 40–1.
24. Hasan, "Muslim Mass Contact Campaign," 2273.
25. Mujeeb, "The Partition of India in Retrospect," in Hasan, *India's Partition*, 405.

26. The Minto-Morley Reforms of 1909 had created separate electorates for Muslims, but the Muslim League won only 108 of 484 available Muslim seats in the General Elections of 1937. 'Seats Captured by the Muslim League and the Congress during the General Elections of 1937, under the Government of India Act of 1935,' in Allan, *Pakistan Movement*, 149.
27. Mohammad Ali Jinnah, 'Presidential Address of the Quaid at the Annual Session of the All-India Muslim league held at Lucknow in October, 1937,' in Allana, *Pakistan Movement*, 153.
28. Khalid bin Sayeed notes that 'there is no clear authoritative account of how Jinnah built up his party machine almost from nothing.' Sayeed, *Pakistan: The Formative Phase*, 90. But according to Reginald Coupland, within a few months of the Lucknow conference 'no less than 100,000 new members were said to have been enlisted in the United Provinces alone.' Coupland, *The Indian Problem*.
29. Mitra, *The Indian Annual Register*, 415–6.
30. Zaman, *Students' Role*, 26–30.
31. Mahdi, 'Pirpur Report: Delhi: End of 1938', in Aziz, *Muslims under Congress Rule*, 310.
32. Masood ul Hasan, Interview with the author, Aligarh, May 1, 2009. Masood ul-Hasan belittled the significance of the events listed in the report, 'What were the atrocities? Nothing as compared to – two people killed there, one head broken there.' Irfan Habib cited the Muslim League's 'Pirpur Report of imaginary assaults against Muslims'. Habib, Personal Interview, June 28, 2009.
33. Masood ul Hasan, Personal Interview, May 1, 2009.
34. A.B.A. Haleem to Maulavi Mohd. Ashiq Saheb Warsi: Report of the P.V.C. To the University Court. October 25, 1938. FMA, F 1094/340–343. PNA.
35. Jinnah, 'Speech Delivered at the Muslim University Union, Aligarh on 6th March, 1940', in Ahmad, *Some Recent Speeches and Writings*, 153.
36. Umar, Interview with the author, Karachi August 8, 2006.
37. Mohammad Ali Jinnah, 'Full Text of the Presidential Address Delivered Extempore at the Fifth Annual Session of the All-India Muslim Students' Federation at Nagpur on December 26, 1941,' in Ahmad, *Some Recent Speeches and Writings*, 347; Wajahat Husain, Interview with the author, June 13, 2005. Mirza, *Muslim Students and Pakistan Movement*, xlvi.
38. Dyan, "Whither Aligarh?," 5. SSR. AMU.
39. To clarify, Pakistan's 1947 territorial reality may not have been what Jinnah had in mind. Ayesha Jalal argues that it included a surprising if not overwhelming measure of sovereignty. Still, territory was key to the Pakistan demand. Jalal, *The Sole Spokesman*.
40. Ahmad, *Some Recent Speeches and Writings*, 247.
41. Jalal, *The Sole Spokesman*. This is the centrepiece of Jalal's argument, but there is also evidence that scholars with League sympathies continued to prepare plans into the 1940s for 'Muslim India' that included 'safeguards and concessions' for a Muslim Minority. M.A.H. Qadri to M.A. Jinnah: Terms of Reference for Education Committee of All India Muslim League. December 19, 1943. SHC. Vol. 51/144–62, PNA; A.B.A. Haleem. Statutory Safeguards for Minorities. May 12, 1946. FMA, F 1122/59–61, PNA. Anita Inder Singh has argued that Pakistan meant 'all things to all Muslims.' Inder Singh, *Origins of the Partition*, 107.
42. One narrator traced the support of Muslim feudal lords back to the founding of the university. 'Sir Sayyid was a great visionary and he has chosen a place which is very near to Delhi and it is surrounded by small Muslim states… they were all feudal lords. They were very helpful in establishment of Aligarh Muslim University.' Zakir Ali Khan, Personal Interview, August 10, 2006.
43. The Nizam accepted his third term as Chancellor in 1941–42. 'Muslim University in the Year 1941–42,' MUG, May 15, 1942, 4.
44. The Nawab accepted his second term as Pro-Chancellor in 1941–42. Ibid.
45. Khaliquzzaman, *Pathway to Pakistan*, 7.
46. Jinnah, 'Full Text of the Presidential Address Delivered Extempore at the Fifth Annual Session of the All-India Muslim Students' Federation at Nagpur on December 26, 1941,' in Ahmad, *Recent Speeches and Writings*, 365.
47. Minault and Lelyveld have shown the effect of this factionalism in an earlier period. Minault and Lelyveld, "Campaign for a Muslim University."
48. Farzande Raza Rizvi to Qaede Azam [M.A. Jinnah], n.d. FMA. F-960/36-37. PNA; Mohd. Asad Suleiman to Nawabzada Liaqat Ali Khan, FMA. Vol. 238/5–6. PNA.

49. Students of the Engineering College to Nawabzada Liaqut Ali Khan: Secretary All India Muslim League, FMA. Vol. 238/9–10. PNA.
50. Manzar-i-Alam to M.A. Jinnah: Student Election Work and Need for Funds, SHC. Vol. 26/146–51. PNA.
51. Ansari, *Choosing to Stay*, 41–2.
52. KPS (Anonymized), Interview with the author, Lucknow, October 8, 2009.
53. Sherwani, Personal Interview, July 6, 2008.
54. Iqtidar Alam Khan, Personal Interview, Aligarh, May 31, 2009. This narrator mentioned those with non-League views getting 'beaten up' in the Aligarh Union. Irfan Habib remembers being pushed off his bike into a ditch by some boys who 'would harass me and say, "Say Pakistan Zindabad!"' Habib, Personal Interview, June 28, 2009.
55. Zaman, *Students' Role*, 38.
56. 'Speech at the Muslim University Union, Aligarh, on March 10, 1941', in Ahmad, *Some Recent Speeches and Writings*, 269.
57. *Daily Anjam* (Delhi), 27 September 1945, cited in Zaman, *Students' Role*, 145.
58. Zakir Ali Khan, Personal Interview, August 10, 2006.
59. Mirza, *Muslim Students and Pakistan Movement*, lviii.
60. Zaman, *Students' Role*, 155. League student workers in areas under the influence of the pro-Congress Jamiat-ul-ulema-e-Hind reported being 'stoned and abused' and heard allegations that Muslim League workers denounced the Deobandi ulema.
61. Shafi, Interview with the author, May 9, 2010.
62. Abdul Rashid Khan, Interview with the author, August 10, 2006.
63. Balrampur was the biggest taluqa of Lucknow District with an income of over five million rupees per annum at the turn of the century. Khaliquzzaman, *Pathway to Pakistan*, 5.
64. Abdul Rashid Khan, Personal Interview, August 10, 2006.
65. Zaman, *Students' Role*, 157.
66. Abdul Rashid Khan, Personal Interview, August 10, 2006.
67. Masood ul Hasan, Personal Interview, May 1, 2009.
68. Siddiqi, Interview with the author, Aligarh, May 11, 2009.
69. Umar, Personal Interview, August 8, 2006.
70. Wajahat Husain, Personal Interview, July 11, 2006.
71. Masood ul Hasan, Personal Interview, May 1, 2009.
72. Siddiqi, Personal Interview, May 11, 2009.
73. (Sd.) Shakir Husain Khan. Shakir H. Khan to Liaqat Ali Khan. February 13, 1941. FMA. F 237/14–15. PNA.
74. Mohammad Ali Jinnah. Pakistan, the Muslim Charter: Speech by Quaid-e-Azam M.A. Jinnah to Muslim University Union, Aligarh. November 2, 1941. FMA. F 237/19 (1–14). PNA.
75. M.A. Jinnah, 'Muslim India Speaks: Speech Delivered by Quaid-E-Azam Mr. M.A. Jinnah President of the All-India Muslim League at a Meeting Held under the Auspices of the Muslim University Union, November 2, 1942.' FMA. 237/21 (1–25). PNA.

Bibliography

Archival collections

Aligarh Magazine; Muslim University Gazette. Aligarh: Sir Syed Room (SSR), Aligarh Muslim University (AMU).
Freedom Movement Archives (FMA). Islamabad: Pakistan National Archives (PNA).
Shamsul Hasan Collection (SHC). PNA.

Interviews cited

Brigadier Iqbal Shafi, (Ret'd, Pakistan Army), Islamabad.
Engineer (Sir Syed University of Engineering and Technology) Abdul Rashid Khan, Karachi.
Major General Ghulam Umar (Ret'd, Pakistan Army), Karachi.
Major General Wajahat Husain (Ret'd, Pakistan Army), Lahore.
KPS (Anonymized), Lucknow.
Professor Emeritus (History, AMU) Irfan Habib, Aligarh.

Retired Professor (Arabic, AMU) Riazur Rahman Sherwani, Aligarh.
Retired Professor (English, AMU) Masood ul Hasan, Aligarh.
Retired Professor (History, Aligarh Muslim University) Iqtidar Alam Khan, Aligarh
Retired Engineer (SSUET) Zakir Ali Khan, Karachi.
Retired Professor (Zoology, AMU) Ather Siddiqi, Aligarh.

Books and articles

Ahmad, Jamil-ud-din, ed. *Some Recent Speeches and Writings of Mr. Jinnah*. 5th ed. Vol. 1. Lahore: Sh. Muhammad Ashraf, 1952.

Ahmad, Ziauddin. *Reply to the Vice Chancellor [Aftab Ahmad Khan]*. Aligarh: Aligarh Muslim University, 1927.

Alavi, M. A. 1930. "A Plea for Sahibzada Memorial Fund." *Aligarh Magazine*, January–August, 44.

Allana, G. ed. *Pakistan Movement: Historical Documents*. Karachi: Paradise Subscription Agency, 1968.

Ansari, Nasim. *Choosing to Stay: Memoirs of an Indian Muslim*. Translated by Ralph Russell. Karachi: City Press, 1999.

Aziz, Khursheed Kamal, ed. *Muslims under Congress Rule 1937–1939*. Vol. 1. Delhi: Renaissance Publishing House, 1978.

Chopra, P. N., ed. *Quit India Movement: British Secret Documents*. Vol. I. New Delhi: Interprint, 1986.

Coupland, Reginald. *The Indian Problem: Report on the Constitutional Problem in India*. Oxford: Oxford University Press, 1944.

Dyan, M. A. 1940. "Whither Aligarh?" *The Muslim University Gazette*, November 1, 5p.

Graham, G. F. I. *The Life and Works of Sir Syed Ahmed Khan*. 2nd ed. Karachi: Oxford University Press, 1974 [1885].

Hasan, Mushirul. *India's Partition: Process, Strategy and Mobilization*. Delhi: Oxford University Press, 1993.

Hasan, Mushirul. "The Muslim Mass Contact Campaign: An Attempt at Political Mobilisation." *Economic and Political Weekly* 21, no. 52 (1986): 2273–75+77–82.

Inder Singh, Anita. *The Origins of the Partition of India, 1936–1947*. Oxford University South Asian Studies Series. Delhi: Oxford University Press, 1987.

Jalal, Ayesha. *The Sole Spokesman: Jinnah, the Muslim League, and the Demand for Pakistan*. Cambridge: Cambridge University Press, 1985.

Khaliquzzaman, Choudhry. *Pathway to Pakistan*. Lahore: Longmans Pakistan Branch, 1961.

Khan, Aftab Ahmad. *A Brief Comment on Dr. Ziauddin's Reply to My Note Dated 28th: December 1926. Re the Aligarh Muslim University*. Aligarh: Aligarh Muslim University, 1927.

Khan, Aftab Ahmad. *Note by Aftab Ahmad Khan on His Work & Experience During the Last Three Years of His Office as Vice-Chancellor of the Aligarh Muslim University: Addressed to Members of the University Court*. Aligarh: Aligarh Muslim University, 1926.

Khan, Hameed-ud-Din. *Aligarh Muslim University: Attitudes and Trends of the M.A.O. College and the Aligarh Muslim University since 1909- Personal Observations and Revelations*. Unpublished pamphlet, Aligarh, 1966.

Lelyveld, David. *Aligarh's First Generation: Muslim Solidarity in British India*. Princeton, NJ: Princeton University Press, 1978.

Malik, Hafeez Khan, ed. *Sir Sayyid Ahmad Khan's Educational Philosophy: A Documentary Record*. Islamabad: National Institute of Historical and Cultural Research, 1989.

Minault, Gail. *Gender, Language and Learning: Essays in Indo-Muslim Cultural History*. Ranikhet: Permanent Black, 2009.

Minault, Gail. *The Khilafat Movement: Religious Symbolism and Political Mobilization in India*. Studies in Oriental Culture. New York: Columbia University Press, 1982.

Minault, Gail. *Secluded Scholars: Women's Education and Muslim Social Reform in Colonial India*. Delhi: Oxford University Press, 1998.

Mirza, Sarfaraz Hussain, ed. *Muslim Students and Pakistan Movement: Selected Documents (1937–1947)*. Vol. 1. Lahore: Pakistan Study Centre, 1988.

Mitra, Nripendra Nath. *The Indian Annual Register: An Annual Digest of Public Affairs of India*. Vol. 1. Calcutta: Annual Register Office, 1937.

Nizami, Khaliq Ahmad. *History of the Aligarh Muslim University (1920–1945)*. Karachi: Sir Syed University Press, 1998.

Pandey, Gyanendra. “Can a Muslim Be an Indian?” *Comparative Studies in Society and History* 41, no. 4 (October 1999): 608–629.

Sayeed, Khalid Bin. *Pakistan: The Formative Phase, 1857–1948*. 2nd ed. London: Oxford University Press, 1968.

Seal, Anil. *The Emergence of Indian Nationalism: Competition and Collaboration in the Later Nineteenth Century, Political Change in Modern South Asia*. London: Cambridge University Press, 1968.

Talbot, Phillips. *An American Witness to India's Partition*. Los Angeles, CA: Sage, 2007.

Tonki, S. M. *Aligarh and Jamia: Fight for National Education System*. New Delhi: People's Publishing House, 1983.

Verma. 1946. “Present Pakistan Plan: Subject to Expansion.” *The Tribune*, Lahore, April 15.

Zaman, Mukhtar. *Students' Role in the Pakistan Movement*. Karachi: Quaid-i-Azam Academy, 1978.

Beyond centre-periphery: qasbahs and Muslim life in South Asia

M. Raisur Rahman

Department of History, Wake Forest University, Winston-Salem, NC, USA

Qasbahs (small towns or large villages) have the dubious distinction of being at the heart of South Asian Islamic history and yet lying on the margins of historiography. It is almost impossible to imagine the central aspects of South Asian Islam without due acknowledgement to qasbahs and the *qasbatis*, their residents. From the Aligarh Movement and the Deoband madrasa to the development of an extensive body of Urdu literature, qasbahs provided not only the rank and file but also crucial leadership. While scholars concur on this fact, qasbahs and qasbati Muslims continue to fall outside of the academic purview. Addressing this lacuna, this article seeks to bring in qasbahs to the heart of debates by arguing that the various institutions and intellectual output of qasbahs were central, not peripheral, to Indo-Muslim life in South Asia. It discusses the evolution of qasbahs and focuses on Chaudhary Muhammad Ali (1882–1959) of the qasbah of Rudauli, a paragon of the learned and literary tradition of the qasbahs. Chaudhary Muhammad Ali, a quintessential qasbati intellectual, has left volumes of writings in Urdu, many of which are being consulted and written about for the first time. A reformer, writer, religious scholar, and activist, his association with the Progressive Writers' Association in its opening days, alongside the likes of Prem Chand and Sajjad Zaheer, speaks of his recognition in the wider circle of writers in South Asia. Because of his many contributions, as those of his qasbati peers, a discussion of him not only brings to the fore the imaginary of the qasbahs, but also further enriches and complicates the discussion on the centres and margins in South Asian Islam.

> The land [of the qasbah] was capable of producing people who excelled.... Speak of lineage, education, health, intelligence, mannerisms and the principles of etiquette – none but this land was the most appropriate. It were people from here who would move to cities to teach rulers rulership and viziers vizierate and would offer themselves on the altar of riches... Take up the history of Muslims in India, every single noted lineage in a city takes pride in their link with some or the other qasbah.
>
> – Chaudhary Muhammad Ali Rudaulvi[1]

Introduction

Given the magnitude of its role in history, the *qasbah* as a theme has barely been covered in existing scholarship. Despite almost a millennium-old history and widely acknowledged significance, it remains on the margins of academic inquiry. Beginning as early as the twelfth, and even eleventh century, as Muslims began to settle in north India and advanced beyond Delhi, they made home semi-rural areas which later developed as qasbahs, in different parts of the country but in the regions of Rohilkhand and Awadh in particular. Qasbahs were neither urbanized nor completely rural, neither far away from urban centres nor distant from villages and farmlands where the majority of the population resided. Many of the early settlers, including several Sufis, served as magnets that attracted more Muslims from around the Islamic world. Their numbers steadily went up, gradually giving these small towns a distinct character which may be defined as what Marshall Hodgson would call 'Islamicate', societies that 'would refer not directly to the religion, Islam, itself, but to the social and cultural complex historically associated with Islam and the Muslims, both among Muslims themselves and even when found among non-Muslims'.[2] Apart from Sufis, landholders, revenue-free grant (*madad-i-ma'ash*) holders, and judges (*qazis*) were the first ones to have settled during the reign of the Delhi sultans. Subsequent governments – including the Mughals and the British – followed suit, and stationed their officials in these locales convenient for purposes of revenue collection and aiding with crop distribution.

Qasbahs thus initially served as a link between towns and villages in commercial terms, but they progressively took on the characteristics of nodal points, traversing the worlds of the local, the larger Indian, and the global Islamic, as the base of the Muslim population expanded with conversion and other associations. Home to revenue officials, they became religious centres, intellectual harbingers, and promoters and preservers of culture. Facilitated in part by a structure of landholding – marked with the presence of zamindars and taluqdars – and patronage within the locality and boosted by family and community, qasbahs provided a critical site for relatively more autonomous forms of cultural production. They became sites for the promotion of literature, Islamic learning, English education, Muslim architecture, and Sufi ideas – that often occurred simultaneously, mirroring the larger social life of South Asia, as reflected in the persona of Chaudhary Muhammad Ali of qasbah Rudauli.

For several centuries, qasbahs and the *qasbatis* – their residents – played a critical role in the Indo-Muslim world. Producing front running writers, poets, bureaucrats, and leaders since early modern times to serving as nodes of Urdu literature and Islamic education, their centrality is writ large. Regardless, only a handful of scholars have ever considered this entity as a field of inquiry, though not an independent one in most cases. C.A. Bayly's article-length study in 1980 on a qasbah called Kara in Allahabad was followed in 1983 by a relatively greater exploration in his magnum opus *Rulers, Townsmen, and Bazaars*; as well, Ravinder Kumar's brief discussion on the social history of qasbahs in the same year serve as the foundation blocks of study. Although both historians were succinct in their approach, relied ordinarily on English sources, and placed the qasbah within their larger works, it was enough to recognize the potential of the subject. Unmistakably, both showed how qasbahs were integral to understanding Indian social and economic history. As also did Gyanendra Pandey's significant article in the *Subaltern Studies* on the qasbah of Mubarakpur in Azamgarh district in which he compellingly argued how primary sources from qasbah give us 'a very different history' when compared with British sources.[3] However, it was not until almost thereafter that Mushirul Hasan published a book engaging the qasbah as a theme, drawing extensively upon materials in Urdu.[4] Yet, as he admits himself, his is more of a family history of the Kidwais of Barabanki than a wide-ranging study of qasbahs as entities. Largely, though the scholars of South Asian Islam concur that qasbahs have been pivotal to the region's history and culture,[5] the topic itself remains vastly unheeded and understudied – a classic case of historical significance encountering historiographical neglect.

Qasbahs have been integral to the local as well as the larger national and Islamic culture. Their residents included individuals who founded the madrasa at Deoband as well as hordes of students, academics, and administrators who joined the Mohammedan Anglo-Oriental College at Aligarh. Qasbatis from the regions of Awadh and Rohilkhand went to urban centres such as Agra, Aligarh, Allahabad, Faizabad, Lucknow, and even Delhi for the sake of higher learning and to cities as far as Rampur and Hyderabad in search of better employment opportunities and careers. But since qasbahs were networked with a range of educational, literary, and public institutions of their own, they offered a congenial and inviting atmosphere attractive enough to get the qasbatis back into their own locales. This phenomenon was quite unlike the unilinear, outward migration from villages and smaller towns to larger, urban centres that is so characteristic of postcolonial South Asian life. Many residents, of course, were educated in qasbahs where they continued to live, further enriching the intellectual ambience of these places. This is well attested in the vastness of literary output emerging from them.

Utilizing a host of literature, this article seeks to complicate our understanding of space in Muslim South Asia as it considers qasbahs – a rather slighted domain – as critical sites of cultural production. It combines British official with indigenous qasbati Urdu sources – materials that have been artificially kept apart hindering our understanding of the holistic importance that qasbahs came to acquire in history. The article thus credits qasbahs their due in South Asian historiography. This is in relation to an approach that considers certain large urban centres such as Aligarh, Delhi, Hyderabad, and Lucknow as 'central' to South Asian Islam, and does so at the expense of discounting the consequential role of qasbahs as spaces that defined and shaped the character of Muslim life in South Asia in substantial ways. The article begins with a brief discussion on the evolution of the qasbah and how it acquired a distinct identity, different from the hinterlands elsewhere. It goes on to highlight the qasbah Rudauli and takes the case of Chaudhary Muhammad Ali (1882–1959) of that same qasbah as an epitome of the qasbati intellectual, literary, and learned traditions and a role model of Muslim South Asia by examining his intellectual and literary contributions. The aim is to dispel the notion that promotes leadership in South Asia Islam as essentially an urban aptitude and that too, concentrated on a few rather well-known personalities such as Saiyid Ahmad Khan (1817–1898) or Saiyid Ameer Ali (1849–1928). The article also counters approaches that attempts to view societies in terms of binaries such as rural-urban and centre-periphery, at the cost of exclusion of more complex entities such as qasbahs. Qasbah as a space was neither peripheral nor parochial; rather, it was as much critical and defining as any other and a discussion on them only contests and obfuscates the very conception of centres and margins in Muslim South Asia.

Qasbah: from marketplace to intellectual hub

One reason why qasbahs fell outside of academic purview for long is how they were viewed in the official British accounts. Seen mostly as small administrative-economic units, official and authoritative British sources purportedly ignored to dwell upon their overall character and instead gave pre-eminence to cities such as Lucknow – a perspective that continues to inform the way towns, cities, and villages are perceived in India, based on their size. The larger the place, the greater is its significance. This British approach also reflects the conceptual myopia inherent in the official sources when it comes to evaluating the standing of qasbahs. As a colonial source states, 'The qasbahs are almost universally the headquarters of parganas, and from them the pargana used to be administered under the native rule.'[6] This underscores nothing more than the administrative importance of the qasbah as a centre for adjoining villages and parganas. More interesting is the definition that comes from a British judge Mr. Capper in connection with a case regarding qasbah Amethi:

> A Musalman settlement in a defensible military position, generally on the site of an ancient Hindu headquarters, town or fort, where, for mutual protection, the Musalmans who had overrun and seized the proprietary of the surrounding villages resided; where the faujdar and his troops, the pargana qanungo and chaudhri, the mufti, qazi and other high dignitaries lived; and, as must be the case where the wealth and power of the Moslem sect was collected in one spot, a large settlement of Sayyad's mosques, dargahs, etc. sprang up. As a rule, there was little land attached, and that was chiefly planted with fruit groves, and held free of rent, whilst each man really had a free hold of the yard of his house and the land occupied by his servants and followers.[7]

Although most British sources present qasbahs as mere economic units, the above statement stresses the worth of qasbahs as a space accented with visible Muslim presence and eminence. Qasbahs housed significant non-Muslim population, but they generally inhabited a conglomeration of Muslim dignitaries and high officials carrying substantial clout within the political, economic, and cultural machinery, both inside and outside of the locales. It were these Muslim luminaries – people of wealth, knowledge, religion, and power – who controlled land rights, made up the service gentry, were builders of institutions, and ran the administrative machinery of the state since the time of the Mughals. There is much evidence of royal decrees (*farmans*) being issued in particular by Emperors Akbar and Aurangzeb, which granted and recognized revenue-free charitable lands (*madad-i-ma'ash*) to people of knowledge and piety.[8] In a number of cases, such lands, located in and around qasbahs, remained in the family for generations beyond the grantee, and tactically, even the British rulers chose not to disturb such arrangements.

While continuing with their Indo-Islamic culture and lifestyle, Muslim zamindars and taluqdars – the landholding classes who numbered many – actively engaged with the new knowledge and aspects of modernity, as the British ascended.[9] From this Muslim gentry soon emerged what historian Francis Robinson has termed the 'new elites' that sought to manage the new economic and political structures as bureaucrats, intellectuals, and in other capacities.[10] The situation was not very different from the Hindu taluqdars and zamindars. In addition to those controlling land and revenue administration, a variety of professional groups typically came to inhabit the qasbahs.

Ranging from teachers serving in madrasas and schools to petty officials and judges, qasbahs produced, invited, and sustained people of myriad qualifications – all of whom helped create and enlarge the vibrant and pulsating qasbati intellectual and social landscape. How people thrived in the qasbahs is apparent in a variety of sources such as genealogical compilations, local histories, biographical dictionaries, and memoirs, to point out a few.[11] It was no wonder then that by the late nineteenth century, an array of professionals were nurtured in qasbahs: teachers, journalists, writers, poets, historians, lawyers, magistrates, and publishers, in addition to people serving on regular administrative positions. Even a cursory glance at biographical dictionaries (*tazkirahs*) or genealogies (*shajrahs*) would uphold this argument. Literacy, as C.A. Bayly has argued, was one of the key foundations on which an ideal Muslim qasbah society was based.[12] Thus, it was none other than the rock-solid economic foundation provided to the qasbahs by the Mughal and the subsequent British administration that ultimately led to the formation of a robust social and intellectual culture that the qasbahs came to espouse.

The emergence of qasbahs from being marketplace and revenue headquarters to centres for various professional classes gave them a unique intellectual ambience. Qasbahs, over time, also grew in significance as centres of religion and spirituality. In some cases, Sufis were settled on madad-e-ma'ash lands and often came upon the invitation of the local gentry. In other cases, Sufis were the first to settle, gradually attracting a host of people around them. As early as the twelfth and thirteenth centuries, almost all qasbahs had one or more Sufi figureheads who arrived from regions as far as Central Asia, Arabia, and modern day Iran and Iraq, showing how well these qasbahs were networked with the global Islamic landscape. In fact, the initial significance some qasbahs attained was due to the presence of the Sufi saints who lived there and it added to the overall influence of the qasbahs among the surrounding populace. Such early Sufis were able to Indianize themselves by adopting local language, literature, and imagery, similar to what Carl Ernst has shown with respect to Khuldabad in the Deccan or Richard Eaton with regard to the Sufis of Bijapur.[13] The shrines built upon their death became sites of devotion for people belonging to different religions and cultures, both within and beyond the qasbah. A qasbah thus often retained its prominence as a religious centre where people from adjacent areas – qasbahs, villages as well as other towns – flocked at least once a year during the *'urs*, the occasion of a saint's death anniversary.

Qasbah: the case of Rudauli

The qasbah of Rudauli in Awadh is a classic case study, demonstrating the aforementioned qualities of qasbahs. About 90 kilometres from Lucknow, Rudauli fell in between Lucknow, the seat of the Mughal suba and later, the kingdom of Awadh, and Faizabad, a one-time capital of Nawab Shuja-ud-Daulah of Awadh. Historically a part of the district of Bara Banki, Rudauli has only recently been moved to the Faizabad district for certain political-administrative reasons. In the records of the United Provinces, Rudauli is recorded both as a pargana and a qasbah, under the tahsil Ramsnehighat of district Bara Banki. The 1881 census noted the population of the pargana Rudauli at 134,050, while that of the qasbah was only 11,617.[14]

With the arrival and settlement in Rudauli of Shaikh Salahuddin Suhrawardi, one of the earliest Suhrawardi Sufis in South Asia, in the fourteenth century, Rudauli grew to be a Sufi and literary node in northern India. Shaikh Abdul Quddus (1456–1537), an eminent Sufi of his time, was born in Rudauli where he also spent his formative years. His brief compilation of Sufi principles *Rushdnama* consists of his own verses, as well as those of other Rudauli saints. He popularized the Sufi doctrine of *Wahdat-ul-Wujud* (Oneness of Being), alluded to Nathapanthi yogic practices, and included a series of Hindi verses in his work. Abdul Quddus later moved to another qasbah, Gangoh, an example of how qasbahs themselves were networked and reflective of how mobility – despite attachment to a place and homely instincts – was not as restrained as one would tend to believe today. Such movements between qasbahs and between a qasbah and a city were not unusual. With such foundation in Sufism, Rudauli emerged as an important centre inhabited by Muslim professionals who were in the service of the Mughals, in the successor state of Awadh and later in colonial India.[15]

Rudauli reinforces the idea of qasbahs as intellectual hubs. Like most qasbahs, Rudauli was a centre of education, with a strong network of different kinds of schools that elevated it to shape up as a cosmopolitan educational centre. While the madrasa Rifah-ul-Muslemin was founded in 1911, several modern schools emerged under the auspices of local government bodies, beginning 1873.[16] There also developed eclectic models such as the Makhdumiya Anglo-Vernacular School, named after Makhdum Saheb, an eminent local Sufi figure. The purpose of Anglo-vernacular schools was to prepare students for the matriculation examination of the Allahabad University, founded in 1860.

Because obtaining education and disseminating knowledge characterized qasbati life, scholars, physicians, intellectuals, and literary personalities dotted places such as Rudauli. A number of leading physicians – *hakims* or practitioners of *Yunani* (Graeco-Arabic) medicine, the traditional Islamic medical system, as well as doctors of modern medicine were in practice. Hakim Muhammad Mirza (1896–1948), son of Hakim Muhammad Askari, was a hakim as well as a poet. Himself a known hakim, Muhammad Askari's grandfather originally belonged to Nishapur in Iran and had moved initially to Delhi on a *madad-i-ma'ash* grant and then to Faizabad. Eventually, the family made their way into the qasbah of Rudauli upon the invitation of Chaudhary Raza Husain (1841–1885), a resident of Rudauli and the taluqdar of the nearby Narauli estate. Hakim Ghulam Hasnain (1864–1944), with higher degrees in Arabic and Persian from Punjab University, had studied medicine upon his return to Rudauli and practiced with notable success. He also trained Hakim Muhammad Mirza and Hakim Muhammad Yunus, in addition to writing books on various topics, including one that discussed human anatomy, diseases, and their possible cures. Later, in the 1930s, physicians from Rudauli acquired formal degrees from Western-style modern medical colleges. Those trained in modern Western medicine included the likes of Dr. Shahenshah Husain Zaidi, who went to Medical College at Lucknow in 1936 for an M.B.B.S degree and later earned an M.D. Thereafter, in 1963, he published a book on the influence of ancient medicinal practices on modern medicine. The book titled *Modern Medicine and Ancient Thought* was one of the few titles available on that topic at the time.[17]

Rudauli also had its literary connections. Having learned Arabic and Persian from his father at home, Maulvi Muhammad Halim Ansari (1877–1939) became one of the most notable Arabic scholars of his time, not only in the subcontinent, but within the larger Islamic world. He published several essays in *al-Hilal*, an Egyptian literary periodical – not to be confused with Maulana Abul Kalam Azad's Urdu weekly of the same name – although he regularly contributed to Maulana Azad's *al-Hilal* and later, *al-Balagh* as well. Mostly an essayist, he wrote a book titled *Safarnama-e-Mazhari* and translated texts from Arabic, the most significant being *al-Alqan 'Ulum al-Qur'an* – a compendium on the history and principles of Quranic exegesis. In addition, a number of Urdu writers emerged beginning in the early twentieth century. For instance, Shah Muinuddin Ahmad Nadwi (1903–1974),[18] with an early education in Rudauli, studied at Madrasa Nizamia of Firangi Mahal in Lucknow and Darul 'Uloom, Nadwat-ul-'Ulama in Lucknow and started his career at Darul Musannifin in Azamgarh as an associate under Syed Sulaiman Nadwi (1884–1953), a well-known scholar and religious leader widely recognized for his biography of Prophet Muhammad, *Sirat-un-Nabi*. In 1927, Muinuddin Ahmad became the editor and publisher of the Urdu monthly *Ma'arif*.

The line of literary persons of Rudauli is stellar, one that includes both women and men. Daughter of Chaudhary Siraj-ul-Haq, the first college graduate from Rudauli, and sister of the famed revolutionary poet Asrar-ul-Haq Majaz (1911–1955), Safia Akhtar (1916–1952) was a writer in her own right. Her collections of letters – *Harf-e-Aashna* and *Zer-e-Lab* – addressed to her husband, Jan Nisar Akhtar (1914–1976), a writer who later became famous as a lyricist in the Bombay film industry, reflected the contemporary life of an educated Muslim woman, and her struggles and experiences.[19] While the husband had shifted base to Bombay, Safia moved to Bhopal where she worked for the Progressive Writers' Association (PWA) and with the likes of Ismat Chughtai (1915–1991), the eminent Urdu writer noted for her feminist views. Majaz, on the other hand, symbolized the revolutionary streak of the Progressive Writers' Movement. His poem '*Mazdoor Hain Hum*' ('*Laborers, We Are*') was a socialist statement calling for a revolution to end class-based society and to break the systems of exploitation.[20] He also wrote romantic poetry for which he was compared with the English romantic poet John Keats (1795–1821).[21]

The learned environment in Rudauli produced intellectuals in various fields – a feature shared by almost all north Indian qasbahs. The qasbah of Amroha in Rohilkhand, for instance, produced hundreds of eminent poets of Persian, Arabic, and Urdu literature. Of them, Muhammad Zaman 'Zaman' Amrohvi (b. 1708), Ghulam Hamdani Mushafi (1750–1824), and Rais Amrohvi (1914–1988) represented the core of Amroha's literary tradition. Among the historical qasbahs of north India, Amroha is well known for its intellectuals, Sufi dargahs, and its rich history, which extended from the time of the Delhi Sultanate and the Mughal Empire through the period of colonial rule. Out of this qasbah emerged educators, administrators, writers, and most notably, poets whose contribution to the larger national and Muslim social life was significant. One of the better-known persons of Amroha was Munshi Mushtaq Husain, popularly referred to as Viqar-ul-Mulk in Aligarh circles. The famous Aligarh movement was spearheaded by the threesome of Sir Saiyid Ahmad Khan (1817–1998), Nawab Muhsin-ul-Mulk (alias Maulvi Saiyid Mehdi Ali) (1837–1907) of Etawah, and Mushtaq Husain. The latter two successfully carried on the movement after Sir Saiyid's death in 1898.

In contrast to bigger cities, the smaller size of qasbahs[22] afforded greater intimacy and camaraderie of the kind usually found in a village. In addition, with enough people, wealth, and resources comparable to those of the bigger towns and cities, they could resolutely embark on and sustain intense social and intellectual activities. The educated and the literati established dialogues in both print and oral culture, and strengthened their ties to the larger society. Their academic conviviality was comparable to cities with a predominant Islamicate culture such as Lucknow, Hyderabad, and Rampur, but their compactness allowed for rather deeper interactions within local society. In Amroha, the *Dost Ali ka Imambara* (Imambara of Dost Ali), although primarily a religious site dedicated to the performance of Shiite rituals during the month of Muharram, also served as a social space where people from the qasbah met, often in the evenings, to engage in conversations. Such gatherings were as quintessential of qasbati life as Bengali *addas* were a marker of Bengali character, as Dipesh Chakrabarty has shown in his study of Calcutta in the first half of the twentieth century.[23] Hakim Rahat Ali Khan (1861–1931), a *rais*, poet, bureaucrat, and hakim of Amroha, spent most of his day at the imambara; beginning his mornings imparting lessons in Yunani medicine to his young students and winding up with intense scholarly and literary discussions in the evenings.[24] Qasbahs were thus defined by their individualistic economic, commercial, religious, and intellectual milieus – making them unique as well as critical to understanding Muslim history in the Indian subcontinent.

Chaudhary Muhammad Ali Rudaulvi: an exemplar of the qasbati learned tradition

There is possibly no better way to understand the role of qasbahs and evaluate their significance within the larger Indian and Islamic context than by the personalities that represented the qasbati ethos. A host of individuals, families, and communities from qasbahs contributed to local qasbati and a larger pan-Islamic intellectual and social ambience. This is borne out by the genre of *tazkirah*, or biographical dictionaries of honoured individuals, that lists and describes individuals related to a particular region, profession, or ideology by compiling their variously sized biographies in book-length works.[25] As a distinct genre of literature of the Indo-Muslim society, tazkirahs provide significant information on qasbati societies that other sources lack. Since the late medieval era, tazkirahs as biographical anthologies appeared in Persian and later in Urdu in good numbers. Recording details of those individuals considered worthy of being mentioned, Urdu tazkirahs are one of the most compelling sources of information on individuals such as those classified as Sufis, ‘ulama, poets, writers, or a group of such combinations belonging to a particular region, sect, or Sufi order. What they include, in general, are the details of an individual's place and date of birth and death, educational background, lineage and upbringing, as well as sample works or contributions. In the course of enumerating attainments, particularly of those deceased, tazkirahs have a proclivity to become hagiographic. Yet, the information that they provide is generally not to be found in other sources, official British sources in particular.

The focus on individuals as in the tazkirahs serves as a window into the qasbati worldview in all its nuances. It was these individuals, such as Chaudhary Muhammad Ali Rudaulvi, who constantly defined and refined the idea and significance of the qasbah. Rudaulvi was born on 15 May 1882 in muhallah Salar of qasbah Rudauli. Known as Chamru Mian among his family and friends, he was the taluqdar of Amirpur estate in the Bara Banki district. His grandfather, Inayat Rasul, was from a renowned Sunni family of the qasbah and was married to the daughter of Lutf Ali, taluqdar of Amirpur and a Shia Muslim.[26] Chaudhary Muhammad Ali's father, Ihsan Rasul, married Murtaza Begum, daughter of Mir Muhammad Abid, the taluqdar of Purai, another famous estate in Awadh. His mother's family was Shia Muslim, and his father, born a Sunni, had also embraced the Shia faith before he died. Upon adulthood, Muhammad Ali took over his father's estate, earlier placed under the Court of Wards.[27] He grew up surrounded by both Shia and Sunni Muslims[28] and married his cousin Abida Begum, a Sunni Muslim. It is interesting to note his mixed ancestry and influences, contrary to popular perceptions of sectarian divides within Islam, and this very eclecticism was in fact symbolic of the contemporary qasbati life. Rudaulvi was of the view that Muslims needed to be recognized as Muslims, not necessarily as Shias and Sunnis – and he referred to himself in this regard. On being asked by a friend whether he had become a Sunni since he was not performing any of the Shia rituals at that time, he wrote:

> I answered: If had I to become a Sunni, why wouldn't I remain a Shia? Oftentimes I was asked about my faith. And, when I would say that I call myself a Muslim and may God consider me as a Muslim, those who heard would not get convinced. A Godsend name, a name brought by the Prophet "Muslim" became insignificant. Until you put the tag of Shia, Sunni, or Wahhabi, people do not understand what your religion is.[29]

Men from landholding families such as Chaudhary Muhammad Ali's went to the cities to be educated. He attended the well-known Colvin Taluqdar School of Lucknow that later became Colvin Taluqdar College: an institution conceived by Sir Auckland Colvin, Lieutenant-Governor of the United Provinces of Agra and Oudh, to impart education to the children of landed aristocracy and British administrators. There, he made friends with peers from other qasbahs and towns, such institutions being spaces where qasbati individuals of gentry background often forged lifelong friendships into the larger world. It was at this school that in 1892 he met his childhood friend Raja Prithvipal Singh.[30] Rudaulvi had to discontinue his studies in 1899, when he was married at the age of 17. However, he continued with his intellectual pursuits, working his way through a wide array of literature, including a selection of works in English. Among others, he read Karl Marx, Oscar Wilde, H.G. Wells, and George Bernard Shaw and would liberally draw upon them in his Urdu writings. While many of his aristocratic contemporaries lived a life of luxury, he became a self-taught writer and an activist. Belonging to a generation of India's Muslims that provided intellectual leadership during the late nineteenth and early twentieth centuries, he was counted as one of the noted progressive writers of his time. His friends included Abdul Majid Daryabadi, eminent writer from his neighbouring qasbah of Daryabad; Neyaz Fatehpuri, editor of the literary monthly *Nigar* of Lucknow; Salahuddin Ahmad, Urdu writer and editor of the magazine *Adabi Duniya* published from Lahore; Muhammad Tufail, editor of the journal *Naqoosh*; Al-e Ahmad Suroor, renowned Urdu critic and Professor of Urdu at Aligarh Muslim University; Shaikh Wilayat Ali Qidwai Bambooq, a zamindar of Bara Banki and an Aligarh graduate; and Raja Prithvipal Singh, the taluqdar of pargana Daryabad.[31]

Writer and intellectual Abdul Majid Daryabadi (1892–1977), for instance, spoke highly of Muhammad Ali Rudaulvi:

> Maulana [Abul Kalam] Azad Sahib of *al-Hilal* once came to Lucknow some time in 1917 and visited me for a meal. At that time, it was known that no one could face him in conversation and that he could easily outdo his opponent. For a debate, Chaudhary Muhammad Ali was asked to come, and when a discussion started exchanging jokes and pleasantries over dinner, spectators could see that they were an equal match.[32]

Rudaulvi was active in bringing some of the best Hindi and Urdu writers of all time together for the very first meeting of the PWA. He chaired the reception committee of the first conference of the PWA in 1936, which was presided over by the famous Hindi writer Munshi Prem Chand (1880–1936).[33] According to Sajjad Zaheer (1904–1973), noted Urdu writer, Marxist thinker, and a founder of the PWA, the Communist Party of India, and later the Communist Party of Pakistan:

> Chaudhry Sahib was a landlord and belonged to the upper classes of Oudh. He was of a generation before us, but his personality was an amalgam of unusual qualities, which made him one of the most interesting people in the land of Oudh. His manners and decorum were like those of the elite of an earlier age, but his clean-cut face and English education bespoke of a modern man. When he wrote Urdu, the elegance, sweetness, and amused irony in his style had the flavor of old Lucknow. However, when he spoke, he could discuss anybody, from Friedrich Nietzsche and Karl Marx, Rabindranath Tagore and Muhammad Iqbal, to Sigmund Freud and Havelock Ellis. When he was with members of the older generation, he would talk to them about the afterlife, property, and their children. When he found himself among young people, he could dwell on the topic of sexology, with such clarity and realism that the boldest of his listeners would stare at him in disbelief… Chaudhry Sahib's first act on joining our reception committee as its chairman was to quietly give us a donation of one hundred rupees. He said he was embarrassed at the smallness of the sum. But what he did not know was that no individual had so far given us an amount exceeding ten rupees, and so his gift was for us a princely sum.[34]

Muhammad Ali's participation in the PWA made him a representative figure among his qasbatis, who participated in the progressive literary movement. Fellow qasbati Asrar-ul-Haq Majaz was a well-known romantic Urdu poet. His poetry compilations *Aahang* and *Saaz-e-Nau* are archetypal voices of the progressive Urdu writing, which included the poet's advocacy of greater equality for women.[35]

Chaudhary Muhammad Ali wrote in Urdu but was well read in English literature and philosophy.[36] His works include short story collection *Ataliq Bibi* (*The Tutor Wife*), which he wrote on the request of noted novelist and essayist Abdul Halim Sharar (1869–1926) of *Guzishta Lucknow*[37] fame. These short stories highlighted women's role in society, placing them as the advocates of reform. A series of female characters through the different stories pinpoint the bad habits of their husbands and seek ways to redeem them. In one story, the wife chides her husband for not taking good care of family finances as he hands out a loan to a friend while more pressing needs await at home; in another story, the wife confronts her husband's habit of hookah smoking. Characterizing husbands as the wrongdoers, Rudaulvi inversed gender roles to an extent that was noteworthy by the standards of contemporary literature. However, his writings lacked the revolutionary zeal of a Majaz or Josh Malihabadi (1894–1982) and fell short of breaking through the mould of gender norms. In another collection of writings titled *Kashkol Muhammad Ali Shah Faqir* (*The Beggar's Bowl of Muhammad Ali Shah*), Muhammad Ali engaged with contemporary social realities. In several essays published in different newspapers and periodicals over an extended period of time and put together as *Kahskol* in 1951, he dealt with women's issues, British attitudes, and poverty to draw his readers' attention to causes of immediate concern. Most essays are satirical in approach and use an interactive format of posing two characters in a dialogue.

However, one of his most striking Urdu writings was a book titled *Salahkaar* (*Advisor*) that he wrote as a study of sex, intended to provide sex education to men. While the West had published 'thousands of books' on sex and sexuality, he felt there was an acute need of such a book for Urdu speakers on 'a topic of extreme importance'. Moreover, he wrote this book on the premise that women were equal to men and hence the need for better education and awareness on the subject for men to treat women with greater dignity. He wrote:

> Today, women's rights (*huquq*) and women's ability (*qabliyat*) are considered at par with those of men. Women sit in the Parliament, women run motors, women work as engineers, women serve as constables, and display excellence in all fields. Therefore, women have become equal to men.[38]

Well aware that a book of this nature would invite the ire of many, he chose to pass on only as much information as he felt would not infringe upon domestic sensibilities.[39] In *Salahkaar*, he provided a detailed account of the anatomy and sexual characteristics of both men and women and dealt with topics considered taboo in the larger Indian public sphere of the time. He referred to kissing as a symbol of love and affection, even among animals, traced the origins of prostitution and noted the significance of marriage and why women's choices should be respected within the institution. In addition, he focused on venereal diseases gonorrhoea (*suzak*) and syphilis (*atishak*) and wrote about their prevention and cure. Descriptive and often didactic in tone and tenor, this work is written in a very direct, accessible language with occasional stories and anecdotes. Throughout, Muhammad Ali cites numerous thinkers and writers, including Gandhi and George Bernard Shaw, and compares and contrasts the Indian and European contexts.

While he made a clear admonition that only men should read *Salaahkar*,[40] Chaudhary Muhammad Ali published and distributed free copies of a booklet on similar themes, meant solely for women. Titled *Parde ki Baat* (*About the Veil*), it was dedicated to 'a daughter, a niece, and a daughter-in-law'[41] and was concerned with women's health and sexuality. A very short piece, it mostly engaged with pregnancy-related issues and covered topics such as conception, fertilization, and child-bearing. Most importantly, it advocated how women could take better control of their own bodies and learn to assume social responsibilities. In this booklet, he purportedly addressed all Indian women. It thus begins:

> The environment of Hindustan [India] is such that people are neither strong nor that hard-working. In places where one has to work to provide such as in Arabia and England, people are extremely persevering. Only in Hindustan can people sustain themselves by begging or by gathering vegetables and fruits in the jungle…. Even marriages take place at a young age… This is why children are born weak and the parents remain frail as well. In these circumstances, women suffer more than men.[42]

The booklet ended with perhaps an oblique note to the ladies of his own qasbah, 'If there occurs a need to ask any questions, I am by all means available. Ladies, Daughters! Read every word carefully of this small booklet.'[43]

Muhammad Ali Rudaulvi's literary persona in its entirety is representative of the eclecticism of qasbati writers and thinkers who strode the local and larger Muslim intellectual and social milieu. In keeping with his progressive ideals, he approved of educating Muslim girls,[44] a stand encouraged by the views of Saiyid Karamat Husain (1854–1917), a foremost leader in promoting Muslim girls' education and the founder of the Muslim Girls' School in Lucknow.[45] He was so greatly impressed by Karamat Husain that he published a book in his memory in 1918, a year after Husain's death.[46] In addition to women's education, Rudaulvi was an ardent advocate of women's rights and status in society, as testified in his following statement: '… she (the woman) is not just equal to man, she is rather superior. The only difference between the two is that both work in different spheres.'[47] His concern for women's advancement was echoed by Hamida Salim's observation that Chaudhary Muhammad Ali did not only send his own girls to the school founded by Karamat Husain in Lucknow, but also prevailed on her parents to send their girls to the same school.[48] The youngest child of Chaudhary Siraj-ul-Haq of Rudauli and a sister of Majaz and Safia Akhtar, Salim's (b. 1922) memoirs – an invaluable source for the study of qasbati life – tell what it was like to grow up in a qasbah at a time when it was a buzzing intellectual hub.

Although rooted in Rudauli, Chaudhary Muhammad Ali maintained consistent ties with Lucknow. Reputed English schools, major government offices, courts, and the offices for fora such as landholders' associations were located in urban centres where people from various qasbahs and towns found common meeting ground. Qasbahs never rivalled cities in this regard. Rather, they complemented cities and even helped the urban centres thrive and succeed. A constant flow of people between, say, Lucknow and Rudauli helped sustain urban institutions while allowing the qasbah and its qasbatis to become well networked.

The partition of India in 1947 rendered many qasbati families divided, as elsewhere in India. Muhammad Ali Rudaulvi remained in India along with his second wife and her children. The children from his first wife left for Pakistan. He continued writing, more as a way to deal with his solitude and the ensuing developments in a new India that abolished the zamindari system in the 1950s, which adversely affected persons of his standing. Although his writings may not represent the very best specimens of Urdu literature, they mirror the breadth of his vision, most so, in terms of its wide-ranging and progressive content. A progressive Muslim, he was ahead of his time on issues of education and the societal standing of women, and possessed a rare ability to accept new ideas while being rooted in his local milieu. Chaudhary Muhammad Ali's intellectual life highlights the intellectual effervescence of the qasbahs where scholarly dialogue and academic exchange with the wider Indo-Muslim world was the norm rather than the exception. Only an inclusive approach with room for such historical actors can make more holistic the academic inquiries that seek to complicate our understandings of the spaces in South Asian Islam.

Conclusion

In a reflective essay, historian Shahid Amin bemoans the loss of the qasbah culture of the yore, and rightly so: 'A carefully swept *imambara*, functional old *kothi*, periodic assemblage of aspiring local poets, even the local production of local lore, legends and histories are poor substitutes for the lost world of the *qasbas*.'[49] The qasbah as discussed in this essay exists no more, not least in its intellectual avatar. The compactness of its size, the intimacy of its residents, the depth of its intellectual life, and the sense of pride have all diminished, if not completely disappeared, in the face of twentieth-century urbanization. What still remains are physical markers of a past identity: buildings, gates, dilapidated *havelis* (mansions), and the Sufi shrines. All reminiscent of a past whose story they tell. New and incongruous are larger populations, motorbike showrooms, large stores and billboards, and concrete buildings overshadowing past structures – exactly like any other small town in South Asia.

The rise and growth of the qasbahs rested on the twin foundations of economic activity and intellectual vivacity. The financial strength of the landed gentry and the patronage that they were able to extend to a cluster of literary, artistic, and humanistic endeavours made qasbahs both intellectually and socially vibrant in Muslim South Asia. The event of the partition of India in 1947 most affected the regions of Awadh and Rohilkhand. It divided families in qasbahs – as with Chaudhary Muhammad Ali's own family – that held significant Muslim populace and had spawned vibrant Islamicate cultures. The flight of individuals who mattered occurred in most qasbahs, crippling the backbone of qasbati life. The second major blow swept away the taluqdars and zamindars with the passage of the UP Zaminadari Abolition and Land Reforms Act of 1950, enforced in 1952. It altered the qasbati structure, for better or worse. Declining financial conditions hit concerned families – families that had once lived and thrived on a sustained source of income, and were able to extend local patronage. This led individuals to flock towards cities and bigger towns, now a more unilinear movement than ever in the past.

Qasbahs were significant since they offered compact and individualistic ambiences for the pursuit of intellectual activity. While qasbatis moved to other qasbahs and larger urban centres of their choosing, many chose to return or to maintain strong link with the native qasbahs. Post-1950s outward migrations were however more definitive. Qasbatis who moved out to larger towns and cities in search of better careers and livelihoods might have returned periodically but not permanently. Not everything from the past era was lost or changed, though. What remained intact was a sense of pride in the qasbah's past, a past from which the space of the qasbahs emerge to challenge any understanding of non-urban areas or contexts as peripheral or parochial. The qasbah's ethos was critical, even as driving force, in the history of Muslim South Asia. No wonder then that erstwhile 'qasbatis' continue to associate themselves with their respective qasbahs. The Bilgramis, the Rudaulvis, the Amrohvis, and the Badaunis are just a few to name.

Notes

1. Rudaulvi, *Gunah ka Khauf*, 10.
2. Hodgson, *The Venture of Islam*, 59.
3. Pandey, "Encounters and Calamities," 89–128.
4. See, Bayly, "The Small Town and Islamic Gentry in North India,"; Bayly, *Rulers, Townsmen and Bazaars*; Kumar, *Essays in the Social History of Modern India*; and Hasan, *From Pluralism to Separatism.*
5. Historians whose works engage with individuals and events from various qasbahs, though they may not be directly dealing with qasbahs as entities include, Metcalf, *Islamic Revival in British India*; Lelyveld, *Aligarh's First Generation*; Robinson, *Separatism*; Minault, *Secluded Scholars*; Alam, *The Crisis of Empire in Mughal North India*; and Sanyal, *Devotional Islam and Politics in British India.* A more recent work uses qasbahs as locales to study Sufism, and rightly so, since Sufism remains at the base and core of the qasbati topography and life. See Liebeskind, *Piety on Its Knees.*
6. *Gazetteer of the Province of Oudh, Vol. II*, 312.
7. Elaborating on the agrarian structure of Awadh and the place of qasbahs within it, this description appears in the *Gazetteer of the Province of Oudh, Vol. II*, 312.
8. Alam, *The Crisis of Empire in Mughal North India*, 110–7; and Jafri, *Studies in the Anatomy of a Transformation*, 49–59.
9. For a detailed analysis of how these groups of people and other professionals dealt with issues of modernity, see Rahman, *Locale, Everyday Islam, and Modernity.*
10. Robinson, "Knowledge, Its Transmission, and the Making of Muslim Societies," 243.
11. While collecting primary sources in the 1920s and earlier, the Urdu historian of Amroha Mahmood Ahmad Abbasi was overwhelmed by the sheer profusion of documents and writings that he amassed from within households. See Abbasi, *Tarikh-e-Amroha*, 10. Such descriptions reflect how a variety of individual backgrounds and professional pursuits flourished in qasbahs, particularly in the aftermath of the revolt of 1857. In fact, several 'ulama left Delhi in this period in favour of their qasbahs of origin. Barbara Metcalf's study of the foundation of the madrasa at Deoband is just one lead in this direction, showing how qasbah Saharanpur witnessed in 1860s the rise of what came to be the centre of Islamic learning in the Indian subcontinent. See Metcalf, *Islamic Revival in British India.*
12. Bayly, *Rulers, Townsmen and Bazaars*, 192.
13. Ernst, *Eternal Garden*, 155–68; and Eaton, *Sufis of Bijapur*, 155–64.
14. *Gazetteer of the Province of Awadh, Vol III*, 273–4.
15. Alam, "Assimilation from a Distance," 166.
16. *Gazetteer of the Province of Awadh, Vol III*, 274.
17. Zaidi, *Apni Yadein*, 299–327.
18. Ibid., 329, 333–7.
19. Akhtar, *Harf-e-Aashna*; and Akhtar, *Zer-e-Lab.* Lately, a Hindi translation of her letters has been published. Akhtar, *Tumhare Naam.*
20. Alvi and Salim, eds., *Majaz: Kuch Yadein*, 28–9.
21. Asar Lakhnawi (1885–1967), another well-known Urdu poet, wrote about Majaz that a Keats was born to Urdu but was lost to the waves of revolution. Pandit, ed., *Majaz aur Uski Sha'iri*, 24.
22. For instance, the population of the town circles of Amroha was 35,230, Badaun 35,372, Bilgram 11,457, and Rudauli 11,767. For details, see *Twenty-Eighth Annual Report of the Sanitary Commissioner*, 74–132.
23. Chakrabarty, *Provincializing Europe*. See chapter 7: "*Adda*: A History of Sociality," 180–213.
24. Khan, *Intekhab Diwan-e-Haziq*, 7.
25. For a history of this genre in Urdu literature, see Pritchett, "A Long History of Urdu Literary Culture," Part 2, 864–911. For a brief analysis of the contribution of South Asia to the Persian *tazkirah* tradition, see Alam, "The Culture and Politics of Persian in Precolonial Hindustan," 174–7.
26. Rudaulvi, *Mera Mazhab*, 10.
27. *Application of Chaudhri Muhammad Ali, Taluqdar, Bara Banki district, to have his estate placed under the Provisions of the Oudh Settled Estates Act, 1900*, File no. 297, Revenue Department, June 1913, Uttar Pradesh State Archives (UPSA).
28. He mentions one Maulvi Wajid Ali as one of his childhood teachers. He adds that when he would not completely follow Shia rituals and practices, others in the house would blame it on

the Maulvi who had instructed his young pupil to follow what his mother would tell him. Rudaulvi, *Mera Mazhab*, 10–11.
29. Rudaulvi, *Mera Mazhab*, 57.
30. Rudaulvi, *Kashkol*, 101.
31. Khan, *Chaudhary Muhammad Ali Rudaulvi*, 41–51.
32. Daryabadi, *Maasirin*, 119.
33. The Progressive Writers' Association was started by, among others, Sajjad Zaheer (1904–1973), a renowned Urdu writer, Marxist thinker and revolutionary. The PWA gathered the crème de la crème of Urdu literature such as Hasrat Mohani, Firaq Gorakhpuri, Rashid Jahan, and Faiz Ahmad Faiz. Interview with Professor Sharib Rudaulvi, Lucknow, July 2004.
34. Zaheer, *The Light*, 55–6.
35. See Majaz's poem titled "Naujawaan Khaatun se", in Pandit, ed., *Majaz aur Uski Sha'iri*, 85–6.
36. In his writings, he frequently quotes from Spencer, Mill, Machiavelli, G.B. Shaw, and H.G. Wells, among others. Rudaulvi, *Kashkol*, 253–61; Rudaulvi, *Mera Mazhab*, 16–17, 74–5; and Rudaulvi, *Goya Dabistan Khul Gaya*, 161.
37. Sharar is famous for his noted work *Guzishta Lucknow* (*Lucknow of the Past*) that laments the bygone era of Lucknow and cherishes the best of Awadhi culture. Sharar, *Guzishta Lakhnau*.
38. Rudaulvi, *Salahkaar*, 119.
39. Ibid., 3–4.
40. Ibid., 111.
41. It is a pocket sized booklet of only 41 pages and mentions no other publication details but the name of the book and the author. Rudaulvi, *Parde ki Baat*, 2.
42. Rudaulvi, *Parde ki Baat*, 3–5.
43. Ibid., 39.
44. His own daughters attended schools in Allahabad and Lucknow. Rudaulvi, *Mera Mazhab*, 16.
45. Saiyid Karamat Husain was a champion of Muslim girls' education, first as a member of the Muhammadan Educational Conference and later, as the founder of a girls' school in Lucknow. He also had a significant impact on the educated Muslims of his generation, and his friends, peers, and followers spread the idea that girls' education was critical to the progress of the Muslim community. Minault, *Secluded Scholars*, 216–28; and Minault, "Sayyid Karamat Husain," 155–64.
46. Rudaulvi, *Yadgar Maulana Saiyid Karamat Husain Marhum*.
47. Rudaulvi, *Salahkaar*, 119.
48. Salim, *Shorish-e-Dauran*, 86.
49. Amin, "Post-Colonial Towns Called Deoria," 48.

Bibliography

Abbasi, Mahmood Ahmad Hashmi. *Tarikh-e-Amroha*. Delhi: Tajalli Printing Works, 1930.
Akhtar, Safia. *Harf-e-Aashna*. Lahore: Maktab-e-Sha'ir-o-Adab, 1958.
Akhtar, Safia. *Tumhare Naam*. Delhi: Rajkamal Prakashan, 2004.
Akhtar, Safia. *Zer-e-Lab*. Delhi: Maktab-e-Jamia, 1955.
Alam, Muzaffar. "Assimilation from a Distance: Confrontation and Sufi Accommodation in Awadh Society." In *Tradition, Dissent and Ideology: Essays in Honour of Romila Thapar*, edited by R. Champakalakshmi and S. Gopal. Delhi: Oxford University Press, 1996.
Alam, Muzaffar. *The Crisis of Empire in Mughal North India: Awadh and the Punjab, 1707–1748*. New Delhi: Oxford University Press, 1986.
Alam, Muzaffar. "The Culture and Politics of Persian in Precolonial Hindustan." In *Literary Cultures in History: Reconstructions from South Asia*, edited by Sheldon Pollock. Berkeley: University of California Press, 2003.
Alvi, Ahmad Ibrahim, and Manzar Salim, eds. *Majaz: Kuch Yadein*. Lucknow: Zia Azimabadi, n.d.
Amin, Shahid, "Post-Colonial Towns Called Deoria." *Sarai Reader* 1 (2001): 47–52.
Askari, Mirza Muhammad. *Mann Kistam*. Lucknow: Uttar Pradesh Urdu Akademi, 1985.
Bayly, C. A. *Rulers, Townsmen and Bazaars: North Indian Society in the Age of British Expansion, 1770–1870*. Cambridge: Cambridge University Press, 1983.
Bayly, C A. "The Small Town and Islamic Gentry in North India: The Case of Kara." In *The City in South Asia: Pre-Modern and Modern*, edited by Kenneth Ballhatchet and John Harrison. London: Curzon Press, 1980.

Chakrabarty, Dipesh. *Provincializing Europe: Postcolonial Thought and Historical Difference.* Princeton, NJ: Princeton University Press, 2000.

Daryabadi, Abdul Majid. *Maasirin.* Calcutta: Idarah-e-Insha-e-Majidi, 1979.

Eaton, Richard. *Sufis of Bijapur, 1300–1700: Social Role of Sufis in Medieval India.* Princeton, NJ: Princeton University Press, 1978.

Ernst, Carl W. *Eternal Garden: Mysticism, History, and Politics at a South Asian Sufi Center.* New Delhi: Oxford University Press, 2004.

Fazl-i-Allami, Abul. *Ain-i-Akbari, Vol II, A Gazetteer and Administrative Manual of Akbar's Empire and Past History of India.* English translation by Colonel H. S. Jarrett. Calcutta: Royal Asiatic Society of Bengal, 1949.

Gazetteer of the Province of Oudh. Vol. II. Delhi: B. R. Publishing Corporation, 1985; originally published 1877–1878.

Gazetteer of the Province of Oudh. Vol. III. Allahabad: Northwestern Provinces and Awadh Government Press, 1878.

Hasan, Mushirul. *From Pluralism to Separatism: Qasbas in Colonial Awadh.* New Delhi: Oxford University Press, 2004.

Hodgson, Marshall. *The Venture of Islam, Vol. I: The Classical Age of Islam.* Chicago: University of Chicago Press, 1974.

Jafri, Syed Zaheer Husain. *Studies in the Anatomy of a Transformation: Awadh, from Mughal to Colonial Rule.* New Delhi: Gyan Publishing House, 1998.

Kessinger, Tom G. "Regional Economy (1757–1857): North India." In *The Cambridge Economic History of India Volume 2: C. 1757–C. 1970*, edited by Dharma Kumar and Meghnad Desai. Cambridge: Cambridge University Press, 1989.

Khan, Anwar Husain. *Chaudhary Muhammad Ali Rudaulvi: Hayat aur Adabi Khidmaat.* Lucknow: Nizami Offset Press, 1992.

Khan, Kazim Ali. *Intekhab Diwan-e-Haziq.* Amroha, n.d.

Kumar, Ravinder. *Essays in the Social History of Modern India.* Delhi: Oxford University Press, 1983.

Lelyveld, David. *Aligarh's First Generation: Muslim Solidarity in British India.* Princeton, NJ: Princeton University Press, 1978.

Liebeskind, Claudia. *Piety on Its Knees: Three Sufi Traditions in South Asia in Modern Times.* Delhi: Oxford University Press, 1998.

Metcalf, Barbara D. *Islamic Revival in British India: Deoband, 1860–1900.* Princeton, NJ: Princeton University Press, 1982.

Minault, Gail. "Sayyid Karamat Husain and Muslim Women's Education." *Lucknow: Memories of City*, edited by Violette Graff. Delhi: Oxford University Press, 1997.

Minault, Gail. *Secluded Scholars: Women's Education and Muslim Social Reform in Colonial India.* Delhi: Oxford University Press, 1998.

Pandey, Gyanendra, "Encounters and Calamities: The History of a North Indian Qasba in the Nineteenth Century." In *Subaltern Studies III*, edited by Ranajit Guha. New Delhi: Oxford University Press, 1984.

Pandit, Prakash, ed. *Majaz aur Uski Sha'iri.* Delhi: Star Pablikeshanz, 1963.

Platts, John T. *A Dictionary of Urdu, Classical Hindi and English.* London: Oxford University Press, 1974.

Pritchett, Frances W. "A Long History of Urdu Literary Culture, Part 2: Histories, Performances, and Masters." In *Literary Cultures in History: Reconstructions from South Asia*, edited by Sheldon Pollock. Berkeley: University of California Press, 2003.

Rahman, M. Raisur, *Locale, Everyday Islam, and Modernity: Qasbah Towns and Muslim Life in Colonial India*, Forthcoming.

Revenue Department Files, Uttar Pradesh State Archives, June 1913.

Robinson, Francis. "Knowledge, Its Transmission, and the Making of Muslim Societies." In *The Cambridge Illustrated History of the Islamic World*, edited by Francis Robinson. Cambridge: Cambridge University Press, 1996.

Robinson, Francis. *Separatism among Indian Muslims: The Politics of the United Provinces' Muslims, 1860–1923.* Cambridge: Cambridge University Press, 1974.

Rudaulvi, Chaudhary Muhammad Ali. *Goya Dabistan Khul Gaya.* Lahore: Punjab Academy, 1956.

Rudaulvi, Muhammad Ali, *Ataliq Bibi*, n.d.

Rudaulvi, Muhammad Ali, *Gunah ka Khauf.* Lucknow: Naya Sansar, n.d.

Rudaulvi, Muhammad Ali. *Kashkol: Muhammad Ali Shah Faqir*. Lucknow: Siddique Book Depot, 1951.
Rudaulvi, Muhammad Ali. *Mera Mazhab*. Patna: Idarah-e-Tehqiqat-e-Urdu, 1991; first published 1951.
Rudaulvi, Muhammad Ali, *Parde ki Baat*, n.d.
Rudaulvi, Muhammad Ali. *Salahkaar*. Lucknow: Sarfaraz Qaumi Press, 1928.
Rudaulvi, Muhammad Ali. *Yadgar Maulana Saiyid Karamat Husain Marhum*. Lucknow: Nawal Kishore Press, 1918.
Salim, Hamida. *Shorish-e-Dauran: Yadein*. New Delhi: Har-Anand Publication, 1995.
Sanyal, Usha. *Devotional Islam and Politics in British India: Ahmad Riza Khan Barelwi and His Movement, 1870–1920*. Delhi: Oxford University Press, 1996.
Sharar, Abdul Halim. *Guzishta Lakhnau*. New Delhi: Maktab-e-Jamia, 2000.
Twenty-Eighth Annual Report of the Sanitary Commissioner of the Northwestern Provinces and Oudh, for the Year Ending 31st December, 1895, V/24/3756, British Library, London, 74–132.
Zaheer, Sajjad. *The Light: A History of the Movement for Progressive Literature in the Indo-Pakistan Subcontinent (A Translation of Roshnai)*. Karachi: Oxford University Press, 2006.
Zaidi, Saiyid Ali Muhammad. *Apni Yadein: Rudauli ki Baatein*. Rudauli: Azmi Publishers, 1977.

Section II:
Literary Culture and the Imagination

Asian and Islamic crossings: Malay writing in nineteenth-century Sri Lanka

Ronit Ricci

School of Culture, History, and Language, College of Asia and the Pacific, Australian National University, Canberra, Australia

This essay explores how a small diasporic Muslim community in the colonial era – known today as the Sri Lankan Malays – maintained its culture through the preservation of language, the transmission of literary and religious texts, the cultivation of genres and of a script. Beginning in the late seventeenth century and throughout the eighteenth, the Dutch United East India Company (VOC) used the island of Ceylon as a site of banishment for those considered rebels in the regions under Company control in the Indonesian archipelago. Criminals from these territories were also sent to Ceylon, as were native troops who served in the Dutch army, and others employed in various capacities. After their takeover of the island in 1796, the British too brought to Ceylon colonial subjects from the archipelago and the Malay Peninsula, primarily to serve in their military. I examine issues of cultural encounter and religious developments through an analysis of a Malay manuscript written in Colombo in the early years of the nineteenth century. I emphasize the referencing of titles and names as well as the text's multilingual character. Through this discussion I question the notion of distinctly defined centres and margins as they pertain to the Sri Lankan Malays – situated physically and figuratively between the Malay and Arab worlds – and suggest that crossroads, connections and movement are more appropriate conceptual categories for considering their case.

Introduction

This article explores some of the ways by which a small diasporic Muslim community in the colonial era – known today as the Sri Lankan Malays – maintained its culture through the preservation of language, the transmission of literary and religious texts, the cultivation of genres and of a script.[1] Such an exploration requires us to imagine the world of the Indian Ocean in the seventeenth and eighteenth centuries: the contours of Dutch Asia that included both the island of Ceylon and parts of present-day Indonesia encompassing, predominantly, the island of Java[2]; the established sea routes of trade and travel at the time, central among them the pilgrimage path from Southeast Asia to Mecca that passed through Ceylon; and the wide-ranging, active networks of Muslim scholars teaching and studying across these regions.

Beginning in the late seventeenth century and throughout the eighteenth, the Dutch United East India Company (VOC) used the island of Ceylon as a site of banishment for those considered rebels in the regions under Company control in the Indonesian archipelago.[3] Criminals from these territories were also sent to Ceylon, as were native troops who served in the Dutch army, and others employed in various capacities. After their takeover of the island in 1796, the British too brought to Ceylon colonial subjects from the archipelago and the Malay Peninsula, primarily to serve in their military. Many of the recruits and their families lived in and around the military cantonments in Colombo, Kandy, Trincomalee and elsewhere, thus settling across the island. From the early political exiles – many of whom were members of ruling families in Java, Sulawesi, Madura and other islands – and the accompanying retinues, soldiers, servants and workers developed the community known as the Sri Lankan Malays.[4]

Manuscripts and books preserved in private collections currently owned by Malay families in Sri Lanka testify to an impressive and ongoing engagement by previous generations with a range of texts written primarily in Malay and Arabic. The majority of these have an 'Islamic character' in that they include theological treatises, manuals on prayer and ritual, well-known hadith, tales written in the Malay genres of *hikayat* (prose) and *syair* (poetry) on the battles of early Islam, heroic figures and adventures, musings on Arabic letters and mystical tracts. A striking feature of these writings, at least to one approaching them from the perspective of Indonesian or Malay Studies, is how similar many of them are to those found in manuscripts now housed in Jakarta, Kuala Lumpur or Leiden. In addition, however, there are works that represent very local agendas, depict events that unfolded in colonial Ceylon or are otherwise not known from the broader eighteenth- and nineteenth-century Malay literature from elsewhere.[5]

Although the ancestors of the Sri Lankan Malays came from a range of places and linguistic and ethnic backgrounds in the Indonesian archipelago and, to a lesser degree, the Malay Peninsula, the Malay language emerged as the single most important language in which they wrote their literary and religious works. Although it is reasonable to assume that they spoke a variety of languages, at least on their arrival in Ceylon – given the different regions from which they came and the strata of society they represented – it is virtually impossible to trace the history of their oral culture. Of their writing practices we know more, but in this area too many questions remain, among them when, how and why Malay gained such prominence, doubtless at the expense of other languages spoken by the diverse communities of exiles.

Malay may have provided an option for communicating across ethnic lines as it served as a lingua franca of trade in Southeast Asia. At least in part its prominence may have derived from the fact that many of those recruited to the Dutch army in the archipelago throughout the eighteenth century, although of diverse origins, had been living in Batavia before being sent to serve in Ceylon and were therefore fluent in Batavian Malay as a result.[6] Clearly, the process by which Malay came to dominate the linguistic and literary life of the Sri Lankan Malays needs further exploration. Whatever its precise trajectory, however, I show in this article that behind or beneath the cloak of Malay lie hints and traces of a more variegated linguistic and cultural past.

Despite Sri Lanka's importance to Arab trade from pre-Islamic times, its role as a stopover site for Southeast Asian pilgrims on their way to perform the hajj and its importance to the Islamic imagination as the place where Adam first fell to earth, Sri Lanka's Muslim population has long constituted a minority among much larger Hindu and especially Buddhist segments of the population and thus, in some ways, has been marginalized both in the country itself and by scholars studying Sri Lanka's cultures, archaeological sites, languages and politics.[7] The Malays, forming as they do a small minority within the country's Muslim minority, fit the category of South Asian Islamic cultures explored in this special issue, ones that have come to be viewed as peripheral.[8] Yet numbers do not tell the full story and numerical minority status does not, by definition, imply negligibility. Considering the history of the Sri Lankan Malays begs the question of whether a community that is descended from many high status individuals and families, that played an important military role in Ceylon's history and that was able to preserve its heritage in the most unlikely circumstances can be considered 'marginal'. Marginal in what sense?

In the following pages, I examine a Malay manuscript written in Colombo in the early years of the nineteenth century. In doing so, I emphasize two important dimensions: the referencing of titles and names, and the multilingual character of the manuscript. The mention of titles of well-known Islamic books and treatises and the names of authors, religious teachers and leaders of sufi brotherhoods represent knowledge circuits and intellectual and spiritual genealogies central to Malay life; the manuscript's use of several languages is typical of Sri Lankan Malay writing and calls attention to the Malays' connections to a range of sources, textual traditions and communities. Through this discussion I wish to question the notion of distinctly defined centres and margins as they pertain to the Sri Lankan Malays – situated physically and figuratively as they are between the Malay and Arab worlds – and to suggest that crossroads, connections and movement are more appropriate conceptual categories for considering their case.

The manuscript

The manuscript, measuring 21.2 × 16 × 3.2 cm, is a 270-page long compendium of texts of different lengths and authorship, inscribed by several hands. Its pages are slightly faded, with several pages torn or stained, but the writing is clear and it is generally well preserved. It belongs to Mr B.D.K. Saldin of Dehiwala, a suburb of Colombo.[9] Mr Saldin (b. 1928) inherited it from his father Tuan Junaideen Saldin, who died in 1955. He does not know how it came to be in his father's possession, whether it was part of a family collection or had been acquired from elsewhere.[10]

The manuscript includes several dates and was written over the course of almost three decades and by several hands, a common practice in compendiums of its kind. The earliest date noted is 1803 while the latest, appearing on the inner back flap of the cover, is 1831. The years 1820 and 1824 are noted as well. The dating used does not conform to a single time reckoning system. The hijri or Gregorian calendar, and sometimes both, are invoked in different instances. Noting the year according to the Gregorian calendar the scribe termed it either *hijra Nasara* ('Christian calendar') or *taun Welanda* ('Dutch year'), the latter a reminder that although the manuscript was written and certainly completed in British Ceylon, its inscription was taking place only several years after the end of Dutch rule in 1796.[11]

The name of the owner (*yang punya ini surat*) appears several times in the manuscript as Enci Sulaiman ibn 'Abd al-Jalil or ibn 'Abdullah Jalil.[12] Enci Sulaiman describes himself as hailing from Ujung Pandang in the land of Makassar, currently in the province of South Sulawesi, Indonesia.[13] Makassar was also the homeland of Sheikh Yusuf, religious scholar, anti-Dutch leader and the most prominent person to be exiled to Ceylon by the Dutch.[14] Enci Sulaiman provides further, highly significant detail about his ancestry: he is descended from Mas Haji 'Abd Allah of the central Javanese kingdom of Mataram.[15]

Haji 'Abd Allah of Mataram is mentioned elsewhere in the manuscript as a renowned sheikh whose writing is being cited, although a title for his work is not provided.[16] Towards the end of the 15-page long cited text it is noted that the text (here *kitab*) itself was transmitted from the realm of Mataram. A warning is added that this text should not be read to those disciples who have not yet engaged in *'ilm nafas* and that the guidance of a guru is essential to a correct understanding of this 'science of the breath'.[17] Indeed, discussions of this form of knowledge are common in Javanese works yet not easily found within the Malay 'classics', a fact that complements the claim that this circulating text derived from a Javanese source.[18]

Enci Sulaiman's familial history links the islands of Sulawesi and Java, and the once-powerful kingdoms of Makassar and Mataram, both of which exhibited strong resistance to Dutch advancement in the seventeenth century. The details of this history and the circumstances under which a descendent of a Javanese haji, who spent at least part of his life in Ujung Pandang, arrived in Sri Lanka remain unknown. And yet the names of places and lineages, reference to a pilgrim who returned home from Arabia, the text illuminating an important and secretive form of knowledge allow us, if we connect these small but significant dots, to view a larger and richer picture of movement and connection in which Sri Lanka was deeply embedded.[19]

Networks of reference: names and titles in the manuscript

Because the manuscript is a compendium it offers a rather broad snapshot of the kinds of texts Sri Lankan Malays were engaging with in the early nineteenth century. It contains sections that are several dozen pages long alongside very brief treatises, diagrams and notes. There are sections on zikr, the five daily prayers, the connection between the letters of the Arabic alphabet and prayer times, prophets, angels and colours; on God's attributes, essence and names, the breath, the afterlife, the shahāda, the importance of studying with the proper guru who will not lead one astray. There are also discussions of the Light of Muhammad, the human body, Adam as first human and prophet, Muhammad's advice to 'Ali, Islamic slaughter, conception and pregnancy, forms of esoteric knowledge (*'ilmu ghaib*) that should not be revealed to all, and correct conduct for women. The list could go on, but rather than focus on an in-depth and detailed analysis of content, I wish to draw attention to what referencing in the manuscript reveals about the physical and figurative location of the Sri Lankan Malays in the early nineteenth century.

Through the mention of texts, authors, religious teachers and *tarekat* affiliations the manuscript allows a glimpse of the religious and literary world of the Sri Lanka Malays, one that was complex and, above all, interconnected. Evidence of contact, circulation and a movement of sources and individuals is abundant. That evidence, however, telling as it may be, is brief and fragmentary, indicating a direction rather than leading the way.

The manner in which titles and authors are mentioned in passing, not mentioned at all or evoked in a general way (a text is said to be 'from Arabia'; transmitted by a 'great sheikh'), is reminiscent of the practice of some of the scribes writing in Malay and Javanese in Southeast Asia during the same period.

The majority of texts cited and authors noted in the manuscript originated in Middle Eastern cities, among them Cairo, Damascus, Mecca and Medina. What I wish to highlight is that, prior to their arrival in Sri Lanka, many of these particular works were transmitted to the Indonesian-Malay world by pilgrims from the archipelago who travelled to perform the hajj, or went to Arabia – especially the Haramayn – for long periods of study and initiation. The works they carried back home circulated in Arabic, in translation, and with local interpretations, making them into pillars of Islam as it was practiced and followed in Southeast Asia. Whereas some texts were no doubt brought to Sri Lanka directly from Arabia – situated as it was on the Southeast Asia-Arabia route of the pilgrimage – others were brought there by exiles and soldiers from Java, Sumatra,

Madura and Sulawesi. The result was a textual sphere that was inextricably linked in both directions.

Let us begin with the foundational sources: citations from the Qur'an and hadith. These appear occasionally, often without referencing to source. For example, sura 112 of the Qur'an, surat al-Ikhlās, is cited in full within a longer untitled section that reads like a string of quotes from various people and texts. The sura and the longer section are written in Arabic, accompanied by an interlinear translation into Malay. The sura is prefaced by *qāla Allah ta'ala* (A. 'thus said God, may He be exalted'), but there is no indication that this is a precise quote nor is there mention of its title or location within the sequence of Qur'anic suras.[20] The well-known hadith *man 'arafa nafsahu faqad 'arafa rabbahu* ('he who knows himself knows his Lord') is cited in Arabic three times, with translations into Tamil, Malay and Javanese, but only once is it attributed to the Prophet Muhammad (see Figure 1).[21]

Other, less canonical and much later sources are mentioned in passing as providing inspiration or content. Among them are the *Kitab Mukhtasar*, Kemas Fakhruddin of Palembang's mid to late eighteenth-century Malay translation of and commentary on

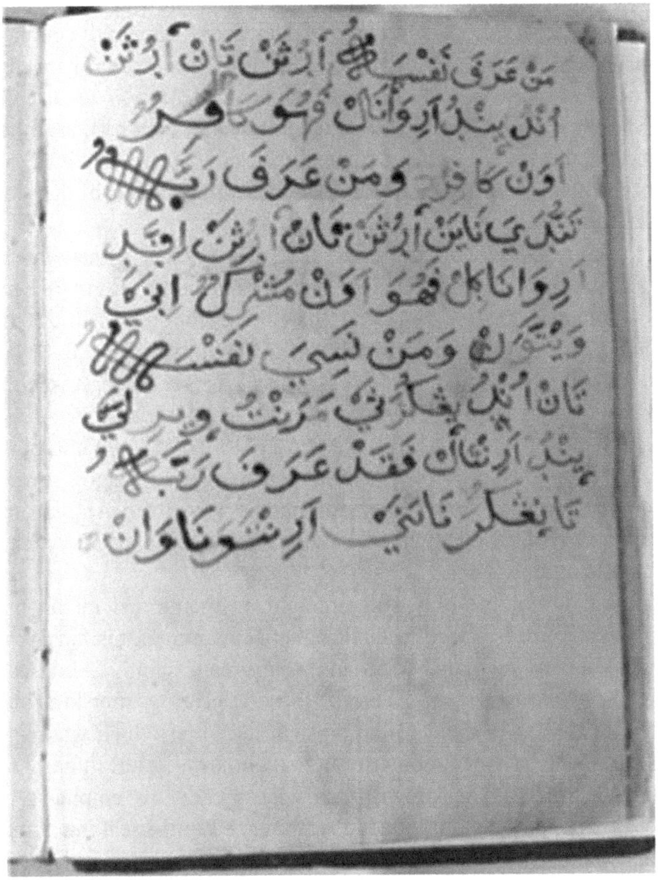

Figure 1. (Colour online) A translation of an Arabic hadith into Arabu-Tamil in the Malay Compendium.

Source: Courtesy B.D.K. Saldin.

Sheikh Raslān al-Dimashqī's twelfth-century *Risāla fī 'l-tawḥīd*. The latter work was widely known in Indonesia in its Arabic original (with interlinear translations into Malay, Javanese and Bugis) as well as via commentaries and adaptations in Malay and Javanese.[22]

A *Kitab Bayanullah* is mentioned twice.[23] A work bearing the same title and discussing sufi teachings through allegory and allusion, written in Sundanese, Javanese and Arabic in the Bandung region of West Java around the mid nineteenth century, is listed in a catalogue of West Javanese manuscripts.[24] If these two works are related, and since the title is not common, this is probable, the mention of a *Bayanullah* in the Sri Lankan compendium may hint at traces of a West Javanese heritage, possibly deriving from the 'Banten connection' in local history, the exile of prince Raja Bagus Abdullah of Banten to Sri Lanka in the mid eighteenth century.[25]

A list consisting of book titles appears towards the end of the manuscript.[26] These books are not cited yet their mention indicates that they were known to the list's compiler. Listed, among others, are the *Kitāb Minhāju al-Qawīm*, a fiqh work deriving from 'Abdallah b. 'Abd al-Karīm Ba-Fadl's fifteenth-century *Al-Muqaddima al-Hadramiyya* and composed by Ibn Ḥajar al-Ḥaytamī in the mid sixteenth century. Van den Berg in his 1886 survey of texts taught in Islamic educational institutions in Java listed the *Kitāb Minhāju al-Qawīm* as a popular work, and it is still well known today[27]; the sixteenth-century *Kitāb Manhāj al-ṭullāb*, a summary of Nawawi's thirteenth-century *Minhāj al-Ṭālibīn* by Zakariyyā al-Anṣārī, the Egyptian scholar whose works were highly popular across the Indonesian-Malay world[28]; al-Ghazzali's *Kitāb Minhāj al-'Ābidīn* (translated into Malay by Sheikh Daud al-Fatani in the late eighteenth century); and the *Kitāb Ṣirāṭ al-Mustaqīm*, considered the earliest work on fiqh produced in Muslim Southeast Asia, written in 1634 by Sheikh Nur al-Din al-Raniri, the leading scholar of the Acehnese court under Sultan Iskandar Thani (r. 1636–1641).

In addition to the titles of works, the mention of a number of scholars and teachers strengthens the impression of a strong Southeast Asia connection. For example, one section of the Compendium is claimed by its author to be based on the fatwas of Sheikh Muhammad al-Zain, possibly referring to Muhammad Zain al-Asyi who served at the Acehnese court under Sultan Mahmud Syah (1760–1781).[29] A scholar of utmost importance to be cited in a section on zikr is Sheikh Muhammad ibn 'Abd al-Karīm al-Sammān al-Madani, better known as al-Sammāni (1718–1775), Medina-born founder of the Sammaniyah.[30] His disciples from the Indonesian archipelago, several of whom became renowned scholars in their homelands upon return from Arabia, introduced his teachings to their own followers, with the Sammaniyah as a result spreading widely, especially in Palembang and Aceh.[31]

The Sammaniyah is not the only sufi order to be mentioned in the manuscript. A *silsila* covering seven pages is traced to the Prophet Muhammad, his family members and other prominent Muslim scholars, including the great 'saint' 'Abd al-Qadir Jilani (d. 1166), founder of the Qadiriyya.[32] Five of those appearing after him in the list bear the nisbah Qadiri, testifying to their affiliation with the order which was popular in Java and Sumatra. Even greater was its popularity in neighbouring south India, where devotion to Sheikh Muhideen (as Jilani is known) was widespread, this emphasis hinting at an important aspect of shared devotional practices amongst Tamil-speaking Muslims in India and Sri Lanka and the Malays.[33] Finally, the owner of the manuscript, Enci Sulaiman ibn 'Abd al-Jalil, describes himself as one who follows the path of the Shatariyya (M. *akan jalan tariqat lishtariyah*), the order that, with its strong speculative tendencies and association with wujudiya teachings, was the dominant sufi order in Southeast Asia in the seventeenth and eighteenth centuries.

The story emerging from this brief and partial overview of the Sri Lankan manuscript corresponds closely with that told by Azra in his seminal study of the ulama networks between the Middle East and the Indonesian archipelago in the seventeenth and eighteenth centuries. Sri Lanka's location in the Indian Ocean, on the maritime route between the two regions, meant that pilgrim ships travelling in both directions docked regularly at her shores. In the late seventeenth century and throughout the eighteenth, both present-day Sri Lanka and Indonesia were governed by the VOC, the Dutch East India Company, with Sri Lanka serving the Dutch as a site of exile, military service and servitude for people from the archipelago, thus forging and cementing ties between colonial subjects on both shores and, intentionally or otherwise, encouraging the creation of new religious networks.[34] Although it is currently impossible to trace precisely the movement of most texts and individuals, the mobility of people, ideas and lineages is almost palpable when reading through the manuscript's pages.

Names of authors, titles of texts and their content are telling. No less important in understanding the religious and literary culture of the Sri Lankan Malays is the prism of language.

The languages of the Sri Lankan Malays

Sri Lankan Malay manuscripts reflect the linguistic multiplicity that characterized the community. Like many Malay manuscripts from Southeast Asia they contain sections in Arabic, often accompanied by interlinear translation or a more holistic form of translation that conveys single sentences or longer sections of the Arabic text in Malay.

In addition to Arabic, some Malay manuscripts contain writing in Arabu-Tamil, Tamil written in the Arabic script and infused with Arabic vocabulary, commonly used by Muslims in Sri Lanka and South India.[35] The inclusion of Arabu-Tamil reflects the close contacts between Malay and Tamil-speaking Muslims in Sri Lanka which formed through inter-marriage, business endeavours, residence in adjoining or shared neighbourhoods, prayer in the same mosques and the use of Tamil for everyday pursuits by members of both communities. The present Malay Compendium contains a single example of the hadith already mentioned and well known in sufi circles – *man 'arafa nafsahu faqad 'arafa rabbahu* – with a translation and brief interpretation in Tamil.

In light of the diasporic history of the Sri Lankan Malays and their diverse roots in the Indonesian archipelago, one might expect some form of writing in an Indonesian language other than Malay to emerge in Sri Lanka. However, Hussainmiya, in his two pioneering books on the Sri Lankan Malays' past, in which he dedicated considerable attention to their writing practices and literary culture based on his access to a large number of manuscripts, mentioned no such finding.[36] Neither did others who have written on the subject.[37] What happened to the multiple languages brought to Sri Lanka by exiles, soldiers and servants, among them Madurese, Buginese, Sundanese, Javanese, Balinese and others? Were they entirely forgotten over time? Were they preserved in speech only, not leaving any written trace?

These are intriguing questions that until recently left much room for speculation. The manuscript I discuss, however, does contain several sections in Javanese and therefore constitutes the first available evidence of its kind attesting to the preservation to some degree of an Indonesian language besides Malay by the descendants of earlier generations, perhaps going back to the early exiles, many of whom were members of Javanese royal families or served them in some capacity. The Javanese appearing in the manuscript can be described under the following headings: two brief self-standing Javanese texts, a

Javanese translation of the Arabic text of a hadith and individual Javanese words scattered throughout the manuscript.[38]

The self-standing Javanese text discussed below is the most striking among these examples, both because it is complete and because of its content and the associations it evokes.[39] It is a well-known poem titled *Kidung Rumeksa ing Wengi* (A Song Guarding in the Night) that, as the title implies, offers its reciter protection from all dangers and evil lurking in the darkness, including jinn, sheytans, fire, water, thieves and others. The poem is traditionally attributed to Sunan Kalijaga, the fifteenth-century leader of the Javanese *wali sanga*, the nine 'saints' to whom is credited the conversion of Java to Islam. Accordingly, it echoes powerfully with foundational events of the Javanese past (see Figure 2).[40]

The poem in the Sri Lankan manuscript is written somewhat differently from the way it is conventionally written in Java (although there are variations there as well). Some of these

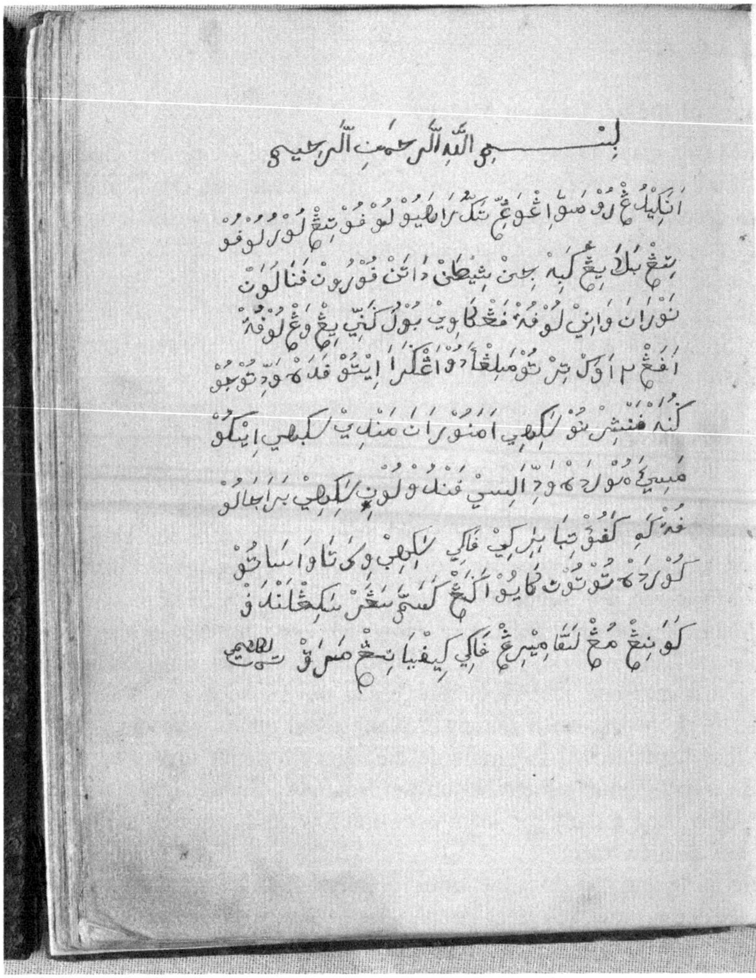

Figure 2. (Colour online) First page of the Kidung Rumeksa ing Wengi in the Malay Compendium.

Source: Courtesy B.D.K. Saldin.

changes relate to features of the phonology of the Sri Lankan Malays, among them a nasalization that occurs at word endings that must have also found its way into what may be considered Sri Lankan Javanese.[41] Thus *bilahing* for *bilahi* (disaster, bad luck), *luputing* for *luput* (miss, escape). As well, the sound 'a' (similar to English 'o' in orange) is sometimes replaced with 'u': *adu* for *adoh* (far), *tirtu* for *tirta* (water). Some words are misspelt or are substituted by others. These features suggest that the poem may have been copied and recopied by scribes who were not well acquainted with Javanese and could not identify and correct the errors. It may also be the case that the poem was written down from memory, with the scribe basing himself on aural memory rather than a written sample.

Not only are the questions of vocabulary and content interesting here. The poem is written in *macapat*, the poetic meters in which much of Javanese literature in the eighteenth and nineteenth centuries was composed and which were not employed in Malay writing. The various macapat meters are differentiated by the number of lines per verse, the number of syllables in each line and the nature of the final syllable in each line. Not only did these meters dictate the way poets structured lines and selected words but they were also closely associated with particular kinds of literary and performative scenes and with certain moods and atmospheres. The *Kidung* is written in dhangdhanggula, a meter which according to Nancy Florida conveys a melodic mood that is lithe and flexible, 'with didactic clarity and romantic allure'.[42] The preservation of the poem's metrical properties also suggests a possible familiarity with, or perhaps distant memory of, Javanese prosody and literary conventions in nineteenth-century Sri Lanka.

Another example of self-standing Javanese writing appears in the form of a list of the numerals from 1 to 40 that fills two pages of the manuscript.[43] Whereas the *Kidung* suggests a certain acquaintance with Javanese literary tradition, the list of numerals signals a more mundane realm of knowledge in which the practical skill of counting and calculating in Javanese may have remained significant or at least worthy of mention. There are several errors in the list that indicate confusion regarding the Javanese numerals or perhaps an attempt to rely on memory with mixed results. The Javanese word for 25, for example, constitutes an exception and differs from the rest of the numerals between 20 and 30 which follow a set pattern. Rather than listing the correct yet anomalous word *selawe*, the scribe used *limalikur* which fits the logic of the sequence but is not conventionally used. After reaching 40 with the numerals listed in the low register of Javanese (*ngoko*), the scribe went back to 31 (rather than 41) and repeated the same numerals using a combination of low and high (*krama*) Javanese that is unconventional.[44] In this instance we find a hint of the complex system of Javanese speech registers that is at the heart of Javanese notions of power and societal hierarchies, albeit only a faint echo that does not constitute conclusive evidence for an in-depth understanding of that system.

The second form Javanese writing takes in the Malay manuscript is that of a brief hadith in Arabic that is translated, line by line, into Javanese.

Arabic and Javanese, both written in the Arabic script, alternate on the page (Arabic in bold, in source and translation):

bism Allah al-raḥmān alraḥīm
utawi pangandikaning Allah Ta'āla
ing ḥadith qudsī ***al insānu sirri***
wa ana sirruhu *tegesé manusa iki rasa*
nisun lan isun iku pawin rasané
In the name of God the compassionate the merciful

And the words of Exalted God
In the ḥadīth qudsī **man is my secret**
And I am his secret this means man is my
Secret and I am his secret[45]

Interestingly the first Arabic phrase, the bismillah, is not translated into Javanese (as occurs occasionally in Javanese and Malay manuscripts) but is left as is, perhaps because it was often included as an almost obligatory opening line for texts and letters and was viewed more as a frame than a part of the text. Also incorporated into the Javanese is the term *ḥadīth qudsī* – sacred, holy traditions – referring to non-Qur'anic divine revelations to the Prophet Muhammad. Writing these Arabic words within a Javanese text composed in the Arabic script (pégon, see below) was straightforward and allowed the reader to recognize them immediately and pronounce them correctly.

The translation of the hadith itself is accurate and concise, not adding or detracting from the source text. It appears that the word *sirr* in Arabic, usually translated as secret or hidden, may have been rendered here not as *rahsa* (J. secret) but as *rasa*, a word that is not easily translated and has a range of meanings including taste, meaning, sense, flavour, sensation, experience and inner feeling of the heart. The latter translation – inner feeling, inner self – may in fact correspond quite closely with the meaning of *sirr* in sufi writings. Whether the translator had *rasa* or *rahsa* decisively in mind is difficult to determine because of spelling variations in these manuscripts, but it may also be that he intentionally played on both possibilities. The translation is followed, suggestively, by a second rendering that closely resembles the first – *manusa iku dhāt ingsun lan isun iku pawan dhāt ing manusa* – except that the key word standing for *sirr* is *dhāt* (from Arabic *dhāt*: being, essence, nature) rather than *rasa*. This appears to represent an attempt to define Arabic *sirr* in a way that complements the meanings of *rasa* or emphasizes them further, interestingly through the use of another key Arabic-Islamic concept – *dhāt* – that was employed as thoroughly Javanese.

Finally, the third manner in which Javanese was incorporated into the manuscript was in the form of individual words that seem to appear randomly throughout, used as part of local Malay vocabulary, perhaps interchangeable with corresponding words in that language. For example, we find *tembung* (word), *sethithik* (a little, few), *tiyang* (person), *iki saking* (on account of), *ojo lali* (do not forget). A diagram that features the points of the compass lists them in Javanese: *lor*, *wétan*, *kidul* and *kulon* (north, east, south and west, respectively).

It is difficult to deduce the precise level of familiarity with Javanese on the basis of these brief examples derived from a single manuscript. Nonetheless, the presence of Javanese in this otherwise predominantly Malay and Arabic compendium is significant. The *Kidung* raises questions about the transmission of Javanese poetic genres and meters to Sri Lanka. Its content – including a list of dangerous entities lurking in the night – evokes popular Javanese notions of one's susceptibility to the host of unseen yet potent beings populating the environment and recalls the foundational belief in the supernatural world that shaped the practices of Javanese kings and laymen alike. As Merle Ricklefs writes in his study of the court of Pakubuwana II (ruler of Mataram, 1726–1749): '…it is clear that to the Javanese court the phenomenal world was a reflection or echo of another world, of an unseen realm which was always present behind, and occasionally became manifest in, the visible world in which humanity lived.'[46] The *Kidung*, opening with the words *ana kidung rumeksa ing wengi* ('There is a song guarding in the night'), also recalls the Javanese notion of the power of particular forms of language and recitation to afford protection and refuge, extending from pre-Islamic mantras to Arabic *lapal*.[47] We might go further to suggest that the cherishing of this particular poem within the Malay community speaks to a desire to be guarded through the 'night' of exile in days past and to the way in which the expression of that earlier sentiment continued to reverberate across the generations as exemplified by the poem's preservation.

The question of script usage has been noted in passing but deserves further attention. Tamil, Malay and Javanese are written in this manuscript and others using modified forms of the Arabic script that accommodate sounds that do not occur in Arabic by adding diacritical marks to existing Arabic letters. The Arabic-Tamil script is known as Arabu-Tamil or arwi, the Arabic-Malay script is referred to as jawi and the Arabic-Javanese one as pégon.[48] The adoption of the Arabic script by speakers of these languages constituted an important dimension of Islamization and allowed for easier and more accurate rendering of Islamic terminology into Tamil, Malay and Javanese. When one looks at a manuscript page that contains alternating lines of, for instance, jawi and Arabic, one is struck by the orthographic continuity across languages and the impression that the two flow from and into one another.[49] That a single manuscript from Sri Lanka contains four languages all written, broadly speaking, in the same script offers one more testimony to the interconnectedness of South Asian Muslim communities with their co-religionists across geographical and linguistic distance.

Concluding reflections

Exploring Enci Sulaiman's early nineteenth-century Malay Compendium along the axes of reference networks and language use, with brief forays into questions of content, prosody and genre offers a glimpse of the religious and intellectual culture of the Sri Lankan Malays. More than anything else the manuscript shows how intertwined with Islamic life in the archipelago and the Middle East (as well as South India via close ties with local Tamil speaking Muslims) were the lives of these descendants of royal exiles, soldiers, servants and their families who as a community adhered both to Islam and the Malay language.

The continuing use of Malay, both spoken and written, constituted the most pivotal connection to the wider Malay-Indonesian world to the southeast. It allowed for the preservation of texts, many of them in translation from Arabic, that were integral to intellectual and spiritual trends in the lands whence came the Malays' forefathers. The insistence on transmitting the jawi/gundul script across generations meant that texts could be recopied when old books disintegrated and that knowledge of specifically Malay genres like pantun and syair was kept alive.[50]

The intriguing questions of why the Malay language came to dominate the speech and writing of the community and how that process took shape in its initial and later stages await further investigation. For now, possessing evidence of the ongoing use of another Indonesian language, Javanese, which was once spoken by many of the early exiles, reveals something of the foundations of a community whose members came from disparate backgrounds in terms of class, language, cultural and (intra-Islamic) religious affiliations. Although still a speculative proposition I believe that future research into Sri Lankan Malay manuscripts will bring to light additional instances of Javanese writing as well as writing in other languages of the archipelago, perhaps Madurese, Sundanese or Buginese.

The Javanese texts in Enci Sulaiman's manuscript go beyond testifying to the capacity to write in that language. The *Kidung Rumeksa ing Wengi* – evoking the period of Java's early Islamization, the walis and their powers of protection and guidance – indicates a certain sense of historical consciousness. The use of *tembang* and the Javanese speech registers, in however fragmentary a manner, represent additional ties to a cultural and literary world beyond Sri Lanka's shores. The numerous Arabic sections of the manuscript, almost always accompanied by detailed translations, cite the Qur'an, hadith and various works composed in Damascus, Cairo and Madina, then translated by men from Pattani, Palembang and Aceh, indicating the Sri Lankan Malays' ties to the historical heartlands of Islam and to the texts and ideas produced over generations of interactions – mutual processes of study, initiation and exchange – between those heartlands and South and Southeast Asia. The biographical information that Enci Sulaiman presents in the Compendium also reflects this history: descended from a Javanese man who travelled on the hajj to Mecca and living across the Java Sea to the northeast in Ujung Pandang, he later – for reasons unknown – continued his life in British Ceylon where he commissioned the writing of a manuscript encapsulating this tapestry of connections.

Such links, through individuals' movement across places and, equally important, through circulating texts, make it difficult to conceive of the Sri Lankan Malays in marginal or peripheral terms. Indeed, their numbers are small and they hold little political power in contemporary Sri Lanka; they are known neither to scholars nor most Indonesians today. Yet their fertile historical connections with Arab, Indonesian and Indian Muslims and their writings and practices, their own creativity in employing Malay writing and literary conventions despite a geographically separate existence from the rest of the Malay world, and their adherence to a spoken form of Malay into the twenty-first century represent a determination and sense of community that is remarkable. Perhaps the use of the Arabic script in Enci Sulaiman's manuscript is symbolic of this larger picture where crossings and contacts loom large: employed to write four different languages – Arabic, Malay, Javanese and Tamil – the script represents a standard, an equivalence across languages and communities that defies ideas of centres and margins and emphasizes the shared, the overlapping and the connected.

Acknowledgements

I wish to express my gratitude to B.D.K. Saldin for allowing me access to the Malay Compendium. I thank professor Tony H. Johns for his suggestions, and for patiently and generously discussing with me many of the Arabic and Malay texts I mention above. I thank Neilesh Bose and the two anonymous reviewers for their helpful and insightful comments on an earlier version of this article; the British Library's Endangered Archives Program for funding the manuscript documentation project (EAP 450) on which this research is based; and the Australian Research Council for supporting the writing of this article through a Distinguished Early Career Research Award.

Notes

1. Although there is evidence that some of the early exiles and servants from the areas under Dutch control in the Indonesian archipelago were non-Muslim, including those arriving from places like Bali and Ambon, the majority were likely Muslim from the start. With time this religious affiliation came to be synonymous with being Malay.
2. Nomenclature is often unstable and telling and this case forms no exception. I use Ceylon to refer specifically to the colonial possession. For the sake of convenience in most cases, I use Sri Lanka as a designation for the island and Sri Lankan Malays when discussing the community, employing the term with which they currently refer to themselves when speaking or writing in English. The appellation 'Malay' was one of several used in the past and present. The issue of nomenclature is beyond the scope of this article.
3. The Dutch United East India Company (*Vereenigde Oost-Indische Companie*) was founded in 1602 and formally dissolved in 1800 when its possessions, territory and debts were taken over

by the government of the Dutch Batavian Republic. Banishment to Ceylon was part of a much wider phenomenon of forced migration in the Company Empire. For an in-depth study of this topic, see Ward, *Networks of Empire*. Chapter 5, 179–238, 'Company and Court Politics in Java: Islam and Exile at the Cape', is particularly relevant to my discussion, dealing as it does with the cases of Javanese exiles in South Africa.

4. For the two most comprehensive books to date on the Sri Lankan Malays' history, see Hussainmiya, *Lost Cousins*; and Hussainmiya, *Orang Rejimen*.
5. For an example of a poem depicting a local event, a squabble between Malay and Bengali soldiers serving in the British army, see Hussainmiya, "Syair Kisahnya Khabar Orang Wolenter Benggali." For an analysis of a text almost unknown in Malay elsewhere (but popular in Javanese), see Ricci, "Remembering Java's Islamization."
6. For the latter theory, see Hussainmiya, *Orang Rejimen*, 51.
7. For a history of Islam in Sri Lanka, see Shukri, *Muslims of Sri Lanka*. For detailed information on three Muslim communities in Sri Lanka, including the Moors, Malays and Memons, see Hussein, *Sarandib. An Ethnological Study*, 309–408.
8. On the politics of being Muslim in Sri Lanka, see McGilvray, "Arabs, Moors and Muslims."
9. I refer to the manuscript as the Malay Compendium throughout and list it as such in the reference list.
10. Mr Saldin and his family trace their roots to Encik Pantasih, who came to Sri Lanka from Sumenep in the eastern part of Madura, Indonesia. For a family history, see Saldin, *Portrait of a Sri Lankan Malay*.
11. For example, the dating on page 227 reads: *Tamat al kalam pada hari Ahad jam pukul tuju dua puluh tuju hari bulan Rabi' awwal tersurat tatkala didalam nakari Kalambu hijrah Nasari seribu dalapan ratus tiga* (The End. [Concluded on] Sunday at seven o'clock, 27 of Rabi' awwal, written while in Colombo, in the Christian year 1803). Transliteration from sources that do not follow a standard spelling system and are written in several languages is a vexed issue. I employ current (diacritic-free) Malay spelling conventions in most cases and use diacritics for citation from Javanese and Arabic, unless a word from the latter (i.e. sura) has entered the English language.
12. *Enci* (sometimes spelt encik or ence') is a title, defined in Wilkinson's dictionary (first published 1901) as 'master; mistress'. Wilkinson, *A Malay-English Dictionary*, 303. Interestingly, a Javanese dictionary defines *enci* as a title for a non-Javanese, especially one from Bawean, Bandar, Sumatra or Malacca, or a term of address for a 'full blooded Chinese' (*Cina singkèk*), see Poerwadarminta, *Baosastra Djawa*, 123.
13. *Orang dari nakarinya Maqashar di Hujung Pandan.* Ujung Pandang was an old pre-colonial fort, captured and rebuilt by the Dutch in 1667 and renamed Fort Rotterdam. The famous Prince Diponegara who led an uprising in Java against Dutch rule in 1825–1830 was exiled to Ujung Pandang and died there. The city that developed on the site, known as Makassar, was renamed Ujung Pandang from 1971 to 1999. The two names are often used interchangeably. Makassar is currently the largest city on the island of Sulawesi.
14. Sheikh Yusuf was exiled in 1684 and remained in Sri Lanka for a decade, during which time he wrote extensively and gained a following. In 1694 he was exiled further to the Cape of Good Hope in South Africa, where he died in 1699.
15. *Turunan daripada Mas haji 'Abd Allah Jawi Mataram.* Mataram was a powerful kingdom from the late sixteenth century to the eighteenth, when it increasingly lost power and territory to the Dutch East India Company. Under Sultan Agung (r. 1613–1645) Mataram was able to expand its territory to include most of Java. It was eventually divided into two, and later three regions in the mid eighteenth century, with the royal courts of Yogyakarta and Surakarta continuing its line.
16. *Inilah risala daripada shaikh kamal mukamal yaitu daripada haji 'Abd Allah nagari Mataram.*
17. *Kitab turun daripada nagari Mataram kepada anaq muridnya jangan engkau berikan membaca kepada orang yang belum mengaji 'ilm nafas ini.*
18. Discussions of the breath (Jav. *napas*) are found, for example, in the extensive Javanese *Serat Samud* corpus. See also Zoetmulder, *Pantheism and Monism*, 142. A search for 'ilm nafas (using a variety of spellings) on the Malay Concordance Project website which documents 170 Malay texts and documents does not result in a single reference, see mcp.anu.edu.au/Q/mcp.html
19. Another name, scribbled in pencil towards the end of the manuscript, is difficult to decipher. This may be the person who either received or bought the manuscript from Enci Sulaiman, perhaps someone related to the Saldin family, the present owners of the manuscript.

20. The manuscript pages are not numbered. For the purpose of clear referencing I have numbered the pages of my copy. The sura is on page 187.
21. Pages 4, 146 and 181, respectively.
22. Page 206. On the Arabic text and its circulation in the Indonesian archipelago from the eighteenth century onwards, its Malay and Javanese adaptations, and translations of the latter, see Drewes, *Directions for Travellers*.
23. Pages 180 and 185.
24. Ekadjati et al., *Katalog Induk,* 474–5.
25. Descendants of the Bantenese prince still reside in Sri Lanka (personal communication, Faiq Doole, June 2011). See also "Arsip Berbahasa Belanda Bawa Doole Ke Sultan Banten," *Banten Pos* (2012), June 21, 2012. bantenpos-online.com/2012/06/13/arsip-berbahasa-belanda-bawa-doole-ke-sultan-banten/
26. Page 271.
27. ʻAbdallah b.'Abd al-Karīm Ba-Fadl's work is known in Java as *Bapadal* (deriving from Ba-Fadl). The Kitāb Minhāju al-Qawīm and its glosses deal with the prescriptions concerning worship (*fiqh al-'ubudiyya*); see van Bruinessen, "Kitab Kuning," 238.
28. Zakariyyā Al-Anṣārī also wrote the *Kitāb Fatḥ Al-Raḥmān*, a commentary on the above-mentioned *Risāla fī 'l-tawḥīd.* He died in Cairo in 1520. See Drewes, *Directions for Travellers*, 26–38. Another one of his works, the *Fatḥ al-wahhāb*, a commentary on his own *Manhāj al-ṭullāb*, also appears in the manuscript's list of titles. An early Malay translation of the *Fatḥ al-wahhāb*, titled *Mir'at al- ṭullāb*, was made by ʻAbd al-Ra'uf of Singkel; see van Bruinessen, "Kitab Kuning," 236.
29. Page 167. On al-Asyi see Azra, *Jaringan Ulama*, 261.
30. Page 248.
31. For a list of some of al-Sammāni's well-known disciples from the archipelago, see Azra, *Jaringan Ulama*, 261–2. These disciples often introduced their fellow countrymen to the teachings while still in Arabia; see Drewes, *Directions for Travellers*, 36–7.
32. Pages 252–7. Jilani is described using multiple honorifics as 'ḥaḍhrat Sulṭān al-ʻArifīn Burhān al'āshiqīn makhdūm Sulṭān Shāh ʻAbd al-Qādir Muḥialdīn Jīlāni raḍi Allah ʻanhu.'
33. See Schomburg, "Reviving Religion." For a list and description of the many Tamil literary works dedicated to al-Jilani, see especially, 248–99.
34. A Javanese perspective on circles of diasporic Islamic teachers and disciples appears in the eighteenth-century *Babad Giyanti*.
35. Shu'ayb ʻAlim, *Arabic, Arwi and Persian*.
36. Hussainmiya, *Lost Cousins*.
37. See, for example, Burah, *Saga of the Exiled*; Hamid, "Islam Dalam Sejarah"; and Mat Piah, "Tradisi Kesusastraan Melayu Sri Lanka."
38. For an expanded discussion of these Javanese sections, see Ricci, "The Discovery of Javanese Writing," 511–18.
39. Pages 45–6.
40. On the walis, see Rinkes, *Nine Saints of Java*.
41. On the nasalization phenomenon, see Saldin, *The Sri Lankan Malays*, 51. Suryadi, in the context of analysing a Malay letter written in early nineteenth-century Ceylon that also exhibits similar added nasalization, suggests that it may point to an author of Buginese ancestry; see Suryadi "Sepucuk Surat," 5. If true this phenomenon may offer additional evidence for the ongoing use of languages other than Malay in the community and to the ways these may have mingled and altered one another.
42. Florida, *Writing the Past*, 90.
43. Pages 266–7.
44. Thus the first series of numerals is telungpuluh siji, telungpuluh dua [another error, should be telungpuluh loro but the Malay word dua, 'two,' is used rather than the Javanese loro], telungpuluh telu, etc. In the repeat series tigangpuluh siji, tigangpuluh dua [as above], tigangpuluh telu etc. appears. Thirty in high Javanese should be tigangdasa rather than tigangpuluh; 31 should be tigangdasa setunggal, etc.
45. Page 181.
46. This world view had roots in both the pre-Islamic Javanese past and the world of Islam. Perhaps most well known in this context is the powerful deity Nyai Rara Kidul – Goddess of

the Southern Ocean – the supernatural spouse and patron of the kings of Java. Ricklefs, *The Seen and Unseen Worlds*, 1–2.

47. *Lapal* are texts comprising Arabic prayers, formulas and spells.
48. The term *gundhul* (bald) is used in Java to refer to the Javanese language written in an unvocalized form of the Arabic script, whereas the more common and vocalized Arabic script used to write Javanese is known as *pégon*. Interestingly, Sri Lankan Malays have retained a Javanese term yet they use it to describe Malay writing. This may attest to the dominance of Javanese among the early exiles.
49. In other instances – and this is true for Javanese manuscripts – Arabic quotes or phrases were written in the traditional Javanese script known as *aksara Jawa* and used concurrently with gundul/pégon over several centuries. Tamil Muslims too continued to employ the Tamil script in their writings. The case of Malay differs. Although a variety of scripts were used to write Malay in Southeast Asia, with Islamization the Arabic script gradually came to dominate while older scripts disappeared. On the recent discovery of a rare Malay manuscript written in a pre-Islamic script, see Kozok, *The Tanjung Tanah Code*.
50. Hussainmiya describes the compulsory jawi lessons given to Malay children whose fathers served in the Ceylon Rifle Regiment of the British Army.

Bibliography

"Arsip Berbahasa Belanda Bawa Doole Ke Sultan Banten." *Banten Pos*. June 21, 2012. Accessed June 27, 2012. http://bantenpos-online.com/2012/06/13/arsip-berbahasa-belanda-bawa-doole-ke-sultan-banten/

Azra, Azyumardi. *Jaringan Ulama: Timur Tengah Dan Kepulauan Nusantara Abad Xvii Dan XVIII*. Bandung: Mizan, 1999.

Burah, Tuan Arifin. *Saga of the Exiled Royal Javanese Unearthed*. Dehiwala: Tuan Arifin Burah, 2006.

Drewes, G. W. J. *Directions for Travellers on the Mystic Path: Zakariyyā Al-Anṣārī's Kitāb Fatḥ Al-Raḥmān and Its Indonesian Adaptations*. vol. 81. Verhandelingen Van Het Koninklijk Instituut Voor Taal-, Land- En Volkenkunde. The Hague: Martinus Nijhoff, 1977.

Ekadjati, Edi S., A. Undang, and Darsa, eds. *Katalog Induk Naskah-Naskah Nusantara. Jawa Barat:Koleksi Lima Lembaga*. Jakarta: Yayasan Obor Indonesia, 1990.

Florida, Nancy K. *Writing the Past, Inscribing the Future: History as Prophecy in Colonial Java*. Durham: Duke University Press, 1995.

Hamid, Ismail. "Islam Dalam Sejarah Dan Masyarakat Melayu Sri Lanka." *Sari* 9 (1991): 25–41.

Hussainmiya, B. A. *Lost Cousins: The Malays of Sri Lanka*. Bangi: Universiti Kebangsaan Malaysia, 1987.

Hussainmiya, B. A. *Orang Rejimen. The Malays of the Ceylon Rifle Regiment*. Bangi: Universiti Kebangsaan Malaysia, 1990.

Hussainmiya, B. A. "Syair Kisahnya Khabar Orang Wolenter Benggali: A Sri Lankan Malay Syair, Introduction and Text." *Sari* 5 (1987): 17–49.

Hussein, Asiff. *Sarandib. An Ethnological Study of the Muslims of Sri Lanka*. Dehiwala: A.J Prints, 2007.

Kozok, Uli. *The Tanjung Tanah Code of Law: The Oldest Extant Malay Manuscript*. Cambridge: St Catharine's College and the University Press, 2004.

Malay Compendium. *Collection of B.D.K. Saldin*. Sri Lanka: Malay Compendium, 1803–1831.

"Malay Concordance Project." Accessed April 20, 2013. http://mcp.anu.edu.au/Q/mcp.html

Mat Piah, Harun. "Tradisi Kesusastraan Melayu Sri Lanka Dalam Konteks Kesusastraan Melayu Tradisional Nusantara: Satu Tinjauan Ringkas." *Sari* 4, no. 2 (1986): 63–82.

McGilvray, Dennis B. "Arabs, Moors and Muslims: Sri Lankan Muslim Ethnicity in Regional Perspective." *Contributions to Indian Sociology* 32, no. 2 (1998): 433–483.

Poerwadarminta, W. J. S. *Baosastra Djawa*. Groningen: J.B. Wolters, 1939.

Ricci, Ronit. "The Discovery of Javanese Writing in a Sri Lankan Malay Manuscript." *Bijdragen tot de-Taal, Land-, en Volkenkunde* 168, no. 4 (2012): 511–518.

Ricci, Ronit. "Remembering Java's Islamization: A View from Sri Lanka." In *Global Islam in the Age of Print and Steam 1850–1930,* edited by Nile Green and James Gelvin. Los Angeles: University of California Press, 2014.

Ricklefs, Merle C. *The Seen and Unseen Worlds in Java. History, Literature and Islam in the Court of Pakubuwana II 1726–1749*. Honolulu: Asian Studies Association of Australia and University of Hawai'i Press, 1998.

Rinkes, D. A. *Nine Saints of Java*. 1910–1913. Translated and edited by H. M. Froger. Kuala Lumpur: Malaysian Sociological Research Institute, 1996.

Saldin, B.D.K. *Portrait of a Sri Lankan Malay*. Dehiwala: B.D.K. Saldin, 2003.

Saldin, B.D.K. *The Sri Lankan Malays and Their Language. Orang Melayu Sri Lanka dan Bahasannya*. Kurunegala: B.D.K. Saldin, 2001.

Schomburg, Susan Elizabeth. "'Reviving Religion': The Qadiri Sufi Order, Popular Devotion to Sufi Saint Muhyiuddin 'Abdul Qadir Al-Gilani, and Processes of 'Islamization' in Tamil." PhD diss., Harvard, 2003.

Shu'ayb 'Alim, Takya. *Arabic, Arwi and Persian in Sarandib and Tamil Nadu*. Madras: Imāmul 'Arūs Trust, 1993.

Shukri, M. A. M. *Muslims of Sri Lanka: Avenues to Antiquity*. Beruwala: Jamiah Naleemia Institute, 1986.

Suryadi, M. A. "Sepucuk Surat Dari Seorang Bangsawan Gowa Di Tanah Pembuangan (Ceylon)." *Wacana: Jurnal ilmu Pengetahuan Budaya* 10, no. 2 (2008): 214–243.

van Bruinessen, Martin. "Kitab Kuning: Books in Arabic Script Used in the Pesantren Milieu." *Bijdragen tot de Taal-, Land- en Volkenkunde* 146 (1990): 226–269.

Ward, Kerry. *Networks of Empire: Forced Migration in the Dutch East India Company*. Cambridge: Cambridge University Press, 2009.

Wilkinson, R. J. *A Malay-English Dictionary*. 2 vols., 1901. London: Macmillan, 1959.

Zoetmulder, P. J. *Pantheism and Monism in Javanese Suluk Literature: Islamic and Indian Mysticism in an Indonesian Setting*. Translated and edited by Merle C. Ricklefs. Leiden: Kitlv, 1995.

Can 'Om' be an Islamic term? Translations, encounters, and Islamic discourse in vernacular South Asia

Torsten Tschacher

Centre for Modern Indian Studies, University of Göttingen, Göttingen, Germany

This article aims at offering a critique of recent approaches to the study of vernacular Islamic literature in South Asia through examples taken from Islamic literature composed in Tamil. First, the article argues that many approaches tend to re-inscribe essentialised religious differences by assuming that specific religious meanings underlie the semantics of a given language. This tendency ignores that both Arabic as well as South Asian vernaculars were employed in multi-religious environments long before Islamic vernacular literature came to be composed in any of these languages. Second, the article seeks to challenge the assumption that the prime aim of vernacular literature was didactic, i.e., that it was composed for the sole purpose of educating a population largely ignorant of religious tenets in Islam. This has led scholars to overemphasize the constraints under which authors composed texts and to ignore the importance of aesthetics in the production of vernacular Islamic literature. Third, the article critiques the portrayal of vernacular Muslim authors as isolated individuals grappling with a non-Muslim environment. Rather, it suggests that many authors responded to other Muslims communicating in the same vernacular, forming a network of poets and texts following similar conventions. In conclusion, the article argues for understanding vernacular Islamic discourse in South Asia as expression of an 'Indic' Islam rather than of an uneasy encounter between Islam and Hinduism.

Introduction

'Can Savitri be a Muslim name?' Encapsulated in this seemingly innocent question is one of the most persistent debates in contemporary Muslim societies as well as among academics studying the Islamic World, namely the problem of the relationship between the universalist claims of Islamic discourse and its specific expressions in idioms particular to a certain time and space. Posing this question in December 2000 in the headline of a short article published by the Bangalore-based English monthly *Islamic Voice*, the author of that article was obviously aware that there was no clear answer to whether Savitri could be a Muslim name or not, for in reply to the question he noted: 'Certainly not in India. But Muslim Indonesians have plenty of Savitris, Gayathris, Leelas, Pushpas, and even Seetas among themselves'.[1] When I first came across this article, it seemed to sum up my own experiences at that time. Having arrived in Singapore to do my PhD in January 2003, I was astonished at the ease with which Muslims in Southeast Asia were using Sanskrit-derived words and phrases such as *guru agama Islam*, 'Islamic religious teacher', which would have engendered heated discussions among Muslims as well as students of Muslim societies in South Asia. How was it possible that something Indonesian Muslims apparently considered being normal was so contested in India?

The wider question of how to make sense of the 'Indic' or even 'Hindu' terminology and imagery encountered in Muslim vernaculars of South Asia has inspired discussions about the 'accommodation', 'rooting', and 'localization' of Islamic traditions in many local South Asian contexts. Earlier scholarship had responded to the presence of the 'local' in vernacular South Asian Islamic texts with the idea of syncretism. Islam, in this perspective, had become 'permeated by indigenous elements' in India,[2] elements that were assumed to be often in conflict with 'orthodox' Islam. The result appeared, depending on the observer, either as a skilful blend of two separate traditions or as a dilution of 'pure' Islam. Conveniently, the idea of 'syncretism' could be applied to literary culture as much as to ritual practice or kinship patterns. Yet in the last two decades, this notion has increasingly been seen as untenable and new models have begun to develop. The most sophisticated models that have been formulated so far have come from translation theory.[3]

In this paper, I will utilize examples from Islamic Tamil literature to interrogate the assumptions which have guided the application of translation theory to other vernacular Islamic literatures of South Asia. This critique is aimed at three aspects of these scholarly approaches. First, I will question the tendency of scholarship to invest terms and images with certain fixed and religiously specific meanings, especially notable in the tendency to reduce 'Indic' elements in texts to 'Hinduism', rather than noting their often multiple religious and non-religious valences.[4] Not only has this led scholars to read their own understandings and evaluations into vernacular Islamic poetry, it has also obscured the degree of agency exercised by poets in their choice of vocabulary and imagery. Secondly, the paper will critique the assumption that the main purpose of vernacular Islamic texts was didactic, i.e., that the transmission of information to an audience ignorant of Arabic and Persian was the prime concern of these texts, and that therefore 'translation' in these contexts was primarily a search for semantic equivalences constrained by the language and knowledge of the audience. I will argue that poetic and literary choices rather than semantic constraints occasioned many of the instances of translation encountered in vernacular Islamic literature in South Asia. Finally, the paper will argue that scholarship has tended to portray vernacular Islamic texts as the products of isolated Muslim authors grappling ever anew with the task of putting Islamic discourse into South Asian vernaculars.[5] In the process, the degree to which Muslim authors communicated with other Muslims writing in the same languages and utilized a shared set of conventions and poetics has been obscured. All in all, I wish to argue that greater attention to vernacular aesthetics and poetics and the values attached to different vernacular idioms is necessary to gain any understanding of the process of 'translating' Islamic discourse into South Asian vernaculars.

Hindu notions or South Asian concepts? Confusing meaning and religion

The roots of Islamic Tamil literature lie in the sixteenth century (the tenth century of the Hijra). In the two hundred and seventy years between the composition of the oldest extant Islamic text in Tamil, the *Āyiramacalā*, in 1572 and the first printing of an Islamic text in Tamil in 1842, poets and scholars created a sizeable corpus of poems and prose texts. This corpus includes highly ornate narrative poetry, songs on 'supreme knowledge' (*meyññāṉam*), often dubbed 'Sufi poetry' in secondary literature, transcripts of oral ballads, and doctrinal treatises.[6] Before proceeding to discuss the questions raised in this paper, let me shortly justify referring to this body of texts as 'Islamic'. Peter

Gottschalk has called attention to the dangers of applying classifications such as 'Hinduism' and 'Islam' without questioning and being aware of the presuppositions which attach to these labels.[7] Using the term 'Islamic' for a whole body of texts indeed seems to come perilously close to arriving at foregone conclusions through the choice of a descriptive label. The reason why I chose to use that label, though, is not simply because the texts in question exhibit certain traits and topics, but because they explicitly and repeatedly align themselves to something they call 'Islam'. Consider the following stanza from the most celebrated of these poems, Umaṟuppulavar's *Cīṟāppurāṇam* of ca. 1700, which describes the conversion of a certain King Ḥabīb of Damascus and his retinue:

> Without ceasing the daily worship according to the custom of scripture,
>
> Venerating God, studying without deficiency the straight path of Islam,
>
> And giving up unbelief that seems attractive but causes only hardships,[8]
>
> They became excellent Muslims unfailing in conduct.[9]

This stanza, like many others that could be quoted, draws a clear demarcation line between 'Islam' (Tamil *iculām*) and 'Muslim' (Tamil *mucilim*) on the one hand, defined through ritual practice and scriptural injunctions, and 'unbelief' (Tamil *kupir*, from Arabic *kufr*) on the other.[10] The alignment of the *Cīṟāppurāṇam* and other Tamil texts with Islam and Muslims justifies in my opinion to call this corpus 'Islamic'. Admittedly, it would be more correct to call this body of texts 'Dīnic', as *tīṉ* (from Arabic *dīn*) is even more commonly used by the texts than 'Islam'. But as these terms appear to be interchangeable,[11] and as 'Islam' is the more recognizable of the two, I opted for 'Islamic'. It should be noted that I do not want to imply by this that each Islamic Tamil text could and should be discussed only in reference to the fact that it is 'Islamic' in this sense. Rather, this note serves to highlight that any discussion which draws on these texts with reference to the category of 'Islam', even if it is to challenge the validity and usefulness of this category, needs to be cognizant of the fact that the texts self-align themselves with such a category.

The most common approach to this corpus of texts has been to stress its supposedly 'local' character to such an extent that almost all other considerations are excluded. While there is no doubt that in diction, imagery and the use of literary convention, Islamic Tamil literature certainly does follow the general rules of Tamil poets regardless of religion, this is hardly surprising and could be said of almost any Islamic literature (including, for example, Persian). The deeper problem with this characterization lies in the strong binary between the 'local' and the 'non-local' that many studies assume and the assumptions about this bifurcation that colour the discussion.[12] As I have noted elsewhere, this tendency to stress the 'local' character of Islamic Tamil literature has mainly served to buttress narratives demonstrating the harmonious inclusivism of Tamil literary culture. Rather than investigating what 'Islamic' meant for the authors of such texts, scholarship has been content with asserting that the 'Islamic' discourse of these texts has not disrupted the unity of Tamil literary culture.[13]

The most common method of demonstrating the adherence of Islamic Tamil texts to local traditions of poetics is by pointing out the use of Tamil words, phrases and imagery in reference to Islamic discourse – in a sense, it consists in pointing out how Islamic discourse is translated or 'rooted…in a Tamil conceptual world'.[14] Noting the use of 'Indic' and other 'local' tropes and idioms in Islamic discourse has been at the root of anxieties over whether a name like Savitri could be a Muslim name as well as the scholarly conceptualization of vernacular Islamic literature as translation. Consider Tony

Stewart's seminal article concerning the use of translation theory in conceptualizing what he calls the 'Muslim-Hindu encounter' in Bengal. Distinguishing his approach from earlier models of syncretism, Stewart proposes:

> ...that we can reconstruct a process by which the premodern Sufi or other Muslim writer, working within the constraints of a Bengali language whose extant technical vocabulary was conditioned largely by Hindu ideational constructs, attempted to imagine an Islamic ideal in a new literary environment. These texts become, then, historical witnesses to the earliest attempts to think Islamic thoughts in the local language, which is to say, to think new thoughts for Bengali, ideas that had never previously been explicitly expressed, otherwise there probably would have been an explicit vocabulary to support them, as there now is.[15]

Through the backdoor of language, Stewart's argument reintroduces some of the problems he had identified with models of syncretism, namely that they 'presuppose essentialized, dehistoricized, monolithic entities'.[16] To say that Bengali was 'conditioned largely by Hindu ideational constructs' and could not have been 'pure in exclusively Islamic terms' because of its Sanskritic roots, while after the eighteenth century, 'a technical terminology derived from Persian and Arabic' would replace Bengali words, ostensibly to provide an 'explicit vocabulary' for Islamic discourse, comes very close to state that Bengali is 'essentially' Hindu while Arabic and Persian are 'essentially' Islamic – something that presupposes an essentialised Islam and Hinduism as well.[17] In reality, both Arabic and Indian languages are religiously plural, having been employed for expressing Jainism, Buddhism, Christianity, Judaism, and Arabic polytheism as well as Hinduism and Islam.

The precise point is that whether authors and audiences consider a language as proper for some sort of religious discourse does not lie in its 'ideational constructs' but in the values attached to the language by historically contingent actors. For many scholars of North India, Persian's status as an Islamic language seems to be unquestionable. Few of them seem to know the invective against the Persian language by none other than the famous scholar Abū al-Raiḥān al-Bīrūnī (973–1048), who described Persian in his book on pharmacology not only as unfit for scientific purposes, but as a veritable danger to Islam and the Caliphate.[18] Not everyone considered Persian with its Zoroastrian and Manichean ancestry a fit medium for Islamic discourse. The awareness that ultimately Persian had no more claims to be 'Islamic' than any other language apart from Arabic was even present among Bengalis, despite the obvious anxieties displayed by Bengali authors to use their own language for Islamic discourse. The celebrated Saiyad Sultān legitimized his use of Bengali in his *Nabīvaṃśa* by depicting Persian as another medium, just like Javanese (*yāvā*) or Tamil (*coliyā*), through which a non-Arabic-speaking population could learn about the Quran.[19]

When we shift our attention to Tamil, the problematic character of Stewart's formulations becomes even more apparent. From Stewart's arguments, it becomes clear that he speaks about situations where authors used either an Arabic term or a Bengali one, but not both together. In contrast, Tamil authors seem to revel in utilizing as many different words for the same concept as they could in close proximity to each other. For example, in *Cīṟāppurāṇam* 1.4.14–16, the beings generally known as 'angels' in English are labelled in turn by the Sanskrit-derived term *amarar*, the Arabic-derived *malakku*, and the Tamil *vāṉavar*. In such a situation, how would one determine which term was semantically dominant: *amarar* with its etymological connection to deathlessness, *malakku*, which seems to derive from a Hebrew word meaning messenger, or *vāṉavar*, 'celestials'? Maybe, the author was aware of all these meanings, or only of some? In any case, he does not seem to have perceived any of these terms to be contradictory to Islam.

This case may alert us to another danger when talking about instances of translation in vernacular Islamic texts. Many scholars seem to think that translation is a two-dimensional process, comprising a translated and a translating idiom. What gets overlooked in this case is that there is a third dimension, namely, what the scholar thinks the terms in the translated and translating languages actually mean in English.[20] Consider the case of the terms *vētam* and *maṟai*, used in Islamic Tamil literature to refer to the revealed scriptures of Islam. While Paula Richman rendered *maṟai* into English as 'revealed texts', Vasudha Narayanan preferred the translation 'Vedas', due to the etymology of the synonymous term *vētam*.[21] It becomes immediately obvious how the choice of English translation predisposes a reader differently to the original Tamil text, for 'revealed texts' seem unobtrusive in an Islamic poem, the 'Vedas' on the other hand appear as rather misplaced. Narayanan's decision to use this translation gives the impression that Muslim authors aimed at setting up a direct analogy between a specific corpus of early Sanskrit texts and the revelations of the Muslim God. But as Narayanan herself shows, by the seventeenth century, thinking about the Veda in the Tamil country had gone a long way towards establishing it as a kind of text with particular characteristics rather than a predefined corpus.[22] She lists some of these characteristics in her discussion: some schools considered it to be authored by God and therefore being infallible, while others stressed that it was eternal and authorless. She concludes: 'Calling the Qur'an a Veda, therefore, includes at least some of these meanings as understood in Hindu writings'.[23] The problem is that to understand the Qur'an as 'infallible', 'eternal', and 'trans-human' is precisely what Sunnī 'orthodoxy' does across the Muslim world. It is indeed no surprise that Muslims seized upon the term *vētam* and have maintained its use until this day: the Tamil translation of the Quran sanctioned by the Ministry of Hajj and Religious Endowments of Saudi Arabia translates the first words of Quran 2.2., *dhālik al-kitāb* ('this is the book') with *itu vētamākum* ('this is *vētam*').[24] Under these conditions, one wonders how to identify specifically 'Hindu' meanings in the use of the term *vētam* by Muslims.

As Stewart himself rightly notes,[25] the translation of Islamic discourse into a South Asian language was actually made possible by the fact that terms were present in these languages which shared much of the conceptual content of Islamic discourse, and we may add that in most cases, translated Arabic terms themselves hardly had only one clearly demarcated meaning. It is important to stress that the semantic fields of most Tamil terms which were adopted in Islamic Tamil literature already had a fairly wide and general application across different religious formations; the tendency to see all South Asian terminology as inherently bound up with 'Hinduism' blinds us to the fact that the extension of a term to translate a Muslim concept was, after all, a completely normal act. A given term may actually have crossed religious boundaries earlier – simply compare the common use of the genre-term *purāṇam* in Śaiva, Vaiṣṇava, and Jain contexts before it was applied to Muslim texts. As the examples given suggest, scholars need to pay careful attention to the whole semantic range of a given term and refrain from identifying specific religions with specific languages on the basis of essentialising assumptions. Yet understanding the semantics of a term, of what it means, is fundamentally tied up to another question, namely, to the term's pragmatics, that is to how and for what purpose is it deployed.

Constraints or choices? The pragmatics of translation

Words and images do not 'mean' in isolation, but rather receive their particular meanings only in relation to context. That Muslim authors are not referring to the Sanskrit Vedas but rather to the revealed scriptures of Islamic history when they use the term *vētam* becomes obvious when one considers the contexts in which this term is used, such as the Caliph Uthmān's efforts to collect Quranic revelations. Given that the importance of the pragmatics of terminology and imagery is obvious, it is actually surprising how little effort scholars have invested to study this pragmatics. In his discussion of the process he calls 'identification', Richard Eaton notes how Bengali Muslim authors 'identified' the Muslim God with different local entities, of which he names for example *prabhu* ('lord'), *nirañjan* ('the one without qualities'), *īśvar* ('lord'), *jagat īśvar* ('lord of the universe'), and *kartā* ('creator').[26] One is immediately struck by the fact that the terms listed are hardly personal names which are applied only to a single deity, but rather descriptive epithets which were applied to several deities together even before Muslims began to use them. As such, it is difficult to see in how far any sort of 'identification' of the Muslim God with a local deity was intended in the first place. Rather, one might argue that the use of these terms by Muslims is another example of what Eaton has called 'displacement', namely, contesting the right of other religious groups to utilize these terms for their own purposes by appropriating them in a Muslim context.[27]

In her excellent study of translation in the Arabic cosmopolis of the Indian Ocean, Ronit Ricci has documented what appears to be precisely such an instance of displacement. Focusing on terms with the basic meaning of 'melting' or 'dissolving', she notes that these terms, which have positive connotations in Tamil Śaiva literature, are employed in the Muslim text most commonly 'in the realm of sheer human terror and suffering', especially in the context of the tortures non-Muslims will have to endure in hell. It seems likely that the author of the *Āyiramacalā* intended a deliberate comment on Śaiva imagery: those who 'melt' for Śiva will ultimately come to 'melt' in hell-fire.[28] Thus, while the text seems to use the same vocabulary as Śaiva texts did, it used them in significantly different ways.

A tendency of many models for understanding vernacular Islamic discourse is to explain this discourse by pointing out constraints which allegedly conditioned authors to produce the texts they did. Earlier models of 'syncretism' tended to blame either the ignorance of the author, whose limited knowledge of Islam made him or her utilize 'Un-Islamic' terms and images, or the ignorance of the audience, who would not understand what was being said if it would not be put into their terms.[29] But the same pattern of explanation is found in studies stressing 'translation' over 'syncretism'. For all his criticism of the value judgments inherent in concepts like 'syncretism', Stewart seems strangely apologetic regarding the choices Bengali authors made in translating Islamic concepts, for he keeps on stressing that the authors were actually constrained by the 'Hindu ideational constructs' which were inherent in Bengali vocabulary. Furthermore he inserts this into a historical narrative consisting of two phases: an earlier one until the eighteenth century characterized by 'the initial experiments of these innovative and adventurous authors' to struggle with the constraints of expressing Islam through Bengali vocabulary, and a later phase when 'a technical terminology derived from Persian and Arabic would take its place in the Bengali of the Muslim author' and the earlier constraints apparently vanished.[30] Thus, while defending the early Bengali Muslim authors, Stewart still apparently feels the need to explain why they tried to express Islamic discourse through Bengali, and to somehow exonerate them from possible criticism by stressing that the constraints imposed by Bengali did not allow them to do differently. Once the massive borrowing of Arabo-Persian terminology became feasible, it was employed, seemingly indicating a sort of provisionality of the earlier practice.

The uneasiness with which scholarship treats vernacular Islamic discourse, namely, as a problem to be explained rather than as an expected phenomenon to be understood, again demonstrates to what degree presuppositions about what is 'proper' from an 'Islamic' point of view colour even those models which attempt to break loose from such presuppositions. For a closer look at the texts we are studying reveals that in many cases, we seem to be dealing with conscious authorial choices rather than with constraints. As part of a possibly seventeenth-century poem entitled *Ñāṉappukaḻcci* ('Praise of Knowledge'), the first Tamil 'Sufi poet', Takkalai Pīrmuhammatu, provided what may be the earliest extant 'translation' of a Quranic text into a South Asian vernacular, a rendering of the first chapter of the Quran, *Sūrat al-fātiḥa*. The text consists simply of a long list of vocatives, in which God is addressed in terms that indicate the meaning of the Quranic words:

> O you who perceives the situation of those who search for much good support
>
> And removes their grief, as they say: '*wa iyyāka nasta'īn*'.[31]

The meaning of the Arabic words, 'and you we ask for help' (Quran 1.5) is indicated by showing God's response to those who utter these words. The rest of the chapter is rendered similarly, with minimal use of Arabic vocabulary outside the actual quotation of the Quranic text. At the same time, the comments adhere closely to the common Muslim interpretation of the *Sūrat al-fātiḥa*. This poem is a good example that Tamil poets were able to render even a Quranic text into Tamil without facing too many constraints. Precisely for this reason, the rendering of the final words of verse 7 of *Sūrat al-fātiḥa*, 'and not those who go astray' (*wa lā al-ḍāllīn*), is all the more surprising. For the *ḍāllūn* are actually described in Tamil as 'those who miss your way without perceiving the lights inside the [syllable] *ōm*'.[32] There is no reason to believe that Pīrmuhammatu was constrained by the level of understanding of his audience in his choice of words – after all, he rendered the rest of the Quranic text without such seemingly 'Hindu' elements. A reference to the syllable *ōm* in an Islamic text may appear problematic to a twenty-first-century observer, but that is immaterial in the context. What needs to be understood is that it was apparently not problematic for Pīrmuhammatu and his intended audience – for them, *ōm* could be an Islamic term, much as Savitri can be a Muslim name for Indonesians.[33]

The question of how Muslim authors translated Islamic discourse into South Asian vernaculars actually needs to be supplemented by the question for what purpose they were translated. Many seem to assume that translation primarily had a didactic purpose, that Islamic discourse was translated so that those who could not access it in Arabic or Persian would still be able to participate in it. Otherwise, it seems, no translation would be necessary. There is no doubt that didacticism played an important role in the composition of many a vernacular text. But it is surprising to what degree the very presence of vernacular literatures in the Muslim World is actually explained by the need to provide information on Islam to the ignorant masses. In the South Asian context, these assumptions are often tied into a narrative of the spread of Islamic discourse among the 'simple folk' of India by Sufi poetry.[34] Vernacular literature in this account serves the singular purpose of teaching simplified and 'translated' versions of Islam to largely ignorant, non-elite populations.

Yet there are some fundamental problems with this association of translation and didacticism. Perhaps the most obvious indicator that something is amiss in this interpretation is the fact that the texts which are most openly didactic are often also the texts which display the least amount of 'translation' in the sense of the complex transposition of imagery, terminology and discourse described by Stewart. Discussions usually focus on the most striking examples of vernacular translation, such as esoteric poetry. At the same time, texts which deal with daily worship or religious law have received much less attention. If the main aim of translating Islamic discourse into Indic terminology and imagery had been transmission of information to an otherwise ignorant population, one would expect precisely these texts to show the greatest amount of such translation – after all, Islamic ritual or law is not necessarily conceptually closer to South Asian terminology than esoteric thought. But at least as far as Tamil is concerned, the Tamil texts which most directly and explicitly translate Arabic discourse for those who did not understand it were also the least 'localized' in terms of imagery and other features. Theological prose texts can often be identified even visually as translations: the copy of the tract *'Iẓām al-fawā'id fī niẓām al-'aqā'id* contained in Leiden University Manuscript OR-7368 makes the succession of Arabic text and Tamil translation visible through the use of red ink for Arabic and black ink for Tamil passages. While even such 'Arabic-Tamil' texts utilize Tamil vocabulary to render Arabic terms, they still follow the Arabic original so closely that it even impacts Tamil syntax. There is little trace in these texts of the elaborate imagery of Tamil poetry that suffuses elite poems such as the *Cīṟāppurāṇam*. Similarly, Bengali texts relating to basic ethical and ritual duties of a Muslim do not seem to be particularly noteworthy for their use of vernacular terminology and imagery; Asim Roy deliberately ignored such texts in his study on 'Islamic Syncretism' because they 'closely conformed to standard Islamic prescriptions'.[35] If 'translation' into Indic terms and images on the one hand and didacticism on the other were two sides of the same coin, why is it that the most basic didactic texts seem to contain comparatively little 'localization' of terminology and imagery?

Of course, not all didactic Islamic literature refrained from using 'translation' in the wider sense of rendering concepts of Middle Eastern Islamic discourse through the vocabulary, imagery, and textual conventions of South Asian languages. Such texts do exist. The oldest Islamic poem in Tamil, the *Āyiramacalā*, in which the Prophet answers the questions of a Jewish scholar, clearly had a didactic purpose. In 1708, the German missionary Bartholomäus Ziegenbalg reported that this text was memorized by children in Muslim schools, indicating that it was indeed utilized as a medium of instruction.[36] But even this text is not only composed in the poetic idiom of 'refined Tamil' (*centamiḻ*) that by the sixteenth century was already quite far removed from the colloquial Tamil of everyday life. It also utilized the literary embellishments and terse allusions common to elite Tamil poetry, and this tendency is far more pronounced in the narrative poetry and devotional songs which were produced during the following three hundred years. Yet it is unlikely that the majority of these poems were meant to educate ignorant Muslims about basic principles of Islam or supply the basics concerning the life of a prophet or saint. A.K. Ramanujan has noted in a celebrated essay that '[i]n India and Southeast Asia, no one ever reads the Rāmāyaṇa or the Mahābhārata for the first time. The stories are there, 'always already''.[37] Similarly, the biography of the Prophet or the events of Karbala did not have to be narrated to Tamil Muslims for a 'first' time through an ornate poem in difficult language. Islamic Tamil poetry was obviously directed largely at an audience capable of decoding the complex literary idiom of elevated Tamil poetry and of making sense of even the most 'opaque' reference.[38] I would therefore disagree with Ronit Ricci,[39] who argued that such allusions in the *Āyiramacalā* had a didactic purpose, and rather assume that, much as in Hindu poetry, they were a sign of erudition of the author and those in the audience who could decode them. In fact, Muslim scholars of the nineteenth century were well aware that the refined narrative poetry of the Tamil tradition was hardly a useful medium for the transmission of information. 'Māppiḷḷai Leppai' Sayyid Muḥammad b. Aḥmad (1816–1898) lamented in his *Hadyāmālai* in 1869 that nothing resulted from the mere recitation of poetry (*kāviyam*).[40] The Ceylonese reformer M.C. Siddi Lebbe (1838–1898) was even more explicit in his criticism of traditional Islamic Tamil poetry:

> Our poets and Tamil-scholars should note: If they were to write and publish in Tamil the necessary sciences contained in many languages *in a manner that everyone can understand them*, rather than to think that it is their duty to comment on the songs of poets who came before them, to turn commentaries into songs, and to sing songs and poems, it would mean fame for them and benefit for the Muslims.[41]

These examples should suffice to indicate the dangers of perceiving 'translation' solely from the perspective of the transmission of information about Islamic discourse to newly Islamized audiences. This perspective perpetuates a negative evaluation of Islamic textual cultures in South Asian vernaculars by reducing the process of translation to the constrained attempts of poets obliged to use problematic non-Islamic terminology and imagery in order to transmit information to ignorant audiences. Yet the way 'translated' terms and imagery are utilized in Islamic Tamil literature points towards a different aspect, that of convention and aesthetics. To discuss these topics, it will be necessary to bring the vernacular textual cultures of Muslim South Asia back into history, as I shall argue in the next and final section.

New thoughts or old conventions? Erasing the history of textual cultures

Perhaps the most striking aspect of many discussions of Islamic texts produced in South Asian languages is the curiously ahistorical nature of the arguments. It seems to be assumed that vernacular Islamic texts from South Asia arose from a situation in which authors were actively creating the terminology and imagery they were utilizing. As mentioned, Stewart claims that the texts he was investigating were 'historical witnesses to the earliest attempts to think Islamic thoughts in the local language, which is to say, to think new thoughts for Bengali, ideas that had never previously been explicitly expressed'.[42] Similar ideas have been expressed for Tamil. The anonymous *Ceytakkātinoṇṭināṭakam* has been described as '*an attempt to develop* a vocabulary appropriate to the context'.[43] The specific vernacular Islamic text in question is highlighted as an unmediated encounter between Muslim thought and non-Muslim vernacular literary tradition, in which the individual poet is credited with innovatively creating or developing the specific Islamic instantiation of vernacular vocabulary and imagery.

These claims are ahistorical in so far as they result in two erasures with rather problematic consequences, both of which are encapsulated in the term 'encounter'. An 'encounter' suggests, firstly, that two or more entities come into sudden contact where there was no contact before. And secondly, an encounter implies a singular event, not a process. The first consequence of perceiving vernacular Islamic textual cultures as the outcome of an 'encounter' is to erase the simple fact that by the time these texts came into being, Muslims and non-Muslims had long lived cheek by jowl in the cities and towns of South Asia. Communities of Muslims speaking a specific South Asian language often came into being a substantial amount of time before the first text on an Islamic topic was written down in that language. For example, inscriptions in Tamil referring to Muslim places of worship date back to the times of the Pāṇḍya-dynasty in the twelfth and thirteenth century, while the first known literary text was composed only in 1572.[44] To claim, then, as Stewart has done, that any written text is a first attempt to think Islamic thoughts in a South Asian language sounds difficult to believe. How did Muslims talk about their religion in a local vernacular if the terminology for that would only be developed by some poet writing centuries later? Even in those cases where Muslims were fundamentally involved in actually creating the idiom in which the texts were written down, as for example in the case of the Avadhi *premākhyāns*, these texts emerged into a world where Muslims had been part of wider society for generations.[45]

The second consequence is to ignore that the texts we are talking about did not exist in isolation, though significantly, this is how they are usually presented to us. When Umaṟuppulavar composed the *Cīṟāppurāṇam* around 1700, not only was it not the first attempt to think Islamic discourse in Tamil, it was not even the first attempt to write such discourse down. Umaṟuppulavar clearly drew on the works of other authors who had come before him. The vocabulary and imagery of the *Cīṟāppurāṇam* was not developed by Umaṟuppulavar, but had been in existence since at least a century. Already the two earliest Islamic poems in Tamil, the *Āyiramacalā* of 1572 and the *Mikuṟācumālai* of 1590, exhibit the same features. It is clear that Islamic Tamil literature does not consist of isolated attempts by similarly isolated authors to produce Muslim inflections of a single Tamil literary culture, though this is how their efforts have usually been presented. Islamic Tamil texts have mostly been discussed in relationship not to each other, but to a supposedly unified corpus of Tamil literature which transcended religious identities. This tendency is exacerbated by the fact that much of the secondary literature, in English at any rate, deals with singular and isolated texts rather than with the literary networks formed by these texts and their authors. This has generated an image of a unified and multi-religious Tamil literary culture to which Muslims strove to contribute, rather than to take note of the way the common language of Tamil poetics served to contest and demarcate religious communities.[46] Conventions shared by the vast majority of Islamic poems in Tamil, but not present in the same form in non-Islamic literature, indicate that Muslim authors more often than not drew on other Islamic texts rather than on non-Islamic ones. This was clearly expressed in the early-eighteenth century by the author of the poem *Tirumaṇakkāṭci*, who described himself as someone 'who listened to have an ear for the erudite poetry of the old books by the people of *dīn*'.[47]

To accept vernacular Islamic texts as part of a textual culture shared among Muslims in a particular region over centuries undermines the assumptions of those scholars who have tried to explain their peculiar imagery and vocabulary by seeing them as pioneering, isolated attempts at 'rooting' or 'grounding' Islamic literature locally. While the oldest extant texts in a given language may indeed contain examples of such pioneering activity, the taking over of vocabulary and imagery demonstrates that soon there were Muslims who had accepted these conventions as proper ways of expressing Islamic discourse in that language. To understand how and why authors utilized these conventions requires us to first ask a number of interrelated questions: how did different genres and types of texts relate to each other? What was the purpose of different types of texts? Why were certain languages and idioms chosen for a text, and what valuations were they imbued with? It is this wider context that needs to be considered before we will really be able to understand how Islamic discourse was translated into South Asian vernaculars. In effect, it will require scholars to shift their attention from semantics to aesthetics and from religion to poetics. It will also require that scholars re-examine the social contexts in which vernacular texts were produced. The use of 'popular' vernacular genres such as certain types of songs is too often facilely associated with an unlettered audience. Carl Ernst has called this equation into question in the case of Dakhani poetry, whose complexity and contextualization in manuscripts containing Arabic and Persian texts seems to indicate an elite rather than a subaltern audience.[48] This would seem to be even truer in the case of Tamil poetry, with its highly archaic (and archaizing) language and complex poetics.

Both earlier scholarship operating with the syncretism-model as well as recent studies have shared a bias towards those texts which show the greatest amount of 'translation' in the form of South Asian terminology and images. The evaluation of this literature may have changed – what the syncretism-model considered to be 'contaminated' texts have been described more recently in positive terms such as 'rooting', 'grounding', or 'sharing' – but both approaches have avoided discussing how this literature may relate to those texts which seem to be closer to patterns expected in Islamic discourse. If we analyse Islamic Tamil poetry as participating in a 'shared' Tamil conceptual culture, then how do we approach the so-called 'Arabic-Tamil' prose texts? Unsurprisingly, these have either been ignored altogether, or been perceived as being in conceptual opposition to more 'localized' texts, with the former indicating a rupture and rejection of 'Tamil culture', the latter signalling respect for and integration into that culture.[49] But a closer look reveals uncomfortably close connections between these different types of Tamil texts. Not only were there authors like Māppiḷḷai Leppai who were as comfortable writing 'Arabic-Tamil' prose as composing Tamil poetry, and not only do these different types of texts share the same terminological conventions. Rather, the most celebrated works of the 'localized' tradition, the poems in the *kāppiyam-* or *purāṇam*-genre, generally claim to be based precisely on the kind of prose texts represented by the so-called 'Arabic-Tamil' tradition.[50]

The relationship between Islamic Tamil poetry and 'Arabic-Tamil' prose is particularly interesting because it seems to invert the hierarchies constructed by scholarship. Instead of popular didactic texts for non-elite Muslims in a localized idiom and an elite literature that is in Arabic or at least in a heavily Arabicized idiom, we find the exact opposite: a textual culture that not only stayed close to Arabic idioms in its most basic didacticism and cherished Tamil imagery in refined poetry, but that actually appears to have conceived of both of these as legitimate expressions of Islamic discourse, even if for different purposes. There was no unidirectional 'diglossic power relationship' between Arabic and Tamil.[51] For a long time, scholars conventionally depicted the relationship between Islamic texts in South Asian vernaculars on the one hand and Arabic and Persian on the other in terms of 'low' or 'popular' folk literatures as opposed to 'high' or 'cultured' elite literatures. Recent work by Sheldon Pollock and others has produced a far more sophisticated tool for conceptualizing these differences, namely that of the vernacular 'local' and that of the cosmopolitan 'translocal' idioms.[52] While this distinction is certainly more helpful than the earlier value-laden terminology, we should not lose sight of the fact that South Asia in the sixteenth to early-nineteenth centuries cannot be easily described in these binaries. Not only were there several cosmopolitan idioms, there was also a large number of vernacular traditions, some just emerging and struggling to define themselves, others, like Tamil, 'cosmopolitan vernaculars' with centuries of history behind them.[53] A language such as Tamil, in contrast to many vernaculars of northern India, carried with it the authority gained through centuries of use as an idiom expressing the power of political, religious, and mercantile elites.

Tamil has been one of the few languages chosen as literary medium by pre-colonial Muslim authors that had not only a long tradition of literature, but also an intensive metadiscourse on literature and language in the form of written grammars and poetics that predated any similar discourse in Arabic or Persian. It was this tradition of grammars, poetics and aesthetics that Muslim poets valued and it is these texts, rather than any specific poems authored by non-Muslims, that are explicitly mentioned in Islamic poetry. The most important Tamil Muslim poet of the nineteenth century, Ceyku Aptul Kātiṟu, whom Tamil Muslims consider even today as the *pulavar nāyakam* or 'Lord of Poets', summed up this sentiment in 1812 when he wrote about himself with the proper humility: 'He does not know the fitting constituents of the *Akattiyam*, the precious *Tolkāppiyam*, the *Yāpparuṅkalam* and the *Naṉṉūl*', thereby mentioning the most important texts of the poetic tradition from the legendary *Akattiyam* to the thirteenth-century *Naṉṉūl*.[54] Similar references to authorities on Tamil grammar and poetics are common in Islamic Tamil literature. Already the two earliest known poems of the late-sixteenth century refer to authorities on Tamil grammar and poetics such as a particular type of treatises on poetics known as *pāṭṭiyal* or the *caṅkam*, the legendary assembly of poets.[55] To adhere to this tradition when composing poetry was not so much a question of the constraints of a religious encounter as a question of aesthetic choice, as the tradition of Tamil poetics transcended the religious boundaries visible in the actual poems.[56] The Tamil case may be peculiar in its details, but the basic lesson to be learned from it is that expressing Islamic discourse in South Asian languages was usually not a spontaneous act of pioneering poets, but followed rules of textual production that had been developed over time.

Conclusion

In a fascinating essay, Shantanu Phukan has recently discussed the encounter of Abdul Wahid of Bilgram, a Persian-educated Mughal intellectual, with Hindi poetry. He details Abdul Wahid's attempt at coming to terms with that poetry and reinterpreting it through the imagery of Persian Sufi thought. Yet that a person like Abdul Wahid would attempt this reinterpretation in the first place demonstrates, as Phukan argues, the extent to which Abdul Wahid 'was moved by Hindi poetry'.[57] Aesthetics, rather than religion, seem to have prompted this encounter. Yet in a manner reminiscent of much scholarship concerning textual cultures in South Asia, Phukan continues to refer to Abdul Wahid primarily as a Muslim, and to the culture he encounters primarily as a Hindu one. There are certainly good reasons for that, not the least being that this seems to have been Abdul Wahid's own perspective. But at the same time, there appears to be something amiss here: why did the Muslim Abdul Wahid consider it to be against Islam to discuss a woman's nipples, but had no such qualms when talking about the Christian bar-boys of Persian poetry, after all hardly a Quranic image either?[58]

The point is that Abdul Wahid, like many of his contemporaries, identified two domains which only recently scholarship has come to disaggregate for analytical purposes. Marshall Hodgson has introduced the term 'Islamicate' to refer to the wider cultural traditions that are associated with Muslim societies, but are not strictly speaking religious.[59] Yet for people like Abdul Wahid, the Islamicate tradition of Persian poetry could not be anything but Islamic at the same time – Islamic and Islamicate merged in his perception. That Abdul Wahid was not able to perceive a conceptual difference between these two aspects is not surprising. What is disconcerting, however, is that the confusion of Islamic and Islamicate still colours so many discussions of Islamic traditions in South Asia, and what is even more disconcerting is that this confusion seems to operate only one way. While scholars have repeatedly pointed out cases of Islamicate practices in non-Islamic contexts, such as the widespread adoption of Persian literary traditions among North Indian Hindu professionals, few seem to be prepared to suggest the existence of the opposite. When encountering 'Indic' textual traditions and conventions being employed for Muslim discourse, scholars appear to be incapable of conceptualizing the 'Indic' elements as anything else but 'Hindu'.[60] Once we are capable of distinguishing 'Indic' and 'Hindu' in the same manner as 'Islamic' and 'Islamicate', it becomes clear that the utilization of Tamil literary conventions in Islamic texts in no way 'transcends any attempt to define clearly bounded Hindu and Muslim identities'.[61] Muslim Tamil authors were as sure about their texts being on the side of Islam as Abdul Wahid was in the case of Persian poetry. Rather, one could describe Islamic Tamil poetry as 'Islamic' texts using 'Indic' conventions. In order to gain a better understanding of the complex processes by which Islamic discourse was translated into South Asian vernaculars, we need to go beyond the presuppositions constructed by two centuries of interaction between scholarship on South Asian Islam and late- or post-Mughal Muslim elites in South Asia, and stop perceiving vernacular Islamic texts as local oddities, but respect their claims to expressing universal Islamic discourse.[62] For this, we will first of all have to accept that to some Muslims, 'Om' can be an Islamic term, much as Savitri can be a Muslim name.

Acknowledgements

I would like to thank A. Azfar Moin, Southern Methodist University, R. Michael Feener, National University of Singapore, and Jon M. Keune, University of Houston, for their comments on an earlier version of this paper.

Notes

1. "Can Savitri Be a Muslim Name?," sec. 1.
2. Schimmel, "Popular Muslim Poetry," 18.
3. In this paper, I will be referring in particular to Stewart, "In Search of Equivalence"; but see also Behl, "Premodern Negotiations"; de Bruijn, "Dialogism"; and Ricci, *Islam Translated.* Finbarr Flood has fruitfully applied the concept to art-history; Flood, *Objects of Translation.*
4. E.g., Narayanan, "Religious Vocabulary"; and Stewart, "In Search of Equivalence"; for further examples from Tamil other than those mentioned in the paper, see Tschacher, "Drowning in the Ocean," 67–71.
5. E.g., Shulman and Subrahmanyam, "Prince of Poets"; Stewart, "In Search of Equivalence." Such a stance is implicit wherever South Asian vernacular Islamic vocabulary is discussed only with reference to non-Muslim texts using the same vocabulary, rather than in the context of other Muslim texts in the same vernacular.
6. The best overview of Islamic Tamil literature in English is still Uwise, *Muslim Contribution*; the most comprehensive survey is Uvais and Ajmalkāṉ, *Islāmiyat tamiḻ ilakkiya varalāṟu*. For a recent study of the *Āyiramacalā*, see Ricci, *Islam Translated.*
7. Gottschalk, "Visions of Incompatibility."
8. A word-play on the double meaning of *arum kupir*, meaning both 'difficult unbelief' and 'precious unbelief'.
9. *maṟai muṟaiyoṭum tiṉavaṇakkam nīṅkilātu/iṟaivaṉait toḻutu iculāmiṉ nēr vaḻi/kuṟaivaṟap paṭittu arum kupirai nīkkiyē/muṟai tavaṟāp perum mucilim āyiṉār*; *Cīṟāppurāṇam* 2.10.7. All translations in this paper are my own unless noted otherwise.
10. Note that these three terms are the only Arabic loanwords in the stanza, while concepts such as 'scripture' (*maṟai*), 'daily worship' (*tiṉavaṇakkam*), 'God' (*iṟaivaṉ*), and even the 'straight path' (*nēr vaḻi*, obviously a translation of the Arabic phrase *al-ṣirāt al-mustaqīm*) are expressed by Tamil terms. For another example of a text aligning itself with 'Islam' in contradistinction to *kufr*, cf. Ricci's excellent discussion of the stark contrast between Muslims and non-Muslims in the *Āyiramacalā*; Ricci, *Islam Translated*, 106–12.
11. Compare the stanza immediately preceding the one discussed here (*Cīṟāppuraṇam* 2.10.6.), where the conversion of Ḥabīb and his retinue is expressed as *tīṉil āyiṉār*, literally 'they became in *dīn*'.

12. For examples and a discussion of this phenomenon, see Tschacher, "Drowning in the Ocean," 63–77.
13. Tschacher, "Drowning in the Ocean," 77–83.
14. Narayanan, "Religious Vocabulary," 92.
15. Stewart, "In Search of Equivalence," 273.
16. Ibid.
17. For quotes see Stewart, "In Search of Equivalence," 268, 273–4.
18. Said, ed. and trans., *Al-Biruni's Book on Pharmacy*, 1:7–8 (English), 1:12–13 (Arabic).
19. Šarīph, *Saiyad Sultān viracit Nabīvaṃśa*, 2:478–9. I thank Hans Harder, University of Heidelberg, for his help with the Bengali text, possibly the first external mention of Islamic Tamil literature. The term *yāvā* might also refer to Malay rather than Javanese, see Milner, *The Malays*, 96–9.
20. Cf. Hart, "Translating the Untranslatable."
21. Narayanan, "Religious Vocabulary," 80; and Richman, *Extraordinary Child*, 146.
22. Narayanan, *The Vernacular Veda*, chap. 2; and Hardy, "A Radical Reassessment."
23. Narayanan, "Religious Vocabulary," 91.
24. Majma' al-Ḥaramayn, *Al-qur'ān al-karīm*.
25. Stewart, "In Search of Equivalence," 269.
26. Eaton, *The Rise of Islam*, 276.
27. Ibid., 281–90.
28. Ricci, *Islam Translated*, 125–7, quote on p. 127.
29. For blaming the author, cf. J.B.P. More's identification of a famous Tamil Sufi poet as a convert in order to explain his apparent 'Hindu' usages; More, *Muslim Identity*, 57. For identifying the needs of the audience as the driving force behind 'syncretism', see Roy, *The Islamic Syncretistic Tradition*, 80–3.
30. Stewart, "In Search of Equivalence," 274.
31. ...*vayyākka//nastakīṉ eṉṟu mika nall' utavi tēṭumavar/kasti pōkkip patavi kāṇpōṉē...*; *Ñāṉappukaḻcci*, 669–70.
32. ...*ōm ataṉul//oḷikaḷ tericitt' uṇarā...uṉ/vaḻi piḷaittār...*; *Ñāṉappukaḻcci*, 676–7.
33. Cf. Laffan, *Makings of Indonesian Islam*, 15 (emphasis in original): 'again and again the defense [of local Islam] will be made in terms of local Islam being the true *Meccan* form'.
34. With regard to Bengali, cf. the otherwise very different accounts in Roy, *The Islamic Syncretistic Tradition*, chap. 2; and Uddin, *Constructing Bangladesh*, 31–40. Generally, see e.g., Eaton, "Sufi Folk Literature"; Green, *Sufism*, 110–2; Levtzion, "Dynamics of Sufi Brotherhoods," 115–16; and Schimmel, "Popular Muslim Poetry."
35. Roy, *The Islamic Syncretistic Tradition*, 82.
36. Quoted in Germann, "Ziegenbalgs Bibliotheca Malabarica," 16–17.
37. Ramanujan, "Three Hundred *Rāmāyaṇas*," 46.
38. Cf. Shulman, "Tamil Praises," 105; Shulman's reference to the Prophet transforming a mass of flesh into a beautiful woman in Kācimpulavar's *Tiruppukaḻ* as 'opaque' would hardly have been opaque to an educated Muslim audience – the miracle of the Prophet turning the horribly ugly daughter of King Ḥabīb of Damascus into a beautiful woman is described in *Cīṟāppurāṇam* 2.9.
39. Ricci, *Islam Translated*, 112–16.
40. *Hadyāmālai* 28; and Tschacher, "How to Die."
41. *namatu pulavamārkaḷum tamiḻppāṣaiyiṉ vittuvāṉkaḷum kavaṉikka veṇṭiyatu, avarkaḷ muṉṉuḷḷa pulavarkaḷ pāṭiya pāṭalkaḷai urai ceyvatum, uraikaḷaip pāṭṭ' ākkuvatum pataṅkaḷ kavikaḷ pāṭuvatumē namatu kaṭamai eṉṟ' irāmal* [sic] *pala pāṣaikaḷilum irukkiṉṟa tēvaiyāṉa ilmukaḷait tamiḻil evarukkum viḷaṅkat takka vitamāy eḻuti veḷiyākkiṉāl avarkaḷukkuk kīrttiyum, muslimkaḷukku naṉmaiyum uṇṭākum*; Cittilevvai, *Asṟāṟul ālam*, 189 (emphasis mine).
42. See note 15.
43. Shulman and Subrahmanyam, "Prince of Poets," 527 (emphasis mine).
44. For example Raja Mohamad, *Islamic Architecture*, 72 (around 1200); Subrahmanya Aiyer, *South Indian Inscriptions*, 211–13 (No. 402, ca. 1225); Raja Mohamad, *Islamic Architecture*, 71 quotes another inscription as dating to the tenth century, but Irācu suggests that this rather stems from the mid-fourteenth century; Irācu, *Tamiḻaka islāmiya varalāṟṟu āvaṇaṅkaḷ*, 111–12 (No. 54.4).

45. Behl, "Premodern Negotiations," 95–6.
46. For a detailed discussion of the secondary literature and the underlying Tamil-nationalist assumptions, see Tschacher, "Drowning in the Ocean."
47. *tīṉāṉōr toṉṉūl/kalvi kavi cevi uṟak kēṭṭaṉaṉ*; *Tirumaṇakkāṭci*, 1.36. For discussions of conventions and usages peculiar to Islamic literature in Tamil; see Tschacher, "Commenting Translation"; and Tschacher, "Convention and Community."
48. Ernst, *Eternal Garden*, 165–8; in his discussion of the use of vernaculars by Sufi authors, Green similarly points out the importance of courtly and scholarly elites for the production of vernacular texts, but he still maintains a model stressing didacticism aimed at unlettered audiences as the main *raison d'être* for vernacular Sufi literature; Green, *Sufism*, 103–12.
49. Tschacher, "Drowning in the Ocean," 71–7.
50. Tschacher, "Commenting Translation," 28–36.
51. Green, *Sufism*, 111.
52. Pollock, *Language of the Gods*, 10–30.
53. Cf. Pollock, "The Cosmopolitan Vernacular."
54. *akattiyam arum tolkāppiyam iyāpparuṅkalam naṉṉūliṉ/takait tiṟam teriyāṉ…*; *Tirukkāraṇappurāṇam*, 1.1.34.
55. … *pāṭṭiyal aṟiyāṉ…*; *Āyiramacalā*, 1.25; *caṅkamuṟṟa pulavar…*; *Mikuṟācumālai*, 22; see Shulman, "First Grammarian, First Poet," 359–69, for a discussion of the *caṅkam*-poets' relation to grammar and poetics; see also Shulman, "Tamil Praises," 100, for further examples of Tamil Muslim poets mentioning treatises of grammar and poetics.
56. Of the four texts mentioned by Ceyku Aptul Kātiṟu, the three latter texts have generally been presumed to have been authored by Jains, while the legend of the *Akattiyam* was present across religious traditions of South India. This should caution us again against the facile identification of South Asian vernaculars and Hinduism which is so often encountered; see Tschacher, "Drowning in the Ocean," 67–71.
57. Phukan, "Path Through Her Hair," 227.
58. Ibid., 214–17.
59. Hodgson, *The Venture of Islam*, 1:57–60.
60. For the use of the term 'Indic' as an equivalent of 'Islamicate', see Gilmartin and Lawrence, "Introduction," 2.
61. Gilmartin and Lawrence, "Introduction," 8.
62. That much of the scholarly image of 'South Asian Islam' was constructed in interaction with Mughal elites and their successors throughout South Asia, i.e., people like Abdul Wahid, seems to have greatly aided the perpetuation of that confusion; concerning the colonial-period construction of Islam in the Madras Presidency in the interaction of Orientalists and late-Mughal rather than Tamil- or Malayalam-speaking Muslim elites, see Vatuk, "Islamic Learning." The hegemony of this image needs to be broken in order to gain a better understanding of vernacular Islamic discourse in South Asia. Cf. Laffan, *Makings of Indonesian Islam*, for a comparable venture.

Bibliography

Islamic Tamil poems

Āyiramacalā by Vaṇṇap Parimaḷap Pulavar. ed. Em. Saiyitu Muhammatu 'Hasaṉ'. Ceṉṉai: Em. Itrīs Maraikkāyar, 1984.

Cīṟāppurāṇam by Umaṟup Pulavar. ed. Em. Ceyyitu Muhammatu 'Hasaṉ'. Ceṉṉai: Maraikkāyar Patippakam, 1987.

Hadyāmālai by 'Māppiḷḷai Leppai' Sayyid Muḥammad b. Aḥmad in: Sayyid Muḥammad b. Aḥmad. *Maghānī mulaḥ al-tibyān fī sharḥ ma'ānī fatḥ al-dayyān*. 2nd ed. Bombay: Maṭba' Gulzār Ḥasanī, 1318 AH.

Mikuṟācumālai by Ālippulavar. ed. Em.Ār.Em. Aptuṟrahīm and Em.Ār.Em Mukammatu Mustapā. Ceṉṉai: Yuṉivarsal Papḷiṣars aṇṭ Pukcellars, 1983.

Ñāṉappukaḻcci by Pīrmuhammatu in: *Ñāṉa māmētai Ṣeyku Pīrmuhammatu Oliyullāh (rali) avarkaḷiṉ meyññāṉap pāṭalkaḷ*. Takkalai: Añcuvaṉṉam Pīrmuhammatiyyā Muslim Acōsiyēṣaṉ, 1995.

Tirukkāraṇappurāṇam by Ceyku Aptul Kātiṟu Nayiṉār Leppai Ālim Pulavar. ed. Mu. Ceyyitu Muhammatu 'Hasaṉ' and Cēmumu. Mukamatali. Ceṉṉai: Ēvi.Em. Jāpartīṉ Nūrjahāṉ Ṭirasṭ, 1999.

Tirumaṇakkāṭci by Vakutai Cēkāti Nayiṉārp Pulavar. ed. Mu. Ceyyitu Muhammatu 'Hasaṉ'. Ceṉṉai: Maraikkāyar Patippakam, 1990.

Books and articles

Behl, Aditya. "Premodern Negotiations: Translating Between Persian and Hindavi." In *Translation, Text and Theory: The Paradigm of India*, edited by Rukmini Bhaya Nair, 89–100. Delhi: Sage, 2002.

"Can Savitri Be a Muslim Name?" *Islamic Voice* 14, no. 12 (December 2000); sec. 1. Accessed April 12, 2013. http://www.islamicvoice.com/december.2000/viewpoint.htm#sav

Cittilevvai, Mukammatukācim. *Asṟāṟul ālam*. Colombo: Star Press, 1897.

de Bruijn, Thomas. "Dialogism in a Medieval Genre: The Case of the Avadhi Epics." In *Before the Divide: Hindi and Urdu Literary Culture*, edited by Francesca Orsini, 121–141. Hyderabad: Orient Blackswan, 2010.

Eaton, Richard M. *The Rise of Islam and the Bengal Frontier, 1204–1760*. Berkeley: University of California Press, 1993.

Eaton, Richard M. "Sufi Folk Literature and the Expansion of Indian Islam." *History of Religions* 14, no. 2 (1974): 117–127.

Ernst, Carl W. *Eternal Garden: Mysticism, History, and Politics at a South Asian Sufi Center*. 2nd ed. Delhi: Oxford University Press, 2004.

Flood, Finbarr B. *Objects of Translation: Material Culture and Medieval 'Hindu-Muslim' Encounter*. Princeton, NJ: Princeton University Press, 2009.

Germann, Wilhelm. "Ziegenbalgs Bibliotheca Malabarica." *Missionsnachrichten der Ostindischen Missionsanstalt zu Halle* 32, no. 1 (1880): 1–20, 61–94.

Gilmartin, David, and Bruce B, Lawrence. "Introduction." In *Beyond Turk and Hindu: Rethinking Religious Identities in Islamicate South Asia*, edited by David Gilmartin and Bruce B. Lawrence, 1–20. Gainesville: University Press of Florida, 2000.

Gottschalk, Peter. "Visions of Incompatibility: Categorizing Islam and Hinduism in Scholarship." In *Incompatible Visions: South Asian Religions in History and Culture: Essays in Honor of David M. Knipe*, edited by James Blumenthal, 1–20. Madison: Center for South Asia, University of Wisconsin-Madison, 2005.

Green, Nile. *Sufism: A Global History*. Chichester: Wiley-Blackwell, 2012.

Hardy, Friedhelm. "A Radical Reassessment of the Vedic Heritage: The Ācāryahṛdayam and Its Wider Implications." In *Representing Hinduism: The Construction of Religious Traditions and National Identity*, edited by Vasudha Dalmia and Heinrich von Stietencron, 35 50. Delhi: Sage, 1995.

Hart, Roger. "Translating the Untranslatable: From Copula to Incommensurable Worlds." In *Tokens of Exchange: The Problem of Translation in Global Circulations*, edited by Lydia H. Liu, 45–73. Durham: Duke University Press, 1999.

Hodgson, Marshall G. S. *The Venture of Islam: Conscience and History in a World Civilization*. 3 vols. Chicago, IL: University of Chicago Press, 1974.

Irācu, Ce., ed. *Tamiḻaka islāmiya varalāṟṟu āvaṇaṅkaḷ*. Īrōṭu: KKSK Kalvi Aṟakkaṭṭaḷai, 2007.

Laffan, Michael. *The Makings of Indonesian Islam: Orientalism and the Narration of a Sufi Past*. Princeton, NJ: Princeton University Press, 2011.

Levtzion, Nehemia. "The Dynamics of Sufi Brotherhoods." In *The Public Sphere in Muslim Societies*, edited by Miriam Hoexter, Shmuel N. Eisenstadt, and Nehemia Levtzion, 109–118. Albany: State University of New York Press, 2002.

Majma' al-Ḥaramayn al-Sharīfayn al-Malik Fahd li-Ṭibā'at al-Muṣḥaf al-Sharīf. *Al-qur'ān al-karīm wa tarjama ma'ānīhi ila al-lughat al-tāmīliyya: Caṅkaimikka kurĀṉ maṟṟum tamiḻ moḻiyil ataṉ karuttukkaḷiṉ moḻipeyarppu*. al-Madīna al-Munawwara: Majma' al-Ḥaramayn al-Sharīfayn al-Malik Fahd li-Ṭibā'at al-Muṣḥaf al-Sharīf, 1414 AH.

Milner, Anthony. *The Malays*. Oxford: Blackwell, 2008.

More, J. B. Prashant. *Muslim Identity, Print Culture and the Dravidian Factor in Tamil Nadu*. Hyderabad: Orient Longman, 2004.

Narayanan, Vasudha. "Religious Vocabulary and Regional Identity: A Study of the Tamil *Cirappuranam*." In *Beyond Turk and Hindu: Rethinking Religious Identities in Islamicate*

South Asia, edited by David Gilmartin and Bruce B. Lawrence, 74–97. Gainesville: University Press of Florida, 2000.

Narayanan, Vasudha. *The Vernacular Veda: Revelation, Recitation, and Ritual*. Columbia: University of South Carolina Press, 1994.

Phukan, Shantanu. "The Path Through Her Dark Hair: Hesitating Muslims and the Hindi Lyric." In *Performing Ecstasy: The Poetics and Politics of Religion in India*, edited by Pallabi Chakravorty and Scott Kugle, 205–231. Delhi: Manohar, 2009.

Pollock, Sheldon. "The Cosmopolitan Vernacular." *The Journal of Asian Studies* 57, no. 1 (1998): 6–37.

Pollock, Sheldon. *The Language of the Gods in the World of Men: Sanskrit, Culture, and Power in Premodern India*. Berkeley: University of California Press, 2006.

Raja Mohamad, J. *Islamic Architecture in Tamil Nadu*. Chennai: Director of Museums, 2004.

Ramanujan, A. K. "Three Hundred *Rāmāyaṇas*: Five Examples and Three Thoughts on Translation." In *Many Rāmāyaṇas: The Diversity of a Narrative Tradition in South Asia*, edited by Paula Richman, 22–49. Berkeley: University of California Press, 1991.

Ricci, Ronit. *Islam Translated: Literature, Conversion, and the Arabic Cosmopolis of South and Southeast Asia*. Chicago, IL: University of Chicago Press, 2011.

Richman, Paula. *Extraordinary Child: Poems from a South Indian Devotional Genre*. Honolulu: University of Hawai'i Press, 1997.

Roy, Asim. *The Islamic Syncretistic Tradition in Bengal*. Princeton, NJ: Princeton University Press, 1983.

Said, Hakim Mohammed., ed. and trans. *Al-Biruni's Book on Pharmacy and Materia Medica*. 2 vols. Karachi: Hamdard National Foundation, 1973.

Śarīph, Āhmad, ed. *Saiyad Sultān viracit Nabīvaṃśa*. 2 vols. Dacca: Bangla Academy, 1978.

Schimmel, Annemarie. "Reflections on Popular Muslim Poetry." *Contributions to Asian Studies* 17 (1982): 17–26.

Shulman, David. "First Grammarian, First Poet: A South Indian Vision of Cultural Origins." *The Indian Economic and Social History Review* 38, no. 4 (2001): 353–373.

Shulman, David. "Tamil Praises of the Prophet: Kācimpulavar's *Tiruppukaḻ*." *Jerusalem Studies in Arabic and Islam* 27 (2002): 86–108.

Shulman, David, and Sanjay, Subrahmanyam. "Prince of Poets and Ports: Cītakkāti, the Maraikkāyars and Ramnad, ca. 1690–1710." In *Islam and Indian Regions*, edited by Anna Libera Dallapiccola and Stephanie Zingel-Avé Lallemant, vol. 1, 497–535. Stuttgart: Franz Steiner Verlag, 1993.

Stewart, Tony. "In Search of Equivalence: Conceiving Muslim-Hindu Encounter Through Translation Theory." *History of Religions* 40, no. 3 (2001): 260–287.

Subrahmanya Aiyer, K. V. ed. *South Indian Inscriptions (Texts) Volume VIII: Miscellaneous Inscriptions from the Tamil, Malayalam, Telugu and Kannada Countries*. Madras: Government Press, 1937.

Tschacher, Torsten. "Commenting Translation: Concepts and Practices of Translation in Islamic Tamil Literature." In *Translation in Asia: Theories, Practices, Histories*, edited by Ronit Ricci and Jan van der Putten, 27–44. Manchester: St. Jerome Publishing, 2011.

Tschacher, Torsten. "Convention and Community: The Poetics of Prefaces to Early Islamic Tamil Literature." *Zeitschrift für Indologie und Südasienstudien* 28 (2011): 183–209.

Tschacher, Torsten. "Drowning in the Ocean of Tamil: Islamic Texts and the Historiography of Tamil Literature." In *Literature and Nationalist Ideology: Writing Histories of Modern Indian Languages*, edited by Hans Harder, 51–83. Delhi: Social Science Press, 2010.

Tschacher, Torsten. "How to Die Before Dying: Šarī'a and Sufism in a Nineteenth-century Tamil Poem." In *Islâm: Collected Essays*, edited by Daniele Cevenini and Svevo D'Onofrio, 433–455. Bologna: I libri di Emil, 2010.

Uddin, Sufia M. *Constructing Bangladesh: Religion, Ethnicity, and Language in an Islamic Nation*. Chapel Hill: University of North Carolina Press, 2006.

Uvais, Mahmūtu Mukammatu, and Pī. Mu. Ajmalkāṉ. *Islāmiyat tamiḻ ilakkiya varalāṟu*. 4 vols. Madurai: Madurai Kamaraj University, 1986–1997.

Uwise, Mahmood Mohamed. *Muslim Contribution to Tamil Literature*. 2nd ed. Madras: Fifth International Islamic Tamil Literary Conference, 1990.

Vatuk, Sylvia. "Islamic Learning at the College of Fort St George in Nineteenth-Century Madras." In *The Madras School of Orientalism: Producing Knowledge in Colonial South India*, edited by Thomas R. Trautmann, 48–73. Delhi: Oxford University Press, 2009.

Remapping Muslim literary culture: folklore, *Bulbul*, and world-making in late colonial Bengal

Neilesh Bose

Department of History, University of North Texas, Denton, TX, USA

Bengali Muslim literary culture comprises a conspicuously under-researched domain of colonial Indian history. That Muslims formed the majority of Bengal's population by the early twentieth century has been recognized in a variety of sources, but the comprehension of this fact within the cultural and literary histories of colonial India has eluded modern historians. Late colonial Bengal saw the rise of a Muslim literary culture that included intense engagements with Hindus, Muslims of other parts of India, and Urdu linguistic and cultural references. These engagements, detailed in this article, include the rise of folklore collection, the creation of a new literary criticism, and critical engagement with pan-Indian Muslim thought in the 1930s. A visible forum for this engagement was the journal *Bulbul* (Nightingale), a 1930s magazine that showcased a specifically Bengali Muslim language, literature, and culture that would draw from both Hindu and Muslim elements and aim to situate Bengali Muslim writing and thought into a 'world-making literature'. In line with recent developments in global intellectual history, this essay argues that Bengali Muslim writers and critics of the inter-war period cultivated 'world-making' practices that sought not to create a separate Muslim nation, but to integrate Bengali Muslim writing into a 'world literature'.

> As much as the Congress leaders put on a Hindu face, I put on more of a 'Muslim' face. This Muslimness of course was not about actual religion nor was it about opposing another religion. I felt only a sense of autonomy, independence, and self-respect.
>
> – Abul Mansur Ahmed, 1938[1]

Introduction

One of the most celebrated Bengali Muslim intellectuals of the late colonial period, Abul Mansur Ahmed would often experience ridicule in Calcutta's streets because of his Muslim identity. His name, patterns of speech, and clothing choices would prompt Calcutta's literary and educational circles to question his credentials, education, and abilities. A Muslim social identity – being labelled a Muslim in public – was for Ahmed a major point of contention in the Hindu-dominated world of Bengali literature and publishing in inter-war Calcutta. By the late 1930s, as a journalist and writer working in both Calcutta and his east Bengali home town of Mymensingh, he came to identify with 'religion' not in the sense of ritual, faith or belief, but as a political strategy in the service of fighting social inequities.[2] One such identification with religion arrived for Bengali Muslim writers through the embrace of a specifically Bengali Muslim variant of Bengali literature.

This article discusses this embrace of a specifically Bengali Muslim variant of Bengali literature through the creation of a Muslim slant on folklore collection in Bengal, the instantiation of a modernist Muslim literary criticism, and a critical appreciation of Muslim intellectuals writing in other languages in other parts of India. These changes were demonstrated most vividly in *Bulbul* (Nightingale),[3] a literary magazine published and in circulation between 1933 and 1938 from Calcutta. Through a focus on the depression decade not for economic change or the hardening of communal identities,[4] I show how Bengali Muslims constructed a specifically Bengali Muslim literature that would draw from both Hindu and Muslim elements and simultaneously provide the seeds for a 'world literature'. Such a 'world literature' was not a form of literature that necessarily transcended its point of origin, as defined by literary critic David Damrosch,[5] but a literature that integrated multiple points of reference and inspiration that both transcended religious community and the traditional binary between Anglocentric English literary criticism and literary criticism in Bengali. Such a literature would be an instance of 'world-making', or including a variety of familiar reference points from both the Bengali Hindu and Indian Islamic landscape as well as engaging with European literary criticism to fashion an unprecedented literary domain, and world view. This domain was not fashioned as 'Muslim' by either the Muslims at the forefront of this construction, or by the many Hindus who also actively participated in it, but did consciously integrate Islamic references as a constituent part of its distinctiveness. From the 1920s, Hindus had been a part of each and every attempt to define Bengali Muslim literature and culture[6] starting from the progressive literary magazines *Dhumketu* (The Comet), *Langol* (The Plough), and *Samyabadi* (The Egalitarian) of early 1920s Calcutta.[7] Additionally, Dacca's Muslim Sahitya Samaj (Muslim Literary Society), an organization of teachers, students, and public intellectuals who debated the contours of modern Islam in the 1920s, included many Hindus and other non-Muslims in their meetings. In the mid-1930s, Bengali Muslims started a new journal, *Bulbul*, which included discussions of folklore, literary criticism, and references to pan-Indian Islam. *Bulbul* was no exception in the literary domain and included Hindu writers in nearly every issue. Through an analysis of the debates in this landmark journal and the writings of those associated with the journal, I argue that the Bengali Muslim experience of authorizing and grappling with literary production in the inter-war period shows not Muslim nationalism, but an iteration of 'world-making' literary criticism. Drawing from similar discussions in global intellectual history[8] and recent literary criticism in the South Asian context,[9] world-making for Bengali Muslim writers of this era included a critical approach to the domination of literary production by the educationally more advanced Hindus. This approach figured in the realms of folklore collection, the creation of a new literary criticism informed by modernist Islam, and finally, in the critical appreciation of pan-Indian Islam from a Bengali point of view.

Folklore collection and world-making

Central to the universe of Bengali Muslim literary critics and writers of the inter-war period was the growing excavation of 'folk' culture that comprised the foundation of a literary past. This excavation was undertaken by East Bengali poets like Jasimuddin (1903–1976) and linguists like Muhammad Shahidullah (1885–1969), the latter a renowned scholar of Sanskrit and linguistics at Dacca University for most of the inter-war period. Both were trained in folklore studies by Dinesh Chandra Sen (1866–1939), the Calcutta University Bengal studies scholar who had initiated such explorations since the early 1920s. The most visible and active folklorist was Abdul Karim Sahityabisharad, a committed amateur collector of Bengali *punthi* manuscripts, who became well known during the 1920s and 1930s with his excavation of the Bengali Muslim literary past. All of these folklorists outlined the contours of a Bengali Muslim literary culture through an investigation of history and forms of language that contributed to a specifically Muslim variant of Bengali literature.

Born in 1863 in the Patiya region of Chittagong, Karim grew up in a home that was a crossroad of different literary cultures inclusive of Bengali, Persian, and Arabic. His family's library included Persian classics like Sa'adi's *Gulistan* alongside the newest Bengali literature of the nineteenth century, including works by Bankim Chandra Chatterjee, Vidyasagar, and Michael Madhusudhan Dutt. As a graduate of his local high school, Abdul Karim studied Sanskrit alongside English in his youth, which prepared him for future work in linguistics and language transmission. Having lost his parents in his teen years, he spent his adolescence and twenties struggling for work instead of pursuing higher education during much of the 1890s. In 1895, he discovered the Vaishnav *padavali* literature through Chittagong friends and from this moment onward he cultivated a personal interest in reading old manuscripts and began on a life-long search for *punthi* manuscripts produced in medieval Bengal. His interest began with a drive towards excavating the history of manuscripts from Chittagong, but it grew to literature from across Bengal.

From the late 1890s through to his death in 1953, Abdul Karim collected approximately 2000 manuscripts and published hundreds of essays in Bengali journals on themes of medieval, or middle period, Bengali literature, and published 11 editions of various *punthis* (manuscripts) during his lifetime.[10] His most well-known edited compilation was the two-volume *Prachin Bangla Punthir Bibaran* (A Description of Ancient Bengali Punthis), published first in 1913. He was not the only *punthi* collector active in the early twentieth century, as Hindu scholars like Haraprasad Sastri (1853–1931) and Nagendranath Basu (1866–1938) were prime movers in this endeavour in this period. But his collection of over 2000 far surpassed that of any other collector in Bengal. Bengali Hindu literary critics were impressed by his editing and linguistic skills. Haraprasad Sastri, the famous Bengali Hindu Sanskritist and prominent member of the Bangiya Sahitya Parishat (Bengali Literary Assembly),[11] commented in 1909 that not only was Abdul Karim's work (commenting on his recently published work *Radhikar Manbhanga*) unparalleled in scholarly grace, but also appeared to bear the influence of German editorial and philological training.[12]

The literal definition of *punthi* is manuscript, and though popularly associated with Muslims in Bengal, the term applies to all middle period Bengali works regardless of authorship. Though no scientific definition has emerged from linguistics or Bengali area studies, the majority of texts called *punthis* use a composite vocabulary drawing from Bengali, Persian, Arabic, and Sanskrit. Finally, the subject matter of *punthis*, though commonly thought of as 'Muslim', often concerned history, romance, mysticism, and folktales. Though he was focused on *punthis* in their broadest manifestation, Abdul Karim also focused on particular authors, like Alaol (1607–1680), as he collected hundreds of editions of his works. Born in Faridpur in East Bengal but a resident of Chittagong for most of his life, Alaol worked often for Arakan courts in Chittagong of the middle and late seventeenth century, primarily as a translator who created free renderings of original works that were travelling throughout northeastern and broader South Asian Islamic literary environments. *Padmavati*, Malik Muhammad Jaisi's Hindi poem about an imaginary love affair between the Khilji emperor Alauddin and Padmini Devi, the queen of

Chitor, was the subject of Alaol's signature work that became famous in late seventeenth-century Bengal. Abdul Karim found and preserved over 30 hand-written copies of the narrative that have been preserved in various institutional locations in contemporary Bangladesh. This poem, like many of his other works,[13] described romance and love in secular terms and cast the narrative in the local milieu of eastern Bengal. Abdul Karim frequently cited Alaol's work to show the vibrancy of early modern Bengali Muslim writers and how they were not solely fascinated with Islam or Islamic themes.

Alaol's *Padmavati* was different from Jayasi's and others for it reflected local politics of the eastern Bengali/Arakenese frontier regions. In Alaol's version, the dying Ratan Sen and Alauddin reconcile, Alauddin becomes the guardian of one of Ratan Sen's sons, and Chandra Sen, Ratan Sen's son, becomes king of Chitor, marking an ideology of reconciliation and rapprochement. Abdul Karim collected 36 versions of Alaol's *Padmavati*, several aspects marking the text's scribes. What appealed to him was the fact that the narrative was sustained through actual recitations, as he found throughout his searches. He discusses in numerous accounts – at speeches during literary societies, as well as published writings – how he would encounter *punthi-majlish* sessions in his childhood reciting the story. He understood this sort of literature through his own life experiences, not through academic research like his formally educated Hindu or European Orientalist colleagues.[14] The living nature of a language, and not an academic commitment, led him to document and preserve.

Abdul Karim believed that Alaol's *Padmavati* was such an important narrative that in the collection of these manuscripts as source material he was evolving an alternative form of history writing than one that was being developed in nineteenth- and early twentieth-century Bengali literary criticism circles. Hindu scholars like Sastri and Basu alongside European collectors like G.A. Grierson (1851–1941), Georg Bühler (1837–1898), and Albrecht Weber (1825–1901) certainly shared the zeal for collecting old manuscripts but for entirely different purposes. These professional scholars saw old manuscripts of value for delineating a sharp distinction between past and present and for dispassionate philological research. Abdul Karim collected them precisely for the opposite purpose of establishing the present's continuity with the past, through living traditions of recitation that would allow Bengali Muslims to reconnect with the sources of more contemporary literature. Near the end of his life, when discussing the past 50 years of his collections, he described himself as literature's *rasik*, container, and lover (punthi sahityer rasher rashik, tar bhandari o premik).[15] Literature was worth preserving for precisely living quality, not because it was a thing of the past. Abdul Karim's approach formed a challenge to the then-dominant understandings of pre-modern literature as lifeless specimens of a past age. Karim's study of past literature also allowed him to construct a Bengali subjectivity that expressly transcended religious differences. In addition to the narrative of *Padmavati*, Abdul Karim was also fixated by *Laila Majnu*, the love story originally written in seventh-century Arabic. He preserved four separate versions of Daulat Wazir Bahram Khan's *Laila Majnu*, which first appeared to historians in the early eighteenth century. Starting in 1913, in his first large-scale edited collection of *punthis*, Abdul Karim claimed that this narrative appealed to all Bengalis, regardless of religion, because its tragedy and hopelessness spoke to the Bengali sensibility of romance and the Bengali heart. It pointed to his investigation into the Muslim Bengali past for constructing a broad, multi-religious Bengali audience in his own time.

Another aspect of Abdul Karim that warrants attention in this context was his personal approach towards *punthi* collection. He saw his work as both devotion and pleasure, but without a professional or scientific anchor. He remarked on this condition throughout his life for unlike most contemporary practitioners he existed as a liminal outsider to the world of professional scholarship. Rather, his commitment wavered between the modern convictions of Hindu fellow collectors and his position as a beleaguered minority subject positioned within two other minorities: a minority within the Bengali literati, dominated by Hindus, and a minority among Urdu-speaking and writing Muslims, who hardly cared for his kind of literary quest. Abdul Karim, on many occasions, stressed that literature was meant for all of humanity, and his literary pursuit was for him a way of countering his liminal status as a Bengali Muslim. Excavating the work of Alaol and others was for him part of a universalist and not a Muslim particularist or communitarian enterprise.

Bulbul: Islamic modernity, literary criticism and a 'world literature'

One of the most significant forums for essay-length deliberations on folklore and language that examined the universalist aspirations of Bengali Muslim literature was the journal *Bulbul*. This landmark magazine of arts and literary criticism was published and in circulation from Calcutta between 1933 and 1938. The phrase 'emancipating the intellect', printed on many of the first year's issues, refers to the 1920s and 1930s Muslim Literary Society of Dacca, of which nearly all of *Bulbul*'s contributors were a part. This society published a journal *Sikha* (Flame), which set its goals of examining Islam, modern education, and gender equity and would term 'emancipating the intellect' as one of its objectives. The phrase itself is taken from Rabindranath Tagore's poem #35 from his 1910 *Gitanjali*, and the first two lines, 'Where the mind is without fear and the head is held high/Where knowledge is free', served as the inspiration and metaphorical goal for the Dacca society's deliberations in the 1920s. Habibullah Bahar, the founder and original editor of *Bulbul*, participated in the 1920s Muslim Sahitya Samaj and carried forth this particular spirit in the production and editing of *Bulbul*. Whereas the discussions of the Muslim Sahitya Samaj focused on Islam and critical discussions of Islam in relation to the politics of the day, *Bulbul*, while continuing such explorations, added the role of literature, and propounded the creation of a new literary criticism inspired by, but not limited to, the experiences of Bengali Muslims.

From its first year in 1933, many essays appeared with a focus on rationalism and Muslim identity. In 1933, M. Wajed Ali's opening essay, 'Jugor Man' (The Feeling of the Age), urged readers to pay heed the current innovations of science and modern thought. Ali was disappointed at how even though science and rationalism was bandied about people were not living scientifically. He urged his readers to find science in an Islamic way, asserting that science and quests for knowledge into nature were cited in Islamic religious texts. Rather than religion holding Muslims back from science, sheer superstition and aversion to change were responsible for obstructing progress.[16]

In the same issue, Abul Hussein, a writer and critic active in earlier deliberations of the Muslim Sahitya Samaj, argued that Islamic tradition dictated rationalism and change. His essay, titled 'Muslim Kalchar O Udar Darshanik Bhitti' (Muslim Culture and its Philosophical Foundations), compared Islam's history with the historical rise of rationalism and science in Europe. He claimed that Islam's entire existence and foundation was based on rational moves away from idol worship and tribalism towards a universal brotherhood and the use of the intellect. Hussein engaged in an extended critique of Ernest Renan's infamous diatribe which stated that 'Islam will perish without striking a blow by the sheer influence of European science'.[17] Young Muslims in Turkey and Egypt of the 1930s were tending towards European science and rationalism, thereby threatening the existence of Islam, for Renan. Hussein agreed with Muslims' embracing of science, but *contra* Renan stated that the avoidance of change would actually be non-Islamic. From the Qur'ānic injunctions regarding *ijtihad* (reason), the foundations of Islam were actually in line with the prevailing European leaning towards some form of socio-economic justice and rational governance. According to Hussein, *zakat*, a pillar of Islam enjoining Muslims to give excess wealth to the poor, resonated with contemporary European discussions of socialism and wealth redistribution. Like M. Wajed Ali's equation of the rationalism undergirding modern European as well as Islamic societies, Hussein argued that 'the foundation of Muslim culture is not eternal, but based on the emancipation of the intellect, which is the foundation of modern Europe'. He defined 'living up to Islam' as a 'yearning for knowledge, change, and experiment' and condemned the Muslims around him for 'not living up to the Islam defined by yearning for change, knowledge, and experimentation',[18] elements that for him also defined European modernity.

Other critics writing in the magazine discussed the social worlds of Bengali Muslims and how literature could aid in a greater understanding of Muslims among the wider Bengali reading public. One of the earliest contributors, Motahar Hussein Choudhury, wrote a lengthy disquisition titled 'Sahitya Sombondhe Nana Katha' (A Few Words on Literature),[19] wherein he critiqued what he perceived to be two poles of the Western literary world: realism and idealism. He invited Bengali writers to steer a middle path, in a way that would be most appropriate for the depiction of Muslims in Bengali literature. The author urged his readers to include the real lives of ordinary Muslims in their writings but also called for greater emotion and feeling. In another essay titled 'Samanbay o Sristhi' (Synthesis and Creation),[20] Abul Kalam Shamsuddin undertook an extensive reading of modern European philosophers Benedetto Croce and Bertrand Russell, who advocated the usage of emotion, passion, and intuition, as opposed to a blind obedience to reason, in the creation of a revolutionary literature. The core question for this writer was the nature of literary creation, and he argued that writers required the input of emotion and impulse for a truly new and revolutionary literary act to take place. He argued that Indian thinkers such as Akbar, Kabir, Nanak, and Bengali reformers like Rammohun Roy had all failed to create revolutionary literature, as they were 'synthesizers…who did not create anew'.[21] Though these inspirational figures had reformed Indian society, they had not actually revolutionized literary representations of that society. Bengali Muslim society required revolutionary writers who could actually depict social life in ways that encouraged substantive change, and no precedent from the past could be the template for such work.

Criticism in the first editions of *Bulbul* was not confined to abstract questions of form but was equally aimed at critiquing existing trends of Bengali literature in order to implant the seeds of a new 'world literature'. Kazi Abdul Wadud contributed a long critique of Bankim Chandra Chatterjee's 'realist' literary style in the second issue of 1933, titled 'Bankim Chandra'. In this essay, he condemned the prevailing Bengali adulation of Bankim as unfounded, not because of his lack of mastery of the Bengali language, but because his standards of realism and character construction would not hold up to the standards of European literature. Tolstoy emerges for Wadud as a prime example of high-standard European literature. Tolstoy's characters, though provincial and often drawn from specific environments, were also constructed so as to make them universally understood. But Bankim's Kamalamani, Chandrasekhar, Matibibi, Jebunessa, Sitaram, popular Hindu heroes and Muslim villains, were too provincial to be appreciated outside of their own contexts. They 'come from ideas, not from reality, and are taken from many places… with an odd sense of the *desh*'.[22] This sense of *desh*, or nation, was critiqued, for its devaluation of Muslims in favour of Hindus,[23] and would have to be recreated – it was argued – for a true world literature to emerge. Wadud ended his essay by declaring love and respect for Bankim's talents, but encouraged readers to understand his contributions in line with a world literature. Without that, it would be impossible to assess the worth, value, and the future of modern Bengali literature. An interest in the possible future, not the past in which Bankim was mired, inspired Wadud's critiques of Bankim.

The future was also linked to a reading of 'world literature'. In his article 'Bartaman Viswa Sahitya' (Today's World Literature),[24] the poet Nazrul Islam reviewed two tracks of literature, one represented by Shelley's 'Skylark' and Milton's 'Birds of Paradise', which saw and celebrated nature and heaven, and the other represented by those who celebrated the real world as it was lived in by people in conditions of cruelty and suffering, such as Dostoyevsky, Gorky, Pushkin, Knut Hamsun, and Johan Bojar. He stated that all of these latter writers, particularly Gorky, 'vowed to take revenge on this cruel world and make the unholy holy',[25] by depicting peasant life and modern turmoil and frustrations. In Nazrul's estimation, these depictions of suffering were important for the representation of a universal humanity. Like Shamsuddin before him, he read Indian literature and history against a critical reading of European novels and European theories and ideas. Against his descriptions of Knut Hamsun's novel *Growth of the Soil* and Bojar's *The Great Hunger and the Swan*, Nazrul claimed that Indian readers would feel the pain of man's helplessness in the modern world. He also argued that a European thinker like Freud, with his emergent theories on desire's relationship to disappointment, meshed with Hindu and Buddhist ideas relating to desire. He ended his essay by looking forward to a new world where Indians may write literature focusing on the problems of peasants, inspired by European precedents but dedicated to making a world anew for Bengali writers. It included self-consciously following the trends of European literary and intellectual production but representing the conditions of Bengali peasant life.

In a second part to his 'Sahitya Sombondhe Nana Katha' (A Few Words on Literature),[26] Motahar Hussein Choudhury lamented the state of cynicism in literature. In this regard, he cited Thomas Hardy as an influence from Europe whose work had infected Bengali writers like Buddhadev Basu and Premendra Mitra. Bengali Muslim writers, according to Choudhury, had to find yet another path towards literary representation. He cites a few lines of an untitled poem by Nazrul which depicted images of sexual desire as a part of being human. Citing Oscar Wilde, Choudhury noted that this humanity[27] needed not be judged as either moral or immoral, but rather just universal. When confronted with the question about religious literature for Bengali Muslims, Choudhury encouraged readers to take account of all literature that asked universal questions, of God, of the soul, of life and death. Universal literature could then also be interpreted as 'religious'. Accordingly, Rabindranath's literature, Vaishnava literature, and *sufi* literature, in addition to traditional commentaries of the Qur'ān or *hadith*, were all 'religious', or rather, as he argued, universalist. He advocated this approach to literature by Bengali Muslims for it would include the totality of life for them, including, but not limited to, matters relating to Islam.

In addition to advocating new styles of writing, *Bulbul* also showcased examples of the new Bengali Muslim 'world literature' 'in action' through the publication of speeches at literary societies by Muslims as well as biographies of Bengali Muslim literary patrons and publishers. Many published speeches from the Bengali Muslim Literary Society of Calcutta, an organization begun in 1911 that met throughout the inter-war period, showcased examples of the burgeoning Bengali Muslim literature. Most important were the Society's speeches that complemented *Bulbul*'s philosophical essays and advocated investigations into folklore and the pre-modern past. Nearly all of Abdul Karim's research and advocacy of folklore appeared as printed speeches in the magazine. In his 1933 speech to the Chittagong Literature Conference, published here in 1934, the Bengali Muslim literary past was excavated to create the foundation for a modern and contemporary Bengali Muslim literature. In this address, Karim had encouraged research on Bengali Muslim literary history, as opposed to Arabic or Persian literary or religious inspirations, for an investment in the specifically Bengali Muslim past. Titled 'Prachin Muslim Sahityer Kromobikash o Boisistho' (The Peculiarities and Evolution of Ancient Muslim Literature),[28] the speech started with the assertion that modern Bengali Muslim writers could hardly discount the history and influence of ancient[29] Bengali Muslim writing from the fifteenth to the eighteenth-century C.E. Writers and texts from these periods, especially of the Muslim sultans predating Mughal rule, must be understood both to clearly grasp Bengali Muslim history but also to shape a literature of the future. He called the late sixteenth and early seventeenth centuries the 'Golden Era' of ancient Bengali Muslim literature, an era of Daulat Kazi, Alaol, Muhammad Khan, Sayyid Sultan, and Nasrullah Khan, among others. Works by these authors included both folk stories of the Muslim tradition, like *Laila Majnu*, as well as religious tracts on Islam, such as Sayyid Sultan's *Nabi-Bangsa*, a text placing the Prophet Muhammad last in a long line of avatars, one of them being Krishna. Karim ended the address by urging the youth of Bengali Muslim society to look to their past literary giants, like Alaol, to buttress their contemporary literature.

In addition to a growing appreciation of literary figures like Alaol, embodied and brought to life by Abdul Karim, Bengali Muslims in the 1930s had contemporary greats like Mozammel Huq, the subject of a biography by Abdul Kadir titled *Mozammel Huq's Devotion to Literature* published in 1934. Huq was a poet, publisher, and literary magnate of the early twentieth century, who started the Bengali Muslim magazine *Muslim Bharat*, a showcase for the talents of individuals like Nazrul and Kaikobad (1857–1951), a prolific Bengali Muslim poet who received positive critical attention from Hindu writers like Nabin Chandra Sen.[30] Kadir placed him in the same class as Rabindranath on the Bengali Hindu side and European literary greats like Shakespeare and Milton. Huq, much in the same way as medieval Bengali Muslims like Alaol, did write on folk Islamic themes like *Hatem Tai* and *Laila Majnu*, but also wrote modern poems and emphasized both the Bengali and Muslim aspects of this literature. By the mid-1930s, therefore, a Bengali Muslim distant past was being evoked, but in the shape of a living tradition out of which a specifically Bengali Muslim literature could be fashioned.

Bengal and pan-Indian Islam

Not only the specifically Bengali Muslim past, but the broader Indian Muslim landscape of ideas and literature was central to the discussions of a Muslim literary movement. Apart from Muslims writing literary criticism alongside poetic and short fiction in Bengali, *Bulbul* in its later years published many works of translation from Urdu into Bengali, showing a confident engagement with the all-India Muslim literary and intellectual trends of the era. These all-India Muslim traditions were represented through Bengali translations of poems by Muhammad Iqbal (1877–1938) and Altaf Husain Hali (1837–1914). Humayun Kabir contributed a translation of 90 verses of Hali's epic poem 'Musaddas e-Madd o-Jazr e-Islam' (The Flow and Ebb of Islam) into Bengali. Muhammad Shahidullah composed a translation from Urdu of 'Iqbal's Petition' rendering a portion of Iqbal's 1930 declaration of Indian Muslim patriotism into Bengali. Mohiuddin translated Iqbal's poem 'Ak Arju' or 'Aakangkha' (Desire) into Bengali and Iqbal's 'Tarana-i-Hind' was anonymously translated. All writers who wrote about Iqbal – including M.

Wajed Ali, Jaminikanta Sen, Golam Moqsud Hilali, S. Wajed Ali, and Abul Mansur Ahmed – praised Iqbal's unique and creative nationalism which simultaneously drew from European philosophical sources and a pride in 'Indian' culture.[31] According to Jaminikanta Sen, Iqbal's inclusion of Arabic and Islamic high culture in his crafting of an Indian patriotic sensibility was a point of pride for all regardless of their religion. S. Wajed Ali, as well, commented on Iqbal's genius in emphasizing Islam's relationship to societal change and progress.

In addition to Hali and Iqbal, the itinerant activist and Muslim political figure Jamal al-din al-Afghani (1838–1897) received several hagiographic outpourings of praise. A famous proponent of modernist Islam in the nineteenth century, al-Afghani was born in Iran and studied in seminaries in Iran and Iraq before travelling throughout the Muslim world in Istanbul, Cairo, and various locations in India. While in India in the 1880s, he delivered a series of speeches in Calcutta's Albert Hall about science and education in early Islamic history. Though a hero of much of Muslim Calcutta and the object of much journalism in the Urdu press, he was not examined in Bengali language forums until this point in *Bulbul*. The appreciation of these figures did not merely show a Bengali fetish of Urdu and Persian literature and culture as it also included critical engagements with the philosophy and political thought of individuals such as Iqbal and al-Afghani. These critiques are important in that they show that Bengalis did not just passively ingest the pan-Indian Muslim cultural milieu but creatively, and critically, reshaped the same in the Bengali language. Iqbal was the focus of several essays of praise and celebration in 1938, soon after his death. A few critics showed a reasoned investigation into the reasons why Iqbal was important at that particular moment, for Bengali Muslims in particular. M. Wajed Ali suggested that Iqbal, like Sir Sayyied Ahmed Khan before him, advocated newness and openness to the outside world, but also encouraged Muslims to keep historical figures like Akbar, Hali, and Ghalib in mind. For Ali, Iqbal was important for Bengali Muslims who had been closed to the best traditions of thought and practice from both the West and the broader Indian Islamic world, the melding of both worlds being the signature of Iqbal.

The most incisive critique came from the pen of Abul Mansur Ahmed. In his 'Philosophical Iqbal',[32] he detailed how Iqbal needed be understood not with reference to his poetry, but with reference to philosophy. Through a reading of his life's trajectory from India to study in Europe at the turn of the twentieth century as well as a reading of his work, 'Sources of the Self', Ahmed concluded that because of Iqbal, 'the day will come when religion and philosophy are indivisible and when materialism and spiritualism are also one'.[33] But the forceful writing of Iqbal showed a danger as well, as Iqbal could be interpreted as 'an emotional essentialist… really standing on fundamental foundations'[34] which could lead to a retreat further only into Muslim identity, not a truly open-minded search for the self without being encumbered by Western or Islamic precedents only. This writer ended his provocative essay by stating that it remained to be seen whether Iqbal was a reactionary in disguise, given his repeated urging of Muslims to focus on the fundamentals of Islam. As with Abul Mansur Ahmed's deconstruction of Iqbal, Kazi Abdul Wadud in 'Syed Jamaluddin Al-Afghani'[35] offered a critical reading of al-Afghani, suggesting that his life and work be seen as an inspiration for the worldwide, and not context-specific, challenges facing Muslims of the day. He creatively compared the Wahabi movement to the Swadeshi movement in Bengal, as both focused on inward-looking sources of inspiration in politics. This was important as he noted that the Muslims of Bengal should 'respect al-Afghani for rousing the feelings and passions of Muslims the world over and for shaking them out of their slavery to foreign cultures',[36] but also that the sources of his inspiration may prove, like the Swadeshi movement, to be dangerously inward looking.

Conclusion

Analysis of South Asian literary cultures (both debates about literature and the actual content of literary texts) has tended towards the study of pre-modern texts and histories.[37] Once the modern world comes into view, the dominant problematic has appeared to be the links between nationalism and literary production.[38] In the case of Bengal, there has yet to emerge a conceptual framework with which to understand the histories of Muslim writing and politics outside of the study of nationalism.[39] Furthermore, most historical investigations of Bengali Muslims have focused on late nineteenth-century reform and 'Islamicization,' the Pakistan movement or the creation of Bangladesh.[40] An important missing element of this history has been the kinds of focus emanating from literary societies and among literary critics in the inter-war period. Through an investigation of these points of interest, I have showed how a significant proportion of Bengali Muslim thought during this time linked not to nationalisms, but to the concept of an inclusive 'world-making'.

Recent work emanating out of the newly designated field of 'global intellectual history' has stressed the need for scholars to focus on how historical actors at different points in time imagine sites beyond the national or imperial, such as the sites of science, utopias, and post-WWII social science, all arenas where intellectuals conjured up visions of the world as a totality. Writing in this tradition, Bell stresses how instantiations of science, utopias or post-war social science are 'world-making practices that seek to articulate a form of universality'.[41] Most important about any world-making practice are the local contexts and understandings of power relations informing such practices. For Bengali Muslim writers and critics, the local context of relative under-development, limited embraces of Western education, and overshadowing by both Bengali Hindus and Muslims of other parts of India formed the backdrop of a creative engagement with Islam. This engagement aimed to introduce Bengali Muslims – via language and literature – into the larger world, and not solely through a 'Bengali Muslim' form of being or narrowly conceived Muslim nation or polity. Not only Bengali Muslims but others in late colonial India engaging with comparable forms of marginalization within their local contexts, such as A. Balakrishna Pillai in the Malayali literary world, approached European and other Indian sources out of such 'world-making' impulses.

Rather than point to a singular, narrowly defined 'Muslim' nation, intellectuals authorized a world where Muslims writing in Bengali belonged, through a recognized kinship with Hindu-authored Bengali literature, a creative appeal to the newly delineated sphere of Muslim folklore, and a critical foothold in the Indian Muslim landscape. This brief study of Muslim Bengalis by way of their own voices shows how rather than a nationalist project, a 'world literature' project arose in Bengal that productively included Hindus and non-Bengali Muslims and therefore complicates historical understandings of later developments, such as singularly 'Muslim' nationalisms and the embrace of a separate state of Pakistan. Though nominal critiques of methodological nationalism maintain a presence in South Asian historiography,[42] these critiques have not integrated the voices of modern Muslim historical actors. Colonial Bengal, as the home of the largest population of Muslims in modern South Asia, comprises an ideal site with which to start this integration.

Notes

1. Ahmed, "Amar Dekha Rajnitir Panchas Bachar," 116.
2. See the discussion on the distinction between 'religion as faith' and 'religion as social identity' in Jalal, *Self and Sovereignty*. For the modern world of late colonial India, this distinction must be understood for a clear picture of social relations between Muslims and non-Muslims, given the importance of 'majority' and 'minority' status granted to various groups in the colonial state at the time.
3. *Bulbul* started the same year that *Poedjangga Boare*/The New Writer, a literary journal in the Dutch East Indies, began to shape a new creative regionalism and cultural regeneration in what became Indonesia.
4. For the political and economic history of inter-war Bengal, see Sugata Bose, *Agrarian Bengal*; Ratnalekha Ray, *Change in Bengal Agrarian Society*, and most recently, Iqbal, *The Bengal Delta*. This article complements the long-standing focus on political, demographic, and environmental history of the period by focusing on changes in the literary sphere relative to Bengali Muslims.
5. See Damrosch, *What is World Literature*, 4.
6. For a detailed discussion of how Hindu bhadralok writers developed a notion of 'culture' in the context of intellectual history, see Sartori, *Bengal in Global Concept History*, 109–35.
7. For a discussion of journals like *Dhumketu* (The Comet), *Langol* (The Lough), and *Samyabadi* (Equality), see Bose, "Muslim Modernism and Trans-regional Consciousness in Bengal, 1911–1925."
8. Sartori and Moyn, *Global Intellectual History*. In particular, Bell's "Making and Taking Worlds," 254–79, discusses 'world making practices that articulate forms of universality' (272) and Bengali Muslim articulations of a 'world literature' could in line with Bell's 'world-making practices'.
9. Menon, "A Local Cosmopolitan", a study of the modernist Malayali critic A. Balakrishna Pillai, offers comparable analysis for the Malayali context.
10. For a complete list with full citations, see Bera, *Abdul Karim Sahityabisharad, 1871–1953*; and Hussain, *Descriptive Catalogue of Bengali Manuscripts*, xiii.
11. The *Bangiya Sahitya Parishat*/Bengali Literary Assembly began in Calcutta in 1893 as an organization designed to promote Bengali literature. The organization sponsored the translation of works from other languages into Bengali, organized research into Bengali literary history, and promoted the writing of original works in Bengali. By the early twentieth century, the organization included many prominent Bengali Hindu writers such as Rabindranath Tagore, Romesh Chunder Dutt, and Nabin Chandra Sen. Abdul Karim was a member of the organization from the 1900s onward and for most of his life was the only Muslim and a member who did not attain a formal higher education.
12. Quoted in Bhadra, *Munshi Abdul Karim Sahityabisharad O Atmiyasattar Rajniti*, 15.
13. Others in this genre include his *Saifulmuluk-Badiujjamal*, another love story, this one taken from the *Arabian Nights*. The story narrates how Sifuan, the king of Egypt, falls in love with Badiujjamal, princess of Iran. This was written after *Padmabati*, under the patronage of Syed Musa in the late 1660s.
14. He mentions this in a 1950 speech made in Chittagong and in several essays published in *Simanto*, a Chittagong periodical published between 1947 and 1952. See Khan, *Abdul Karim Sahityabisharad*.
15. Quoted from a 1951 speech to the Chittagong Literary Society, preserved in Khan, *Abdul Karim Sahityabisharad*, 121.
16. M. Wajed Ali, 'Juger Man' (The Feeling of the Age), Baisakh/Sraban, 1340 B.S./1933 in Shums, *Nirbachita Bulbul*, 10–12.
17. Abul Hussein, 'Muslim Kalchar O Udar Darshanik Bhitti' (Muslim Culture and its Philosophical Foundations) in Shums, *Nirbachita Bulbul*, 43. Jamaluddin al-Afghani had responded to a lecture Renan had given at the Sorbonne in which the French author stated that Arabs were incapable of science and philosophy. In this letter, published in the *Journal des Debats* in 1883, al-Afghani offered a host of examples to demonstrate how Muslims from the beginning of Islam had been thinking scientifically and philosophically. See Keddie, *Islamic Response to Imperialism*, 183. Though Hussein referenced al-Afghani's speeches delivered in Calcutta in other works, he never mentioned this specific exchange between al-Afghani and Renan in the late nineteenth century.

18. Hussein, 'Muslim Kalchar O Udar Darshanik Bhitti' (Muslim Culture and Its Philosophical Foundations) in Shums, *Nirbachita Bulbul*, 43.
19. Motahar Hussein Choudhury, 'Sahitya Sommondhe Nana Katha' (A Few Words on Literature) Baisak – Sraban 1340 B.S./1933, reprinted in Shums, *Nirbachita Bulbul*, 47–50.
20. Abul Kalam Shamsuddin, 'Samanbay o Sristhi' (Synthesis and Creation) Baisakh – Sraban 1340 B.S./1933, reprinted in Shums, *Nirbachita Bulbul*, 56–9.
21. Ibid.
22. Kazi Abdul Wadud, 'Bankim Chandra,' Bhadra-Agrahan 1340 B.S./1934, reprinted in Shums, *Nirbachita Bulbul*, 82–3.
23. See Bose, *Recasting the Region*, for a discussion of earlier criticisms.
24. Paush – Chaitra 1340 B.S./1933, reprinted in Shums, *Nirbachita Bulbul*, 182–4.
25. Ibid., 182.
26. Bhadra – Agrahan, 1340 B.S./1933, reprinted in Shums, *Nirbachita Bulbul*, 84–9.
27. He repeatedly refers to Oscar Wilde when discussing morality and immorality.
28. 'Prachin Muslim Sahityer Kromobikash o Boisistho' (The Peculiarities and Evolution of Ancient Muslim Literature) Baisakh-Sraban 1340 B.S./1933, reprinted in Shums, *Nirbachita Bulbul*, 51–5.
29. What he terms 'ancient' would correspond to medieval in contemporary historical language.
30. Kaikobad was the pen name for Mohammed Kazem Ali Qureshi. He authored several books of poetry, including *Asrumala* (Garland of Tears) in 1895 and the 1904 epic *Mahashmashan* (The Great Crematorium), about the third Panipat War in 1761, modelled after the style of Nabin Chandra Sen and Bankim Chandra Chatterjee. Upon reading *Asrumala*, Nabin Chandra Sen wrote in 1896, 'Had I not received your gift, I would not have believed that a Muslim can compose such beautiful poems in Bengali'. This letter was cited in Ahmed, *Unish Shatake Bangali Mussalmaner Chinta O Chetanar Dhara*, 248.
31. These critical commentaries included M. Wajed Ali's 'Iqbal,' Sri Jaminikanta Sen's 'Great Poet Sir Muhammad Iqbal,' Golum Maqsud Hilali's 'Saint Iqbal,' S. Wajed Ali's 'Iqbal,' and Abul Mansur Ahmed's 'Philosophical Iqbal,' all in a special section titled 'Iqbal's Memorial,' in the Baisakh edition of 1345 B.S./1938, reprinted in Shums, *Nirbachita Bulbul*, 421–40.
32. 'Philosophical Iqbal' in Shums, *Nirbachita Bulbul*, 439–41.
33. Ibid., 440.
34. Ibid., 441.
35. Reprinted in Shums, *Nirbachita Bulbul*, 442.
36. Ibid.
37. The 1066 page, 17 chapter volume, *Literary Cultures in History: Reconstructions from South Asia*, focuses most of its essays on pre-modern literature. Work on modern literature, regarding Hindi, Urdu, and Gujarati, remains largely within the ambit of nationalism studies.
38. See Orsini, *The Hindi Public Sphere, 1920–1940*, for an example of this approach.
39. In *Literary Cultures in History*, Kaviraj's 'The Two Histories of Literary Culture in Bengal' focuses primarily on pre-modern materials. Also, his essay omits any substantive discussion of works by Muslim authors without providing any analytical reason for such an omission.
40. See Ahmed's *Bengal Muslims, 1871–1906*; Hashmi's *Pakistan as Peasant Utopia*; and Umar's *The Emergence of Bangladesh.*
41. Bell, "Making and Taking Worlds," 272.
42. See Goswami, *Producing India*, and Bose, "Post-Colonial Histories of South Asia," for calls to dismantle nationalist methodologies to the modern South Asian past.

Bibliography

Ahmed, Abul Mansur. "Amar Dekha Rajnitir Panchas Bachar" [50 years of politics as I have seen it]. In *Abul Mansur Ahmed Rachanabali, Tritiya Khanda* [The collected works of Abul Mansur Ahmed, third volume], edited by Rafiqul Islam. Dhaka: Bangla Academy, 2001.

Ahmed, Rafiuddin. *Bengal Muslims, 1871–1906: A Quest for Identity.* New Delhi: Oxford University, 1981.

Ahmed, Rafiuddin, ed. *Understanding the Bengali Muslims: Interpretive Essays*. New Delhi: Oxford University Press, 2001.

Ahmed, Sufia. *Muslim Community in Bengal, 1884–1912*. Dhaka: Oxford University Press, 1974.

Ahmed, Wakil. *Unish Shatake Bangali Mussalmaner Chinta O Chetanar Dhara* [The thoughts and ideas of Bengali Muslims in the nineteenth century]. Dhaka: Bangla Academy, 1997.
Bell, Duncan. "Making and Taking Worlds." In *Global Intellectual History*, edited by Andrew Sartori and Samuel Moyn, 254–279. New York: Columbia University Press, 2013.
Bera, Manjula. *Abdul Karim Sahityabisharad, 1871–1953*. Kolkata: Bangiya Sahitya Parishad, 2005.
Bhadra, Gautam. *Munshi Abdul Karim Sahityabisharad O Atmiyasattar Rajniti* [Munshi Abdul Karim Sahityabisharad and the politics of identity]. Dhaka: Sanhati Prakashan, 2007.
Bose, Neilesh. "Muslim Modernism and Trans-regional Consciousness in Bengal, 1911–1925: The Wide World of *Samyabadi*." *South Asia Research* 31, no. 3 (2011): 231–248.
Bose, Neilesh. "Purba Pakistan Zindabad: Bengali Visions of Pakistan, 1940–1947." *Modern Asian Studies* 48, no. 1 (2014): 1–36.
Bose, Neilesh. *Recasting the Region: Language, Culture, and Islam in Colonial Bengal*. New Delhi: Oxford University Press, 2014.
Bose, Sugata. *Agrarian Bengal: Economics, Social Structure, and Politics, 1919–1947*. Cambridge: Cambridge University Press, 1986.
Bose, Sugata. "Post-Colonial Histories of South Asia: Some Reflections." *Journal of Contemporary History* 38, no. 1 (2003): 133–146.
Chatterji, Joya. *Bengal Divided: Hindu Communalism and Partition, 1932–1947*. Cambridge: Cambridge University Press, 1994.
Chaudhuri, N. C. "The Politics of Poetry: An Investigation into Hindu-Muslim Representation in Nabinchandra Sen's Palashir Yuddha." *Studies in History* 24, no. 1 (2008): 1–25.
Damrosch, David. *What is World Literature?* Princeton, NJ: Princeton University Press, 2003.
Datta, P. K. *Carving Blocs: Communal Ideology in Early Twentieth-Century Bengal*. New Delhi: Oxford University Press, 1999.
Devji, Faisal. *Muslim Zion: Pakistan as a Political Idea*. Cambridge, MA: Harvard University Press, 2013.
Gilmartin, David. *Empire and Islam: Punjab and the Making of Pakistan*. Berkeley: University of California Press, 1988.
Goswami, Manu. *Producing India: From Colonial Economy to National Space*. Chicago, IL: University of Chicago Press, 2004.
Hashmi, Taj-ul. *Pakistan as Peasant Utopia: The Communalization of Class Politics in East Bengal, 1920–1947*. Boulder, CO: Westview Press, 1992.
Hussain, Syed Sajjad, ed. *A Descriptive Catalogue of Bengali Manuscripts in Munshi Abdul Karim's Collection*. Dhaka: Asiatic Society of Pakistan, 1960.
Iqbal, Iftekhar. *The Bengal Delta: Ecology, State, and Social Change*. Basingstoke: Palgrave Macmillan, 2010.
Islam, Rafiqul, ed. *Abul Mansur Ahmed Rachanabali Tritiya Khanda* [Complete works of Abul Mansur Ahmed Vol. 3]. Dhaka: Bangla Academy, 2001.
Jackson, Lawrence. *An Indignant Generation: A Narrative History of African American Writers and Critics, 1934–1960*. Princeton, NJ: Princeton University Press, 2010.
Jalal, Ayesha. *Self and Sovereignty: Individual and Community in South Asian Islam since 1800*. New York: Routledge, 2000.
Jalal, Ayesha. *The Sole Spokesman: Jinnah, the Muslim League, and the Demand for Pakistan*. Cambridge: Cambridge University Press, 1985.
Kaviraj, Sudipta. "The Two Histories of Literary Culture in Bengal." In *Literary Cultures in History: Reconstructions from South Asia*, edited by Sheldon Pollock. Berkeley: University of California Press, 2003.
Keddie, Nikkie. *An Islamic Response to Imperialism: Political and Religious Writings of Jamaluddin al-Afghani*. Berkeley: University of California Press, 1968.
Khan, Israil, ed. *Abdul Karim Sahityabisharad: Abhibhasan Samagra* [Collected speeches of Abdul Karim Sahityabisharad]. Dhaka: Bangla Academy, 2010.
Majeed, Javed. "Literary History: The Case of South Asia." *History Compass* 3 (2005): 1–13.
Menon, Dilip. "A Local Cosmopolitan: 'Kesari' Balakrishna Pillai and the Invention of Europe for a Modern Kerala." In *Cosmopolitan Thought Zones: South Asia and the Global Circulation of Ideas*, edited by Kris Manjapra and Sugata Bose. New York: Palgrave, 2010.
Orsini, Francesca. *The Hindi Public Sphere, 1920–1940: Language and Literature in the Age of Nationalism*. Delhi: Oxford University Press, 2002.

Pollock, Sheldon, ed. *Literary Cultures in History: Reconstructions from South Asia*. Berkeley: University of California Press, 2003.
Ray, Ratnalekha. *Change in Bengal Agrarian Society, 1760–1850*. Delhi: Manohar, 1979.
Sartori, Andrew. *Bengal in Global Concept History*. Chicago: University of Chicago Press, 2008.
Sartori, Andrew, and Samuel Moyn, eds. *Global Intellectual History*. New York: Columbia University Press, 2013.
Shamsuddin, Abul Kalam. *Atit Diner Smriti* [Memories of old days]. Dhaka: Bangla Academy, 1994.
Shums, Nasreen, ed. *Nirbachita Bulbul/Selected Articles from Bulbul*. Kolkata: Bulbul Publishing House, 2005.
Singh, Jaswant. *Jinnah – Partition – Independence*. New York: Oxford University Press, 2010.
Trilling, Lionel. *The Liberal Imagination: Essays on Literature and Society*. New York: New York Review of Books, 1950.
Tschacher, Torsten. "Can 'Om' Be an Islamic Term?" Paper delivered at the Margins and Centers in South Asian Islam: An Interdisciplinary Inquiry Conference, University of North Texas, Denton, TX, March 11, 2011.
Umar, Badruddin. *The Emergence of Bangladesh: Class and Political Struggles in East Pakistan, 1947–1958*. Karachi: Oxford University Press, 2004.

Section III:

Reform and Modern South Asian Islam

Breaking the begging bowl: morals, drugs, and madness in the fate of the Muslim *faqīr*

Nile Green

Department of History, UCLA, Los Angeles, CA, USA

This article follows a set of developments that transformed the meaning and value of begging as a religious pursuit in colonial India. Focusing on the Muslim *faqīrs*, the article argues that missionaries, colonial officials, and physicians joined together in a moral and then medical critique of the *faqīrs* as venerated idlers and sanctified drug users. The moral dimensions of the critique were then taken up by Muslim and Hindu reformists. Positioned at the centre of an immoral nexus, for their British critics the *faqīrs* were key to the spread of drug abuse and in turn insanity among their followers. For Indian reformists and then nationalists, this nexus also connected the *faqīrs* to the moral, economic, and physical weakening of the nation. In both of these critical visions, the begging mendicant was seen as an actively harmful figure whose misdeeds ranged from promoting the inversed morality of an anti-work ethic to peddling the evils of drug addiction and rousing the riotous masses on holy days. By drawing on a range of missionary, medical and Muslim reformist texts, the article shows how from around 1870 the discourses of Islamic reform and Indian nationalism gradually joined forces with the medical and moral discipline of empire such that by the 1920s the *faqīrs* had gained an assembly of powerful enemies. In this way, the colonial period is seen as a crucial period of transition in the meanings of begging and drug use that would leave the venerated mendicants of former times disempowered in post-colonial South Asia.

Faqir, s. m. a *beggar*, a dervis: adj. poor, indigent.
– *A Romanized Hindústání and English Dictionary* (Baptist Mission Press, 1847)

Introduction

One of the most important but least recognized religious transformations in modern South Asia has been the 'fall from grace' of the holy beggar or *faqīr*. In pre-colonial India, the *faqīr* (and, less commonly, his female counterpart, the *faqīra*) enjoyed an unusual degree of autonomy from the norms of religious institutions that was based in large part on the economic independence brought by begging. The viability of such begging as a religious no less than financial strategy was in turn based on the widespread valorization of begging as a dignified and moral pursuit for the godly. Indeed, such was the strength of the semantic connection between spirituality and beggary that the latter often served as sufficient proof of the former. This was particularly the case with regard to the subcategory of *faqīrs* who displayed signs of madness which, conceived as *jazb* ('rapture, divine intoxication'), was in turn read as further proof of a beggar's spiritual status. Alongside begging and rapture, the third common attribute of the *faqīr* was drug use, chiefly preparations of cannabis or opium, which was likewise lent religious value as evidence for renouncing this world and as an instrument for reaching the other world. What is crucial to grasp is the way in which three anti-social states – the rejection of work in favour of begging, the mental incapacity to engage coherently with fellow humans and the deliberate pursuit of drugged states of consciousness – were rendered respectable through the attribution of moral value and epistemological meaning. In pre-colonial India, begging, drugging and madness meant something different than they came to mean in post-colonial India and Pakistan. With its induction of new forms of knowledge and morality, the colonial period marked this transition in the meaning and value of the *faqīr*'s lifestyle.

The aims of this article are, first, to identify this problematic as a research topic and, second, to suggest a set of developments that were central to this transformation of the meaning and value of begging as a religious pursuit. However, before moving forward, certain provisos are necessary at the outset. To begin with, it is important to distinguish begging from asceticism and renunciation which, in relying on quite different moral and epistemic foundations from begging, have followed quite different trajectories in the period surveyed in this article.[1] Moreover, no claim is made here that the values assigned to begging in the pre-colonial and colonial periods were universal. There were critics of begging in pre-colonial India just as there still remain some supporters of *faqīrs* in post-colonial South Asia.[2] By extension, it is clear that in both the pre-colonial and colonial periods there were different forms of religious mendicant no less than there were different moral communities that supported them. Neither the beggar, his critics nor his supporters were univocal. Within the remit of a short article, then, the main focus is on a specific type of beggar and a specific set of critics, namely the Muslim *faqīr* and his critics among British missionaries and medics, on the one hand, and middle-class Muslim reformists, on the other hand.

In outline, the argument made here is that the diminished status of the *faqīr* in post-colonial South Asia is the legacy of a transformation during the colonial era in the meanings of voluntary poverty (and thence begging) and self-inflicted madness (and thence drugging). This transformation took place through the trickle down effect of colonial morals, laws and scientific discourses that, for those classes of Indians most exposed to them, undermined both the moral and epistemological foundations of 'holy beggary' (*faqīrī*) as a legitimate religious path. Central to this shared opposition to the *faqīr* among middle-class colonialists and reformists alike were new attitudes to the value of work and the morality of wage-earning. These 'bourgeois' values were in turn reinforced by colonial attitudes – and, indeed, laws – concerning 'native' drug use which were internalized by the reformist Muslim middle classes as well as their Hindu counterparts, who levelled similar attacks on the begging and drug using Yogi. As both morally and medically the beggary of the *faqīr* was increasingly linked to the indolence of the drug user, he became the dual focus of wider social anxieties concerning poverty and drug use. As drugs became associated with 'insanity' under the impetus of such major commissions as the Indian Hemp Drugs Commission of 1893–1894, the *faqīr* was faced with a moral and epistemological triple whammy that explained both his behaviour and conditions as not the result of devotion to and absorption in God, but instead as the voluntary degradation of the work-shy drug addict.[3]

Since the 'colonial knowledge' that undermined the *faqīrs*' status also served as a discursive weapon in the hands of their religious competitors, there was also a strategic dimension to their deployment by Muslim reformists seeking to draw followers (and resources) away from miracle-working beggars towards their own organizations. This is not to say that the *faqīrs* were without their defenders in the face of such competition: the soldiers of the Indian Army and the notables of the princely states remained important supporters of holy beggars for much of the colonial period.[4] Rather than paint an outmoded picture of one-sided colonial domination then, the point here is to highlight epistemic and moral conflict. As the following sections hope to show, the core century of colonial rule introduced to India a powerful set of moral, legal and scientific arguments against the old respectability of the begging bowl that reformists and other religious competitors of the *faqīrs* were happy to adopt for their own purposes.

What follows is neither a detailed survey nor an individual case study. Instead, the following sections present a schematic overview, with selected examples, of increasingly hostile attitudes towards the *faqīrs* between around 1870 and 1930. By suggesting that two crucial parties of critics by way of colonial personnel and Muslim reformists – both largely from middle class, professional/bureaucratic backgrounds – shared and reinforced one another's attitudes, this article aims to provoke further research on this important but neglected socio-religious transformation.

The holy poverty of the pre-colonial *faqīr*

In pre-colonial India as in other Muslim contexts, the *faqīr* had a long history dating back to at least the middle ages.[5] At the level of popular practice, if not necessarily theological discourse, there is little doubt that the high status of the *faqīr* built on much older traditions of venerating renunciants, even if for analytical purposes the issues of begging and drug use need to be disaggregated from renunciation at large. Some sense of the widespread status of the beggar can be gleaned from the number of devotional or descriptive miniature paintings made of *faqīrs* under the Deccan sultanates, the Mughals and their successor states.[6] Similar material evidence is seen in the number of decorative begging bowls (*kashkūls*) that were patronized for such *faqīrs*, particularly from engraved *cocos-de-mer* or embossed metal-work.[7] As practical tools no less than cultural symbols and miraculous relics, such *kashkūls* serve as material evidence for the high status enjoyed by not only *faqīrs* but by the very act of begging. It was not unusual for *kashkūls* that were presented to celebrated *faqīrs* by wealthy devotees to be made entirely from silver and be embossed in gold. What this in turn points to is the paradoxical wealth of many *faqīrs* in pre-colonial India, not only through the patronage of wealthy elites but through their own collective engagement in trade and warfare.[8]

While Islamic law has always opposed the use of alcohol, its relationship to other intoxicants was more complex. As commodities, such drugs played an important part in the social life of religion in which in all its abundance of raw materials the natural world has served as the arsenal and atelier of the soul. If drug use was always contested in Islam, it did have its powerful and influential supporters, who were substantially silenced as Victorian morals sided with the sober trends of Muslim reform. Though regarded with more ambiguity than begging, drug use was supported by textual and theological bolsters, most famously in the *Bangāb-nāma* ('Book of Cannabis Infusions') of Mahmūd Bahrī (d. 1718).[9] Drugs such as cannabis and opium were quite simply part of the *materia medica* of the *faqīr* life, however much the Christian missionaries and Muslim reformists of the colonial era came to deny the role of intoxicants in the practice of 'true religion'.

Although Arabo-Persian texts explicitly devoted to drug use were always few, far more works devoted sections to discussions of begging (*faqīrī, gadā'ī*). The moral importance of individual begging to the Muslim life was discussed in numerous Persian texts from the Mughal period, not least in the *Kashkūl-e Kalīmī* of Kalīmullāh Jahānābādī (d. 1729), which based its entire outline of the Sufi life around a series of illustrative 'morsels' (*loqmah*) of wisdom taken from the metaphorical begging bowl of its title.[10] Another example comes from the circle of Shāh Musāfir (d. 1715) in the late Mughal Deccan, as testified in the *Malfūzāt-e Naqshbandiyya*. There the claim that a *faqīr* who does not go begging (*gadā'ī*) for 3 days should no longer be considered a *faqīr* was weighed up against the fact that the institutional wealth of Sufi life under the Mughals meant that for the patronized few begging was no longer needed as a source of income.[11] In Mughal as in British India, the morality of begging was clearly calculated against alternative sources of income, but the fact remained that in the pre-colonial period the act of begging was upheld by a discursive tradition that morally positioned it at as a pious action. After all, the Prophet Muhammad had himself declared that 'Poverty is my pride (*al-faqr fakhrī*)', a phrase that Sufis had been fond of quoting in their Persian writings since the days of 'Abdullah Ansari (d. 1089).[12]

Supported by such discursive pillars, the *faqīr* enjoyed a kind of *Narrenfreiheit* or 'clown's freedom' that allowed him to avoid many of the obligations of normative Muslim life, including marriage. Even as they came under attack in the colonial period, some *faqīrs* continued to enjoy these freedoms, as in the case of Banē Miyān (d. 1921), whose Urdu hagiography, written in the year of his death, affords rare precise detail on the lifestyle of a *faqīr*.[13] A former colonial soldier whose insanity saw him discharged from the Hyderabad Contingent before he commenced on a second career as a holy beggar, in his hagiographical *A'zam al-Karāmāt* Banē Miyān, was lovingly depicted in many subversive anecdotes. In numerous episodes in the Urdu text, we read of Banē Miyān begging in the bazaars, spending time in the company of courtesans (*tawā'if*), summoning musicians and leaning back to enjoy the pleasures of his *gānjā* pipe.[14] In such ways, *A'zam al-Karāmāt* upheld the value of begging, drug use and madness in a period when such activities were coming under increasing reformist critique and colonial control. Emerging among a distinct social group set apart from the middle-class reformers, the cult of Banē Miyān – and the text that it produced – was formed by low-class Indian soldiers whose collective values, choices and incomes supported the *faqīr* throughout his lifetime. Institutionalized within the colonial army, the enclosed religious economy of the sepoys was able to maintain such *faqīrs* as Banē Miyān at the same time that they were coming under increasing attack from other – British and Indian – sections of colonial society. But as we will see in the following sections, even as such particular pockets of support were maintained as late as the 1920s, the colonial period more generally saw the rise of an influential new class of Muslim critics who built their own moral and epistemological arsenal from the discursive and institutional resources of empire.

Christian and Muslim companions in criticism

The marginalization of the *faqīrs* was a long and slow process which had already been set in motion by the defeat and disarming of the so-called *faqīr* and *sannyāsī* rebellions in Bengal during the 1770s.[15] As the nineteenth century wore on, the widespread resort of the *faqīrs* to begging was in some respects the result of the removal of their former alternative revenue sources by way of soldiering and trading. By the second half of the nineteenth century, the attacks on the *faqīrs* were first moral (and then, as we will see below, medical) as the religious ideology championed by Protestant missionaries favoured action over contemplation by bringing to India critiques that had earlier been levelled against the 'indolence' of the European poor.[16] 'Busy-ness' was the key to the moral no less than the fiscal economy of the Victorian empire. These attitudes were in turn taken up by Muslim reformists.[17] For colonial critics of 'oriental' societies no less than the indigenous reformists who responded to their critique, indolence and introspection were the twin cancers of Asiatic society. The most famous visual image of the connection between opium, sloth and degeneration was the famous photograph of the exiled last Mughal ruler, Bahādur Shāh Zafar (r. 1837–1857), a withered and ragged figure shown lying back smoking his opium pipe. For both colonial critics and Muslim reformists alike, the literal degeneration of the body politic seen in popular images of the effete emperors of Islam was a root and branch decay that affected both the upper and lower echelons of Muslim society.

On a more day-to-day basis, the Protestant activism of these bourgeois social critics could be favourably measured against an ideological critique of Asian societies most potently epitomized by the figure of the drugged and idle *faqīr*. In the early 1870s, K. Raghunathji, a Bombay government servant working for the gazetteer office, described the various ways in which the 'large number of Musulmân faqirs in Bombay' made money, principally through begging, but also through jugglery and the purveying of blessings.[18] Even amid his tone of ethnographic detachment, the *faqīrs'* immorality was as clear to Raghunathji as it was to his Indian and British readers, for 'many... are reputed to be drunkards, smokers of *ganja*, *chandol*, smugglers of opium, and it is generally believed that not a few are addicted to pilfering'.[19] By the time of the 1891 imperial census, the *faqīrs* were officially categorized among other 'Miscellaneous and Disreputable Vagrants' and as such liable for suspicion at best and prosecution at worst.[20] In colonial eyes, both British and Indian, the *faqīr* was the very embodiment of eastern backwardness, proof even for the most sympathetic of overseers that Indian Islam had long since entered its age of decadence. This same critique – indeed the very language of decadence – was shared by the new Muslim reformists re-envisioning Islam as an ideology of social activism. As the Salvation Army missionary Major Frederic Tucker phrased the matter in an article entitled 'Lazy Saints' that attacked religious sloth and begging, 'There is no laziness, no love of ease, no live-as-you-please about Holiness.'[21]

With their background as clerks and lawyers, journalists and teachers, the new Muslim reformists who emerged in dialogue with the Christian missionaries represented a new breed of middle-class moralists whose social ascent would dislodge the *faqīr* from his long-held position of noble impoverishment.[22] From the late nineteenth century, the old Arabic saying of the Prophet to which the *faqīr*'s name alluded – 'Poverty is my pride (*al-faqr fakhrī*)' – was being neglected in favour of an image of Muhammad as the morally perfected merchant, an acute apotheosis of the values of the aspiring Muslim middle class which the reformists were leading.[23] Like the colonial attitudes they echoed, such forms of Islam had little sympathy for the begging of the *faqīrs* and the shirking of social responsibility that was, paradoxically, the *faqīr*'s very road to freedom. Through the combination of the preaching and publishing efforts of a new generation of Muslim moralists and the social and economic impact of a powerful colonial ideology championing the virtues of work and 'busy-ness', the moral underpinnings which had long lent the *faqīrs* credibility as men of faith were rotting away. In India as elsewhere, there would emerge a new Islam which like its protestant predecessor in the Christian west was inseparable from the wider changes in political economy that were reconstituting the experience of daily life the world over.

These attitudes were reflected in the celebrated Urdu poetry of the influential reformist and poet Altāf Husayn Hālī (1837–1914). In his chosen terms, Indian Islam had passed through an era of mighty 'flow' (*madd*) into a miserable 'ebb' (*jazr*).[24] First published in 1879, Hālī's *Madd ū Jazr-e Islām* (better known by its generic title of *Musaddas*) placed considerable emphasis on the theme of begging as both a social and moral condition to which the Indian Muslims had been reduced in his time. For Hālī, one of the chief symptoms of the 'ebb' (*jazr*) of Islam was 'beggary'.

> There is not just a single method of begging (*māngnē*) here.
>
> There are ever new ways of mendicancy (*gadā'ī*) here.
>
> Here mendicity is not restricted to the destitute.
>
> If anyone will give, there is no lack of mendicants here.
>
> Many have stretched out their hands beneath the cloak.
>
> Whether in secret or in open guise, most are beggars (*gadā*).[25]

For Hālī, then, begging was not merely the modus operandi of the *faqīrs*, but was more generalizable as both a condition and a metaphor for the Indian Muslims at large. In pointing to this state of beggary in which India's Muslims found themselves, Hālī was not developing a critique of British rule. Indeed, he devoted a section of his *Musaddas* to 'the blessings of British rule'.[26] Rather, like other Muslim reformists, his approach was moral and self-critical, asking what Muslims had done to bring this condition upon themselves. In his search for an answer to this prevalence of beggary, Hālī identified the cause of the 'ebb of Islam' (*jazr-e islām*) as lying in the Indian Muslims' rejection of learning, public spiritedness and work. He emphasized the latter point – a concern with a 'work ethic' that he shared with his British Protestant interlocutors – several times over in his poem. The section on begging quoted above was thus followed with this warning about the dangers of devaluing labour:

> Those who think hard work (*mashaqqat*) and effort (*mihnat*) disgraceful,
>
> Craft and profession demeaning,
>
> Trade and agriculture difficult…
>
> That people will sink today,
>
> If it has not already sunk yesterday.[27]

Contrasting the moral decay of India's contemporary Muslims with what he proclaimed to be the teachings of their faith elsewhere in the *Musaddas*, Hālī depicted the Prophet Muhammad as having taught the first Muslims the moral value of work:

> He made them realize the value and worth of time (*vaqt*),
>
> And imparted to them the keen desire and urge to work (*kām*).[28]
>
> And elsewhere,
>
> He gave the poor the urge to work hard (*mihnat*),
>
> Saying, 'Earn your money by your arm.
>
> 'So long as you support your own and strangers,
>
> 'You will not have to beg (*gadā'ī*) from door to door.'[29]

Such was Hālī's combined ethic and aesthetic of plain speaking that, in view of the semantic range of the term *faqīr* in Urdu, he chose the less ambiguous term *gadā* to refer to beggars. In doing so, he was able to avoid invoking in his readers' minds any of the positive associations with begging linked with the term *faqīr*. *Gadā'ī*, then, was a more general degenerative condition of which the *faqīrs* were merely the most evident protagonists. What Hālī's enormously influential *Musaddas* shows, then, is how important a question begging had become and how in turn it was linked to the moral 'ebb' of true religion in India. An overlooked manifesto for this new moral focus on begging and labour is found in the supposedly anonymous 'diary' of an Indian Muslim student published in 1909 by the celebrated public intellectual Salāhuddīn Khudā Bakhsh (1877–1931). Among the many reformist sentiments expressed in the diary was the following attack on religious customs that wasted human and financial resources. Here it was the *faqīrs* who were explicitly the target of critique, for Indian customary Islam:

> has neglected the material for spiritual interests; it has set at nought the pressing necessities of the day for the everlasting happiness awaiting the faithful in Paradise. Hence pious endowments, lavish expenditures over the erection of *mosques* and foundation of *caravansarai*s, enormous waste of money in feeding able-bodied *faquirs*...[30]

Alongside such self-confessed modernists as Khudā Bakhsh, in the early twentieth century a new generation of reformists was coming of age that would recreate Islam by shunning the older morality of the *faqīrs* to embrace a capitalist ethic of the nobility of work. In Aurangabad, where the *faqīr* Banē Miyān was seen wandering drugged and naked through the streets, the new value lent to labour and personal effort was being promoted in his lifetime among the new industrial workers at the city's textile mills by the reformist Muslim missionary, Mu'īnullāh Shāh (d. 1926).[31] While the *faqīr* Banē Miyān lay drugged and lazy, throwing bones or pebbles in blessing at his admirers, around him the followers of Mu'īnullāh Shāh were keeping themselves busy, whether working at the city's mills or touring the country to purify the religious ways of the country people. Mu'īnullāh's followers linked his emphasis on the value of work (*kām*) and spiritual action (*'amal*) to the activist ideology propounded by Muhammad Iqbāl.[32] At the same time, in the surrounding regions of Hyderabad State more generally the gift-giving of 'offerings' (*nazar*) that had long supported the *faqīr* no less than the royal economy was falling into popular disrepute, not least through widespread criticism of the extortionate demands for *nazar* made by the last Nizam, 'Usmān 'Alī Khān (r. 1911–1948).

These Muslim debates about the morality of begging and the status of its key exponents, the *faqīrs*, were greatly influenced by the widespread critique of the *faqīr* as charlatan, imposter and idle squanderer of the earnings of others. As *faqīr* became a term of abuse (most famously in Churchill's 1931 reference to Gandhi as 'a seditious fakir of a type well known in the East'), the denigration of the religious mendicant moved from the writings of travellers to the diatribes of missionaries and the wider reading public, for whom the *faqīr* became a synecdoche for India's backwardness at large. Nor was this critique unique to India; further to the west in Iran, Christian missionaries were similarly influencing Muslim reformers in denouncing the old ways of the holy beggar. There, another such negative characterization of the wandering *faqīr* was made by John Wishard, the director of the American Presbyterian Hospital in Tehran:

> [The *faqīrs*'] dress, consisting often of skins, their disheveled hair, their great clubs, and their unique receptacle for alms, make them striking figures. They may often be seen asleep on the doorstep when the weather is severely cold, oblivious to all the elements, having taken a heavy dose of opium or Indian hemp. Some writers have thought that they were the religious leaders of the people, but such is not the case. They are the religious tramps and wanderers of the Orient, with little or no influence.[33]

Wishard illustrates well the connection between Protestant morality and the criticism of the intoxicated beggar as spurious man of faith, as well as the application of this critique beyond the borders of India. A few years later, the critique of the *faqīrs* levelled by Wishard and scores of other European visitors to India and Iran would find expression in the virulently anti-Sufi modernism of the reformist Ahmad Kasravī (1890–1946), for whom idleness lay at the heart of the moral cancer that had destroyed Iran's economy and society.[34] As a symbol of this cancer, the *kashkūl* was an embarrassment and under such criticism, whether in India or Iran, the begging bowl could not survive as a symbol of Muslim piety. The *kashkūl* gradually lost all practical purpose and, even where it did survive, was reinterpreted as a symbol of the moral quality of humility rather than as an accessory of the act of begging.

While the begging bowl had no place in the universe of such new Indian Muslim organizations as the Tablīghī Jamā'at, the old *faqīr* custom of high-minded 'wayfaring' (*sayr ū safar*) did survive, albeit in new evangelical guises.[35] The followers of Muhammad Ilyās and his Tablīghī Jamā'at, founded near the shrine of Nizām al-Dīn Awliyā in Delhi in 1926, transformed the old *faqīr* culture of religious itinerancy from introspective tramping to lengthy tours of doorstep evangelism. The Muslim was still to wander from door to door in the name of faith, but unlike the traditional 'door-lurker' (literally *dar-wīsh*), the new missionary Muslims were not to beg charity so much as offer it. For these new Muslim itinerants no longer begged but instead gave, taking on the Victorian ethic of social work among the urban poor. In the same decade, having absorbed the colonial critique of the indolent 'native' through his European education, Muhammad Iqbāl (1877–1938) mounted a defence of the *faqīrs* as part of his larger attempt to reclaim the language and meanings of Islamic tradition from the depredations of European power and knowledge. In Iqbāl's poetry, the *faqīr* thus figured as an ideal moral type, the man who had found true existential freedom through his non-attachment to worldly riches.[36] Yet the very irony was that in reclaiming the term *faqīr* and endowing it with new moral meanings drawn in part from his readings in Western physics and socialism, Iqbāl divorced this idealized, existential *faqīr* from both the living persons and the physical acts of begging that had been the focus of colonial critique. Iqbāl's *faqīrs* were not beggars; indeed, in the persons of Muslim monarchs such as Amanullah, Nadir Shah or Zahir Shah of Afghanistan or Farouk of Egypt, Iqbal was more likely to use the term *faqīrī* as a virtue of kings. Abandoned even as he was rescued, the living, begging *faqīr* was a lost cause for even the brightest and bravest of Indian Muslims who responded to the colonial critique of their religion.

From the begging to the drugging mendicant

This eagerness of middle-class reformists such as Iqbāl to abandon the embarrassing association of their religion with the practices of the living *faqīrs* was not fuelled merely by their dislike of begging and its Victorian moral connection to workshyness. It was also crucially linked to the *faqīrs*' use of drugs – more specifically low-class 'native' drugs such as cannabis (*gānjā, charas*) and opium (*afyūn, tiryāq*) – that the Indian middle classes had similarly abandoned in favour of temperance or alcohol. Like the use of the begging bowl, the smoking of cannabis and opium had been an important part of Indian religious practice for centuries.[37] But as in the case of begging, missionary and other colonial critics focused on the *faqīrs*' drug use as proof of their moral degradation.[38] When the Salvation Army missionary Major Frederic Tucker visited 'a Mahommedan *faqīr* of considerable celebrity,' for example, he reported to the Salvation Army's magazine how he had found 'him and some of his disciples smoking an intoxicating drug called *charas*'.[39] Tucker's response – 'I urged them as religious leaders of the people to set a good example by giving up so bad a habit' – was one that was axiomatic to his fellow Christian missionaries, for whom the use of drugs was irreconcilable with 'true religion', whether Muslim or Christian. In this logic, if the *faqīr* used drugs, then he could not be 'truly religious' and must instead be a charlatan. As Colonel Robert Blackham (1868–1951) phrased the matter, such *faqīrs* were merely 'imposters who go the rounds for a free subsistence and remain in a state of stupid indifference to their surroundings by means of the use of intoxicating drugs'.[40] So widespread was the *faqīrs*' association with drugs that it also entered the pages of colonial pulp fiction. In one of the most dramatic scenes of F.E. Penny's 1915 novel, *Love in a Palace*, the British heroine was confronted by 'a group of faqirs... with bloodshot eyes revealing the use of hemp and opium', such that 'if they were not actually insane when they entered on their career they had become so with the use of drugs'.[41] Reinforcing the link between drugs, indolence and begging, the threatening *faqīrs* only let the heroine and her Indian lover pass when presented with an increasingly expensive sequence of Indian and then British coins in copper, silver and then gold.[42]

These attitudes towards the corruption of the *faqīrs* would in turn be adopted by Muslim reformists for their own critiques of the moral decay and imposture of their popular *faqīr* rivals. The reformists were helped by the spread to India of a powerful new moral discourse: temperance.[43] From the 1880s, missionary critiques of *faqīr* immorality combined with the spread to India of the international temperance movement, on the one hand, and new colonial regulations of drug use and the link of drug use to the expanding asylum system, on the other hand. Here too the value of the working life lay at the centre of the moral debate over intoxication in India. For in polemical presentations of the drugged and idle *faqīr*, intoxication was widely seen as the moral antithesis of work which was so central a concern of the temperance movement among the urban poor of London no less than Bombay. At the same time that it was spreading through India's major colonial cities in the 1890s, the temperance movement was also expanding into princely states such as Hyderabad, leading to the foundation of such local temperance societies as the *Bazm-e Tahzīb*, formed in 1894.[44] As it was adapted from its original American and British contexts to its new Indian ones, the temperance movement impacted attitudes to the use of 'native drugs' as well as alcohol. Nor was the celebration of sobriety linked solely to religious specialists such as *faqīrs*, for new workers' organizations, like the Kāmgār Hitwardhak Sabhhā founded in Bombay in 1909, justified their workers' temperance drives through reference to the increased productivity of the Indian worker. As one of the Sabhhā's official publications explained, 'Operatives regularly attending these [workers'] gymnasium for physical training after their day's work not only turn out better men by keeping away from the drink evil but improve in their capacity for working and in efficiency.'[45]

In the wake of the missionary and indigenous promotion of temperance, by the 1900s a range of religious authorities were taking up the anti-drug cause in India and elsewhere. In Iran, this was seen in the publication of a condemnation of *faqīrs*' opium habits by the prominent Sufi, Nūr 'Alī Shāh of Gunabad (d. 1918), while influential Hadrami Arab shaykhs also took up the cause among the Muslims under Dutch rule.[46] In the early twentieth century, the most influential Hadrami critic of intoxicated *faqīrs* was Sayyid 'Usmān ibn 'Āqil ibn Yahyā, who occupied no less an influential position than grand *muftī* of the Netherlands East Indies.[47] A similar ideological suppression of intoxication took place in colonial reformulations of Yoga, whose pre-colonial practitioners had echoed their Muslim counterparts in making liberal use of cannabis and opium.[48] When Lieutenant Postans visited the famous Yogis of Kachchh in 1839, he found their leader to have 'a peculiarly melancholy and painful expression of countenance, the effect of the excessive use of opium', which, he noted, was 'common to this sect'.[49] Yet by half a century later, like the religious sobriety of Indo-Islamic reform, the virtues of temperance also became an important part of middle-class Hindu reform. In their search for 'classical' authenticity, figures like Swami Vivekananda (1863–1902) and Aurobindo Ghose (1872–1950) ignored the living practice of large numbers of Yoga practitioners to create a sober and restrained Yoga based instead on what they presented as scriptural precedent and the archaically obscure 'authenticity' of Patanjali's *Yoga Sutra*.[50] In contrast to the intoxicated breaths of the pre-colonial Nath Yogis, the pure *prānayāma* breathing of the colonial Yoga revivalists was in this way a rejection of the 'drugged' and 'idle' mendicants who, like the Christian missionaries, the Hindu reformers likewise saw as the antithesis of 'true religion'. For like their reformist Muslim counterparts, the colonial proponents of Yoga were sober, respectable and indeed Victorian figures. As David Gordon White has pointedly written of the 'reinvention' of the Yogi during this period, among urban middle class Indians 'the bogey of the wild, naked, drug-crazed warrior ascetic was gradually airbrushed into the far more congenial image of a forest-dwelling meditative, spiritual renouncer'.[51] Here was the birth of the '420 Yogi' (*chār sau bīs jōgī*), the demeaning and criminalizing label for supposedly fraudulent mendicants given in reference to Article 420 of the Indian Penal Code.[52] Given the extent of collaboration of reformists such as Vivekananda and Ghose with European occultists, this moral overlap is hardly surprising. Like other elements of Hindu and Muslim reformist thought, their attitude to the intoxicated begging of the Yogis reflected wider moral and intellectual changes in Indian society that responded to the moral – but as we will see, also the medical – impact of empire.

From the 1880s, the link between cannabis, loaferism and moral collapse meant that the *faqīr*'s culture of opium and cannabis use came under new state scrutiny and control. Official attitudes towards *faqīr* drug use were linked to a wider denigration of lower class cultures of pleasure and leisure that were played out on an incremental and daily basis in countless minor incidents and attitudes. As the lazy days of the English nabobs were replaced by the working day of a new breed of professional administrators and bureaucrats, new systems of bourgeois regulations sought to police prostitution, intoxication, carnivals, 'barbaric' sports and other lower class practices of pleasure.[53] Such attitudes were not only directed towards Indians, for through the introduction to India of the workhouse system lower class Britons in India were also subjected to the new moral discipline of labour.[54] Low-ranking British soldiers serving in the Indian Army were similarly subjected to a host of behavioural regulations attempting to bring their sexual and bibulous pastimes into conformity with bourgeois morals.[55] But it was 'native' drugs that were the subject of greatest concern, particularly in relation to their great religious promoters, the *faqīrs*. At the same time as the temperance movement promoted internal moral restraints on the use of intoxicants, the colonial state began to consider external legal restraints on the use of 'native' drugs in particular. Despite the profitability of taxes on certain cannabis preparations, as early as 1881 the use of *gānjā* among the general population of British India was officially restricted by law.[56] Caught in the quagmire between advocates of a traditionalist and a reformist vision of India, the colonial government tried to tread carefully by investigating the religious sensibilities of those who did use cannabis before following the recommendations of the advocates of temperance.[57]

The earliest major outcome of these moral and medical pressures was the drawing up of the Indian Hemp Drug Commission of 1893–1894 to investigate the purposes and practicalities of prohibiting cannabis.[58] Though including medical and statistical enquiries, the Commission was prompted by missionary concerns and conceptions about Indian drug use.[59] Despite the rhetoric of the temperance movement and broader British as well as Indian opinion, the report was pragmatic in its findings. It ultimately led to a series of laws (such as the 1910 United Provinces Excise Act IV) restricting and taxing rather than outright banning the sale of cannabis preparations. Yet, even those British officials who opposed the evangelical politics that sought to extend temperance to the outright banning of India's indigenous drugs were forced to phrase their defence in terms of the moral discourse of labour. In his *Report on the Cultivation and Use of Gánjá*, compiled alongside the great survey of Indian cannabis use as part of which Parliament in London also established the Indian Hemp Drugs Commission in the 1890s, Sir David Prain, Curator of the Herbarium at the Royal Botanic Garden in Calcutta, was sceptical of the evidence connecting cannabis with insanity that lay at the heart of the scientific (rather than moral) rhetoric in favour of its control.[60] Yet his tacit rejection of outright prohibition was voiced through the fact that cannabis could 'give staying power' to the manual labourer in India.[61] The proper and respectable *use* of cannabis should not, he argued, be compared with its systematic *abuse* by the 'jaded sensualist'.[62] Here as elsewhere, intoxication was framed in the terms of the moral value lent to 'busy-ness' and labour.

These policies were not uniform. Despite the spread of a new critical ideology towards drugs, in princely states such as Hyderabad the official position towards intoxicants was different. Though an agreement was made with Calcutta in 1881 to prohibit the cultivation of poppy in the Nizam's Dominions, the sale and use of opium and cannabis remained legal, albeit only through limited local-monopoly licences to sell the drugs auctioned after 1882 by the Hyderabad government.[63] Perhaps it was no surprise that it was in Hyderabad that F.E. Penny had set her 1915 novel with its dramatic scenes of *faqīrs* involved in flagrant public drug abuse and that it was in the Nizam's second city of Aurangabad where in the same decade the opium-loving *faqīr* Banē Miyān had risen to fame on the dividends of sepoys and local land owners. However, even where the sale of drugs was tolerated, drug use that could now be reduced in medical terms to 'insanity' was not, and even in Hyderabad State the new institution of the colonial asylum began to expand. Negative attitudes towards cannabis and opium were thus put into institutional effect through asylums to which the usage of drugs formed a key index of entry.[64]

Drug use, moral collapse and madness

As a result of the associations made between begging, drug use and 'insanity', numerous *faqīrs* and beggars more generally found themselves incarcerated in colonial asylums. Indeed, in the 'native-only' asylums that expanded from the 1870s, 'faqīr' and 'beggar' formed either one of, or often the most populous category of inmate. By 1895, there were some 71 'beggars, fukeers, mendicants and paupers' confined in the asylums of the Bombay Presidency, more than double the number of inmates listed under the next categories of 'no occupation' or 'merchants'.[65] One outcome of this policy was the spread of various tales of *faqīr* escapes from colonial asylums, tales that in both spoken and printed form served as narrative weapons of the weak against this policy of locking up men whom the Indian Medical Service saw as 'insanes' but at least part of the Indian population saw as 'holy fools' or *majzūbs*. Stories of the asylum – or rather, the 'mad house' (*pāgal-khāna*) – thus came to feature in a range of Urdu hagiographies, including those of the 'insane' *faqīrs* Banē Miyān (d. 1921) of Aurangabad and Tāj al-Dīn Bābā (d. 1925) of Nagpur.[66] Indeed, so deeply had the asylum entered the Indian imagination by the late colonial period that the *pāgal-khāna* formed the setting for the most famous Urdu short story about Partition, *Tōba Tēk Singh* by Sa'adat Hasan Manto (1912–1955).[67]

As a result of the expansion of the asylum system, and its discursive partner of colonial psychiatry, the *faqīrs*' drug use became increasingly associated with the spread of 'insanity'. That the *faqīrs* were not merely individual drop outs but revered collective figures in whose corrupting company ordinary working Indians could frequently be found made them all the more dangerous. The *faqīrs* were not only a bad moral influence through their promotion of an anti-work ethic; they were also a social threat through their promotion of drug use. The links between opium use and *faqīrs* and, in turn, madness and beggary were clearly not without foundation and were already recognized in several popular Urdu proverbs collected by S.W. Fallon (1817–1880) and his Indian assistants. According to one such proverb, '*Afīm yā khā'ē amīr, yā khā'ē faqīr* ("Only a beggar or a rich man can eat opium")', suggesting that without great wealth, opium was the road to ruin; according to another, focusing on the link between opium and madness, '*Afyūnī, janūnī* ("Opium user, madman")'.[68] The decades from around 1860 were a period in which there spread throughout British India what Waltraud Ernst has called 'the medicalization of madness'.[69] As it turned its focus away from its original concern with European 'insanes' towards Indian victims and, indeed, causes of 'insanity', colonial psychiatry increasingly came to focus on the impact of 'native' drugs. While the massive, multidisciplinary endeavour of the 1893 Indian Hemp Drug Commission was partly concerned with the link between drugs and madness, its concerns were primarily legal in asking whether the colonial state should regulate or even ban the use of cannabis. However, serving as they were on the frontlines of a battle with Indian insanity, in the years both before and after the Commission it was the colonial psychiatrists who continued to pursue and in some cases very vocally promote the link between madness and drug use.

The most prominent medical figure to propound the link between insanity and 'native' drug use was Major George Francis William Ewens (d. 1913), who published widely on the topic. A Cambridge graduate, influential member of the Indian Medical Service and superintendent of the Punjab Lunatic Asylum, Ewens promoted the theory that drug use was less a moral matter for the private conscience than a social disease caused by *faqīrs* who pushed drugs onto their trusting devotees.[70] The *faqīrs* were not only morally contemptible, as in the language of the missionaries and Muslim reformists, but they were also medically and scientifically dangerous. For Ewens, it was the *faqīr* who was positioned most clearly at the centre of a drug-pushing axis spreading the use of cannabis – and thence both disorder and madness – amid wider Indian society. As he wrote in his enquiry into the link between insanity and popular *charas* (cannabis) use in the official *Indian Medical Gazette* in 1904, '*charas…* is very largely consumed by 'faqirs;' and many of the sufferers [of insanity] met with here ascribe the origin of their habit to association with these men'.[71] Pointing the finger even more firmly at the *faqīrs* as mongers of madness, Ewens went on to declare squarely that he had 'repeatedly met with instances in which after recovery a man has attributed his insanity to a single large dose of *bhang* or *charas* generally stated to have been administered by a *faqir*'.[72]

The intoxication of the *faqīr* thus had much higher stakes, since in the colonial psychology it accounted for the spread of drug use among the wider population. And nowhere was the mass emulation of such practices more widespread than during the popular religious festivals, particularly those associated with the shrines of the Sufi saints.

The *faqīr*, then, was the lynchpin of a mass popular culture of disorderliness that erupted on holy days, including shrine *'urs* festivals and the larger festival of Muharram. As early as the 1850s, attempts to control these festivals had led to riots and rebellions, as in the sepoy 'mutiny' at Bolarum in 1856.[73] As the century progressed, the increasingly vast numbers of urban proletarians taking part in disorderly Muharram revelries in cities such as Bombay raised the stakes still higher. Towards the end of the century, the efforts of colonial administrators to control such popular bacchanals were being echoed by Muslim reformists and Sufi pietists alike as figures such as Habīb 'Alī Shāh (d. 1904) preached on the importance of proper etiquette (*adab*) when attending the city's religious festivals.[74] Within a few years, the colonial medic Major Ewens was going one step further than the likes of Habīb 'Alī Shāh by making a case in his 1908 book for the connection between *faqīrs*, drug use, insanity and in turn crime.[75]

These attitudes and transformations were not unique to India, but were echoed in other colonial and diasporic contexts. For during the same period, the attack on the unruly celebrations of Muharram in India was being echoed on the far side of the British Empire in the Caribbean. In the decades after the first indentured labourers were shipped to the Caribbean from India in 1845, the Muharram carnivals found a new home in the plantation colonies of such islands as Trinidad and in British Guiana and Suriname on the continental mainland.[76] Like the rebellious sepoys of Bolarum, for the indentured labourers in the Caribbean the Muharram holy day of *'āshūrā* – which, through a creolization of the name of the martyred Hussayn, became known as 'Hosay' – was similarly one that blended piety with bacchanalia. In addition to the carnival floats, jesters and cannabis associated with Muharram in India, the new Caribbean context added its own characteristic ingredient of rum alongside the *gānjā* that Indian labourers had introduced to the Caribbean. Yet as in India, the Caribbean celebrations were by no means an entirely happy affair and the British feared the potentially insurrectional character of the carnival for the drunken plantation workers it brought together. As a result, Hosay was banned outright in Suriname, while efforts were also made to legislate a similar ban in British Guiana.[77] As in India again, the bans and restrictions of the Caribbean Muharram were legitimized through assertions that the carnivals had nothing to do with true religion, Islamic or otherwise, and were nothing more than underclass debauches in disguise.[78] In 1882 in Trinidad, these tensions led to an alliance between the respectable classes of Sunni Muslims and the Canadian evangelical missionary Revd Kenneth Grant, who jointly petitioned the island's governor to ban Hosay on the grounds that it was fundamentally irreligious. As a result of the pressure to suppress the carnival, in 1884 a riot broke out at the Trinidad Muharram which resulted in the killing of several celebrants by colonial police and soldiers.[79] Such were the high stakes of a popular religiosity that lent moral value to a nexus of intoxication, carnival and disorder that, in the words of one Christian commentator, added up to nothing more pious than 'a saturnalia of fiends'.[80]

A parallel process was occurring at this time in Egypt, where from the 1880s onwards British colonial administrators and Muslim reformers similarly joined force in their attempts to suppress the customary *mawlid* carnivals that had for centuries celebrated the 'birthdays' (*mawlids*) of Egypt's hundreds of Muslim saints. As Samuli Schielke has noted of these festivals, 'an old (although throughout much of Islamic history, marginal) Islamic tradition of suspicion towards ecstatic emotional states, ambivalent festive traditions, and anything that would compromise a rigid and purified state of the body and soul, comes together with the radically novel concepts borrowed from European intellectual traditions'.[81] Again, the colonial dimension of these attempts to control popular festivities cannot be separated from the wider effort to control Egyptian society after the British annexation of 1882. Nor from the fact that the 1890s saw the extension of colonial psychiatry – and its concern with 'native drugs' – into Egypt, where in 1895 some 41% of the residents of the Cairo asylum were reported as having been turned 'insane' through their use of cannabis, which in Egypt as in India was the stock in trade of the *faqīr*.[82] In such ways, the nexus that colonial missionaries and medics detected between begging, drug use and insanity was seen to have rather higher stakes than individual drug use. Just as the *faqīrs* were regarded as the perennial instigators of anti-colonial rebellions – recollect Churchill's evocation of their 'seditious' character – through their promotion of popular drug use and their rousing of religious festivals, they were also conceived as both synecdoche and subverter of the Muslim masses.

By the 1920s, in different but related ways, the nationalist movement had also adopted a vociferously critical approach to drug use that also undermined its older sanctified status as a religious activity. To many members of the Congress, popular drug use was not a danger to colonial rule but part of its apparatus. In moral terms likewise, drugs were less proof of Indian immorality than of the moral bankruptcy of colonial rule. The clear implication, then, was that the use of drugs (and of opium in particular) was an anti-national activity. The missionary and indigenous temperance movement (which counted among its ranks Gandhi's close friend and supporter Revd Charles Andrews) targeted intoxication of all kinds, with 'native' drugs regarded as especially pernicious.[83] In the wake of Gandhi's anti-opium campaign in Assam in 1921, the nationalist angle on drugs came to present the colonial state as not only morally corrupted through its soft policy on opium but as a moral corrupter of the Indian lower classes. By suggesting, as it were, that opium was the religion of the people, then in allowing its trade the colonial state was implicated in a kind of religio-narcotic pacifying of the lower classes. Of course, the real policy picture was much more complex, but the fact remained that Gandhi and the Congress turned opium and intoxicants more generally into a major moral weapon in their critique of British rule.[84] In this way, the rise of nationalist politics added further weight to the opprobrium of drug use that no amount of religio-cultural nativism would assuage.[85] Gandhi may have transformed himself into some kind of *faqīr*, but he was an emphatically sober one. If Jinnah was ironically quite the opposite, his weakness was tellingly for Scottish whiskey rather than the *gānjā* of the *faqīrs*, still less the opium of the last Mughal, Bahādur Shāh. For the nationalists too, then, drugs had no more role to play in Indian 'true religion' than they had in patriotic politics.

Conclusions

As venerated idlers and sanctified drug users, the *faqīrs* were seen by both the British and Indian middle classes as standing at the centre of an immoral nexus. For the colonists, this nexus connected them to the spread of drug abuse and insanity among their followers and to the disorder of popular holy days that saw drug use and religious fervour combust on a riotous scale. For the nationalists, the nexus connected them to the moral, economic, and physical weakening of the nation to the point that, in the reverse of the British critique, the *faqīr* was almost the colonists' lackey. In both cases, the begging mendicant was seen as more than a cultural relic of superstition: he was an actively harmful figure whose misdeeds ranged from promoting the inversed morality of an anti-work ethic to peddling the evils of drug addiction to even stirring rebellions among Indian soldiers.[86] For colonial missionaries and medics no less than the Muslim reformists and nationalists who absorbed and adapted these critiques to their own purposes, the *faqīr* was a figure of widespread and pernicious influence. As the discourses of Islamic reform and Indian nationalism joined forces with the medical and moral discipline of empire, by the 1920s, the *faqīrs* had gained an assembly of powerful enemies.

While such mendicants did not disappear in the decades that followed, they did as a result cede much of the influence they had enjoyed in former times. Among Hindus, the Sadhu *akhāras* remained an important institutional support for the old ways of the Śaiva mendicant, but aside from the occasional shrine in which to lodge, for the Muslim *faqīrs* there were no institutional supports to compare with the *akhāras*' wealth and connections. What David Gordon White has written of the Yogis applies equally to the Muslim *faqīrs*: 'In postindependence India, when their last remaining princely patrons fell, virtually all of South Asia's yogis were reduced to beggar status.'[87] Through the gradual absorption and normalizing of what were once alien meanings of mendicancy, intoxication, and madness among India's (and then Pakistan's) middle classes, the *faqīr* became an increasingly maligned and then marginal figure.

The set of developments outlined in the previous sections transformed the value of begging and drug use as religious pursuits. But ultimately, the attention devoted to the *faqīrs* by Britons and Indians alike was a response to the visible poverty of Indian (and especially Indian Muslim) society and a debate about its causes. In the period surveyed here, the debate was framed primarily in moral and medical terms. But in the wake of Dadabhai Naoroji's *Poverty and Un-British Rule in India* (1901), these terms gradually shifted to economic ones as increasing participation in nationalist and then socialist political parties spread new economic terms of debate that reframed the discussion of Indian poverty.[88] Rather than being conceived in moral and medical terms, seeing poverty as being caused by internal cultural practices that demeaned the value of labour and replaced it with an apotheosis of begging and drugging, the debate was increasingly conceived in external economic terms, presenting Indian poverty – indeed, impoverishment – as the systematic outcome of colonial policy. The latter, of course, remains the default explanation today. What we have seen in outline in this article is an older and less familiar framing of that ongoing debate.

Notes

1. Jonathan, "Sacrificial Death"; and van der Veer, *Gods on Earth.*
2. On the post-colonial *faqīr* Qurbī, see Frembgen, "Divine Madness."
3. Mills, "Cannabis in the Commons."
4. Green, *Islam and the Army.*
5. Karamustafa, *God's Unruly Friends.* On changing Islamic practices of charity, see Bonner, Ener and Singer *Poverty and Charity in Middle Eastern Contexts*; and Sabra, *Poverty and Charity in Medieval Islam.*
6. For examples, see Topsfield, *Indian Paintings.*
7. On *faqīr* begging bowls, see Frembgen, *Kleidung und Ausrüstung*, 57–101; and Frembgen, *Nahrung für die Seele*, 36–7.
8. Pinch, *Warrior Ascetics.*
9. On this work and other literary accounts of pre-colonial *faqīr* cannabis use, see Eaton, *Sufis of Bijapur*, 256–78. On other literary references, see Grierson, "On References to the Hemp Plant"; and Prain, *Report on the Cultivation*, 39–48. On religious attitudes to drug use in the medieval Middle East, see Rosenthal, *The Herb*; and Taymiyya, *Le Haschich.*
10. Jahānābādī, *Kashkūl.* The text is discussed further in Green, *Indian Sufism*, 22, 42.
11. Awrangābādī, *Malfūzāt-e Naqshbandiyya*, 117 (Persian text); and Digby, *Sufis and Soldiers*, 177–8 (translation).
12. Ibn 'Ataullah/Kwaja Abdullah Ansari, *The Book of Wisdom/Intimate Conversations*, 222.
13. Green, "Jack Sepoy and the Dervishes"; and Green, *Islam and the Army.*

14. Qādirī, *A'zam al-Karāmāt*, 28–9, 51–2. Relevant sections of the text are translated in Green, "Transgressions of a Holy Fool."
15. Islam, "The Contribution of Majnū Shāh."
16. Ewing, *Arguing Sainthood*, 57–61; and Fischer-Tiné, "Britain's Other Civilising Mission."
17. The point is argued further in Robinson, "Other-Worldly and This-Worldly Islam."
18. Raghunathji, "Bombay Beggars," with the focus on Muslim beggars on 172–4.
19. Ibid., 172.
20. Green, *Islam and the Army*, 108–10; and White, *Sinister Yogis*, 240.
21. Tucker, "Lazy Saints," 21.
22. On the middle class context of reformism, see Daechsel, *Politics of Self-Expression.*
23. On changing biographical depictions of Muhammad, see Waugh, "The Popular Muhammad."
24. Hālī, *Hali's Musaddas.*
25. Ibid., 156 [Urdu], 157 [translation].
26. Ibid., 156, 158 [Urdu], 157, 159 [translation].
27. Ibid., 156 [Urdu], 157 [translation].
28. Ibid., 116 [Urdu], 117 [translation].
29. Ibid., 118 [Urdu], 119 [translation].
30. Khuda Bukhsh, "Some Pages," 138.
31. Green, "Mystical Missionaries."
32. Ibid. On Iqbal's role in Islamic reformism, see Schimmel, "Iqbal in the Context."
33. Wishard, *Twenty Years in Persia*, 161–2.
34. Ridgeon, *Sufi Castigator*, 53–5.
35. Metcalf, "Meandering Madrasas."
36. For the fullest discussion of Iqbāl's use of the term *faqīr*, see Schimmel, *Gabriel's Wing*, 140–3.
37. Ewing, "Malangs of the Punjab"; Fisher, "Cannabis in Nepal"; and Vetschera and Pillai, "The Use of Hemp."
38. Ewing, *Arguing Sainthood*, 50–2.
39. Tucker, "A Tour in the Punjab," 191.
40. Blackham, *Incomparable India*, 112.
41. Penny, *Love in a Palace*, 228. On the wider associations between Indian religious cults and criminality made by fiction writers, see Mukherjee, *Crime and Empire*, chapter 5.
42. Penny, *Love in a Palace*, 228–32.
43. Carroll, "Temperance Movement in India"; and Colvard, "A World Without Drink." On the colonial reshaping of the culture and consumption of lower-class alcohol use, see Hardiman, "From Custom to Crime."
44. Leonard, *Social History of an Indian Caste*, 205.
45. Tacherkar, *Brief Sketch*, 7. On the huge scale of opium use among Bombay's lower classes at this time, see Jehangir, *Short History of the Lives.*
46. On Hadrami scholarly opposition to opium and alcohol use, see Moor, *Notices of the Indian Archipelago*, appendix, 16, 66; and van den Berg, *Le Hadhramout*, 130, 144, 186.
47. Azra, "Hadhrami Religious Scholar."
48. Khakhar, "History of the Kânphâtâs," 78; and Postans, "Account of the Kânphatîs," 270–1.
49. Postans, "Account of the Kânphatîs," 270–1.
50. Green, "Breathing in India."
51. White, *Sinister Yogis*, 244.
52. Ibid., 82–3.
53. Fischer-Tiné, "White Women Degrading Themselves"; and Oddie, *Popular Religion.*
54. Fischer-Tiné, "Britain's Other Civilising Mission."
55. Peers, "Imperial Vice."
56. For overviews of colonial cannabis policy, see Mills, *Cannabis Britannica*; and Mookerjee, "India's Hemp-Drug Policy."
57. Campbell, "On the Religion of Hemp."
58. *Indian Hemp Drugs Commission Report.* The Report was only one of a series of earlier governmental reports assessing the cultivation, use and taxability of cannabis. See also Prain, *Report on the Cultivation*; and Kerr, *Report on the Cultivation.*
59. Mills, "Colonialism, Cannabis and the Christians."
60. Prain, *Report on the Cultivation*, especially his conclusions, where the evidence for *gānjā*'s links to insanity was characterised as 'slight' (77). On the earlier relationship of Calcutta's

botanic garden to colonial knowledge, see Thomas, "The Establishment of the Calcutta Botanic Garden."

61. Prain, *Report on the Cultivation*, 66–9.
62. Ibid., 72.
63. *Hyderabad State Gazetteer*, 61.
64. Mills, *Cannabis Britannica*.
65. For statistical data and fuller discussion, see Green, *Islam and the Army*, 108–9.
66. For fuller discussion of these Urdu texts, see Green, "Making a 'Muslim' Saint" and Green, *Islam and the Army*, 112–7, 120–6.
67. Mantō, "*Tōba Tēk Singh*."
68. Fallon, *Dictionary of Hindustani Proverbs*, 4.
69. Ernst, *Mad Tales from the Raj*, 77–8.
70. Ewens, *Insanity in India*.
71. Ewens, "Insanity Following the Use of Indian Hemp," 401.
72. Ibid., 404.
73. Green, *Islam and the Army*, 62–85.
74. Green, "Muslim Bodies and Urban Festivals."
75. Ewens, *Insanity in India*, 1, 6, 130–1, 136, 158, 161, 287, 291–4, 300, 307, 323, 338.
76. Korom, *Hosay Trinidad*.
77. Ibid., 109.
78. Ibid., 110.
79. Ibid., 112–14.
80. Mitchell, *Indian Missions*, 7, cited in Green, *Islam and the Army*, 73.
81. Schielke, "Mawlids and Modernists," 6.
82. Clouston, "The Cairo Asylum." As Arthur Silva White reported in 1899 of the inmates of the Cairo Lunatic Hospital, 'a large proportion of the patients suffer from hashish insanities. It has been found difficult to restrict the sale of this *drug*, which may freely be bought in every town of Egypt'. See White, *Expansion of Egypt*, 270.
83. Andrews, *Opium Evil in India*; and Anonymous, *Devastation of India's Millions*.
84. For context, see Blue, "Opium for China," 44 *et passim*.
85. Cf. Chatterjee, *Nation and Its Fragments*.
86. On the rebellions, see Green, *Islam and the Army*, chapter 2.
87. White, *Sinister Yogis*, 243.
88. Naoroji, *Poverty and Un-British Rule*.

Bibliography

Andrews, Revd Charles F. *The Opium Evil in India: Britain's Responsibility*. London: Student Christian Movement, 1926.

Anonymous ('A Resident in India'). *Devastation of India's Millions by Opium under British Rule: Will God Permit Its Continuance?* London: Morgan & Scott, 1895.

Awrangābādī, Mahmūd. *Malfūzāt-e Naqshbandiyya: Hālāt-e Hazrat Bābā Shāh Musāfir Sāhib*. Hyderabad: Nizāmat-e 'Umūr-e Mazhabī-e Sarkār-e 'Ālī, 1358/1939-40. Translated by Simon Digby as *Sufis and Soldiers in Aurangzeb's Deccan*. Delhi: Oxford University Press, 2001.

Azra, Azyumardi. "A Hadhrami Religious Scholar in Indonesia: Sayyid 'Uthman'." In *Hadhrami Traders, Scholars, and Statesmen in the Indian Ocean, 1750s–1960s*, edited by Ulrike Freitag and William G. Clarence-Smith, 249–263. Leiden: E.J. Brill, 1997.

Blackham, Colonel Robert J. *Incomparable India: Tradition; Superstition; Truth*. London: S. Low, Marston, 1933.

Blue, Gregory. "Opium for China: The British Connection." In *Opium Regimes: China, Britain, and Japan, 1839–1952*, edited by Timothy Brook and Bob Tadashi Wakabayashi, 31–54, Berkeley: University of California Press, 2000.

Bonner, Michael, Mine Ener, and Amy Singer, eds. *Poverty and Charity in Middle Eastern Contexts*. Albany: State University of New York Press, 2003.

Campbell, J. M. "On the Religion of Hemp." *Indian Hemp Drugs Commission Report*. Calcutta: Government of India Stationary Office, 1893–94, vol. 2.

Carroll, Lucy. "The Temperance Movement in India: Politics and Social Reform." *Modern Asian Studies* 10, no. 3 (1976): 417–447.

Chatterjee, Partha. *The Nation and Its Fragments: Colonial and Postcolonial Histories*. Princeton, NJ: Princeton University Press, 1993.

Clouston, T. S. "The Cairo Asylum: Dr Warnock on Hashish Insanity." *Journal of Mental Science* 42, no. 179 (1896): 790–795.

Colvard, Robert Eric. "A World Without Drink: Temperance in Modern India, 1880–1940." PhD diss., University of Iowa, 2013.

Daechsel, Markus. *The Politics of Self-Expression: The Urdu Middle-Class Milieu in Mid-Twentieth Century India and Pakistan*. London: Routledge, 2006.

Eaton, Richard M. *Sufis of Bijapur, 1300–1700: Social Roles of Sufis in Medieval India*. Princeton, NJ: Princeton University Press, 1978.

Ernst, Waltraud. *Mad Tales from the Raj: The European Insane in British India, 1800–1858*. London: Routledge, 1991.

Ewens, Major G. F. W. "Insanity Following the Use of Indian Hemp." *Indian Medical Gazette* 39 (1904): 401–413.

Ewens, Major G. F. W. *Insanity in India: Its Symptoms and Diagnosis, with Reference to the Relation of Crime and Insanity*. Calcutta: Thacker, Spink, 1908.

Ewing, Katherine Pratt. *Arguing Sainthood: Modernity, Psychoanalysis and Islam*. Durham: Duke University Press, 1997.

Ewing, Katherine Pratt. "Malangs of the Punjab: Intoxication or Adab as the Path to God." In *Moral Conduct and Authority: The Place of Adab in South Asian Islam*, edited by Barbara D. Metcalf, 357–371, Berkeley: University of California Press, 1984.

Fallon, S. W. *A Dictionary of Hindustani Proverbs, Including Many Marwari, Panjabi, Maggah, Bhojpuri and Tirhuti Proverbs, Sayings, Emblems, Aphorisms, Maxims and Similes*, edited by R. C. Temple and Dihlavi Fakir Chand, Benares: Medical Hall Press, 1886.

Fischer-Tiné, Harald. "Britain's Other Civilising Mission: Class Prejudice, European 'Loaferism' and the Workhouse-System in Colonial India." *Indian Economic and Social History Review* 42, no. 3 (2005): 295–338.

Fischer-Tiné, Harald. "'White Women Degrading Themselves to the Lowest Depths': European Networks of Prostitution and Colonial Anxieties in British India and Ceylon, ca.1880–1914." *Indian Economic and Social History Review* 40, no. 2 (2003): 163–190.

Fisher, James. "Cannabis in Nepal: An Overview." In *Cannabis and Culture*, edited by Vera Rubin, 247–256. The Hague: Mouton, 1975.

Frembgen, Jürgen W. "Divine Madness and Cultural Otherness: *Dīwānas* and *Faqīrs* in Northern Pakistan." *South Asia Research* 26, no. 3 (2006): 235–248.

Frembgen, Jürgen W. *Kleidung und Ausrüstung islamischer Gottsucher: Ein Beitrag zur materiellen Kultur des Derwischenwesens*. Wiesbaden: Harrassowitz, 1999.

Frembgen, Jürgen W. *Nahrung für die Seele: Welten des Islam*. Munich: Staatliches Museum für Völkerkunde, 2003.

Green, Nile. "Breathing in India, c.1890." *Modern Asian Studies* 42, no. 2–3 (2008): 283–315.

Green, Nile. *Indian Sufism since the Seventeenth Century: Saints, Books and Empires in the Muslim Deccan*. London: Routledge, 2006.

Green, Nile. *Islam and the Army in Colonial India: Sepoy Religion in the Service of Empire*. Cambridge: Cambridge University Press, 2009.

Green, Nile. "Jack Sepoy and the Dervishes: Islam and the Indian Soldier in Princely Hyderabad." *Journal of the Royal Asiatic Society* 18, no. 1 (2008): 31–46.

Green, Nile. "Making a 'Muslim' Saint: Writing Customary Religion in an Indian Princely State." *Comparative Studies of South Asia, Africa and the Middle East* 25, no. 3 (2005): 617–633.

Green, Nile. "Muslim Bodies and Urban Festivals: Sufis, Workers and Pleasures in Colonial Bombay." In *Sufism since the Eighteenth Century: Learning, Debate and Reform in Islam*, edited by Syed Farid Alatas and Terenjit Sevea, Singapore: Institute of Southeast Asian Studies, forthcoming.

Green, Nile. "Mystical Missionaries in Hyderabad State: Mu'in Allah Shah and his Sufi Reform Movement." *Indian Economic and Social History Review* 41, no. 2 (2005): 187—212.

Green, Nile. "Transgressions of a Holy Fool: A Majzub in Colonial India." In *Islam in South Asia in Practice*, edited by Barbara D. Metcalf, 173–185, Princeton, NJ: Princeton University Press, 2009.

Grierson, G. A. "On References to the Hemp Plant Occurring in Sanskrit and Hindi Literature." In *Indian Hemp Drugs Commission Report*, 7 vols. Calcutta: Government of India Stationary Office, 1893–1894.

Hālī, Altāf Husayn. *Hali's Musaddas: The Flow and Ebb of Islam*. Edited and translated by Christopher Shackle and Javed Majeed. Delhi: Oxford University Press, 1997.
Hardiman, David. "From Custom to Crime: The Politics of Drinking in Colonial South Gujarat." In *Subaltern Studies*. 4. Edited by Ranajit Guha, 165–228. Delhi: Oxford University Press, 1985.
Hyderabad State Gazetteer. Imperial Gazetteer of India: Provincial Series. Calcutta: Superintendent of Government Printing, 1909.
Ibn 'Ataullah/Khwaja Abdullah Ansari. *The Book of Wisdom/Intimate Conversations*. Translated by Victor Danner and Wheeler M. Thackston. New York: Paulist Press, 1978.
Indian Hemp Drugs Commission Report, 7 vols. Calcutta: Government of India Stationary Office, 1893–94.
Islam, Nurul. "The Contribution of Majnū Shāh to Fakīr and Sannyāsī Rebellion: An Appraisal." *Journal of the Pakistan Historical Society* 54, no. 1 (2006): 99–110.
Jahānābādī, Kalīmullāh. *Kashkūl*, ms Tas. 130. Hyderabad: Salar Jung Library.
Jehangir, Rustom Pestanji. *A Short History of the Lives of Bombay Opium Smokers*. Bombay: J.B. Marzban & Steam Printing Works, 1893.
Jonathan, Parry. "Sacrificial Death and the Necrophagous Ascetic." In *Death and the Regeneration of Life*, edited by Maurice Bloch and Jonathan Parry, 74–110, Cambridge: Cambridge University Press, 1982.
Karamustafa, Ahmet. *God's Unruly Friends: Dervish Groups in the Later Middle Period, 1200–1550*. Salt Lake City: University of Utah Press, 1994.
Kerr, H. C. *Report on the Cultivation of, and Trade in, of Gānjā in Bengal*. Simla: Government Central Printing Office, 1877.
Khakhar, Dalpatrâm Prânjivan. "History of the Kânphâtâs of Kachh." *The Indian Antiquary* 7 (1878).
Khuda Bukhsh, S. 1909. "Some Pages from the Diary of an Indian Student." *Modern Review*, August.
Korom, Frank J. *Hosay Trinidad: Muharram Performances in an Indo-Caribbean Diaspora*. Philadelphia: University of Pennsylvania Press, 2003.
Leonard, Karen I. *Social History of an Indian Caste: The Kayasths of Hyderabad*. Berkeley: University of California Press, 1978.
Mantō, Sa'ādat Hasan. "*Tōba Tēk Singh*." In *idem., Phundnī*. Lahore: Maktaba-ye Jadīd, 1955.
Metcalf, Barbara D. "Meandering Madrasas: Knowledge and Short-Term Itinerancy in the Tablighi Jama'at." In *The Transmission of Knowledge in South Asia: Essays on Education, Religion, History, and Politics*, edited by Nigel Crook, 49–61, Delhi: Oxford University Press, 1996.
Mills, James H. *Cannabis Britannica: Empire, Trade, and Prohibition 1800–1928*. Oxford: Oxford University Press, 2003.
Mills, James H. "Cannabis in the Commons: Colonial Networks, Missionary Politics and the Origins of the Indian Hemp Drugs Commission, 1893–4." *Journal of Colonialism and Colonial History* 6, no. 1 (2005). http://muse.jhu.edu/journals/journal_of_colonialism_and_colonial_history/v006/6.1mills.html.
Mills, James H. "Colonialism, Cannabis and the Christians: Mission Medical Knowledge and the Indian Hemp Drugs Commission of 1893–41." In *Healing Bodies, Saving Souls: Medical Missions in Asia and Africa*, edited by David Hardiman, 169–192, Amsterdam: Rodopi, 2006.
Mitchell, Revd J. R. *Indian Missions; Viewed in Connexion with the Mutiny and Other Recent Events*. London: James Nesbit, 1859.
Mookerjee, H. C. "India's Hemp-Drug Policy under British Rule." *Modern Review* 84 (1948): 446–454.
Moor, J. H. ed. *Notices of the Indian Archipelago and Adjacent Countries*. London: Frank Cass, 1968 [1837].
Mukherjee, Pablo. *Crime and Empire: The Colony in Nineteenth-Century Fictions of Crime*. Oxford: Oxford University Press, 2003.
Naoroji, Dadabhai. *Poverty and Un-British Rule in India*. London: S. Sonnenschein, 1901.
Oddie, Geoffrey A. *Popular Religion, Elites, and Reform: Hook-Swinging and Its Prohibition in Colonial India, 1800–1894*. Delhi: Manohar, 1995.
Peers, Douglas. "Imperial Vice: Sex, Drink and the Health of British Troops in North Indian Cantonments, 1800–1858." In *Guardians of Empire*, edited by David Killingray and David Omissi, 25–52, Manchester: Manchester University Press, 1999.
Penny, F. E. *Love in a Palace*. London: Chatto & Windus, 1915.

Pinch, William R. *Warrior Ascetics and Indian Empires*. Cambridge: Cambridge University Press, 2006.

Postans, Lieutenant T. "An Account of the Kánphatis of Danodhár, in Cutch, with the Legend of Dharamnáth, Their Founder." *Journal of the Royal Asiatic Society* 5 (1839): 268–271.

Prain, Surgeon-Captain David. *Report on the Cultivation and Use of Gánjá*. Calcutta: Bengal Secretariat Press, 1893.

Qādirī, Muhammad Ismā'īl Shāh. *A'zam al-Karāmāt*. Aurangabad: Mu'īn Prēs, n.d. 1921.

Raghunathji, K. "Bombay Beggars and Criers." *Indian Antiquary* 11–12 (1872): 22–24, 44–47, 141–146, 172–174.

Ridgeon, Lloyd. *Sufi Castigator: Ahmad Kasravi and the Iranian Mystical Tradition*. London: Routledge, 2006.

Robinson, Francis. "Other-Worldly and This-Worldly Islam and the Islamic Revival." *Journal of the Royal Asiatic Society* 14, no. 1 (2004): 47–58.

Rosenthal, Franz. *The Herb: Hashish Versus Medieval Muslim Society*. Leiden: E.J. Brill, 1971.

Sabra, Adam. *Poverty and Charity in Medieval Islam*. Cambridge: Cambridge University Press, 2001.

Schielke, Samuli. "Mawlids and Modernists: Dangers of Fun." *International Institute for the Study of Islam in the Modern World Review* 17 (2006): 6–7.

Schimmel, Annemarie. *Gabriel's Wing: A Study into the Religious Ideas of Sir Muhammad Iqbal*. Leiden: E.J. Brill, 1963.

Schimmel, Annemarie. "Iqbal in the Context of Indo-Muslim Mystical Reform Movements." In *Islam in Asia*, Vol. 1 *South Asia*, edited by Yohanan Friedmann, 208–226. Jerusalem: Magnes Press, 1984.

Tacherkar, H. A. and others. *A Brief Sketch of the Work of the Kāmgār Hitwardhak Sabhha, Bombay*. Bombay: Indu-Prakash Press, 1919.

Taymiyya, Ibn. *Le Haschich et l'extase*. Translated by Yahya Michot. Beirut: Albouraq, 2001.

Thomas, Adrian P. "The Establishment of the Calcutta Botanic Garden: Plant Transfer, Science and the East India Company, 1786–1806." *Journal of the Royal Asiatic Society* 16, no. 2 (2006): 165–177.

Topsfield, Andrew. *Indian Paintings from Oxford Collections: A Selection of the Mughal Period (c.1500–1850) Paintings from the Ashmolean Museum and the Bodleian Library*. Oxford: Ashmolean Museum, 1994.

Tucker, Major Frederic. "Lazy Saints." *All the World: A Monthly Record of the Work of the Salvation Army in All Lands* 1, no. 2 (1884–1885): 20–21.

Tucker, Major Frederic. "A Tour in the Punjab." *All the World: A Monthly Record of the Work of the Salvation Army in All Lands* 1, no. 10 (1884–1885): 191–193.

van den Berg, Lodewijk Willem Christiaan. *Le Hadhramout et les colonies arabes dans l'archipel indien*. Batavia: Imprimerie du Gouvernement, 1886.

van der Veer, Peter. *Gods on Earth: The Management of Religious Experience and Identity in a North Indian Pilgrimage Centre*. London: Athlone Press, 1988.

Vetschera, Traude, and Alfonso Pillai. "The Use of Hemp and Opium in India." *Ethnomedezin* 5, no. 1–2 (1978): 11–23.

Waugh, Earl H. "The Popular Muhammad: Models in the Interpretation of an Islamic Paradigm." In *Approaches to Islam in Religious Studies*, edited by Richard C. Martin, 41–58, Tucson: University of Arizona Press, 1985.

White, A. S. *The Expansion of Egypt under Anglo-Egyptian Condominium*. London: Methuen, 1899.

White, David Gordon. *Sinister Yogis*. Chicago, IL: University of Chicago Press, 2009.

Wishard, John G. *Twenty Years in Persia: A Narrative of Life under the Last Three Shahs*. New York: Fleming H. Revell, 1908.

A matrilineal Sufi shaykh in Sri Lanka

Dennis B. McGilvray

Department of Anthropology, University of Colorado, Boulder, CO, USA

This article explores the influence of local concepts of matrilineal kinship and descent through women in the construction of a modern Sufi *silsila* (an authorized 'chain' of spiritual and genealogical ancestry) in Sri Lanka. Makkattar Vappa, a popular Sufi shaykh in the Tamil-speaking eastern region of the island, asserts hereditary *maulana* (sayyid) status as a member of the Prophet's household descent group (*ahlul bayt*) by means of close genealogical linkages to a locally enshrined saint of Yemeni family ancestry traced through several women, including his mother, his father's mother, and his wife. The kinship system here is Dravidian in structure, but with a matrilineal emphasis that is seen today in the administration of Hindu temples and Muslim mosques by matrilineal clan elders, and in the negotiation of matrilocal marriages based upon women's pre-mortem acquisition of dowry property in the form of houses and paddy lands. The shaykh in question is himself the successor Kālifā of a Sufi order (*tāriqā*) based in Androth Island, Lakshadweep, a similarly matrilineal society located off the west coast of India. In his prior career, he was an art and drama teacher in a local government school, and his style of Sufi leadership continues to be pastoral and pedagogical in tone. This, together with a strong base of support from former students, has enabled him to escape the sort of stridently anti-Sufi violence that has erupted in Muslim communities elsewhere in the region. His awareness of anthropological research on matrilineal kinship and marriage patterns in this part of the island may have encouraged him to trace his sayyid *silsila* through both male and female genealogical connections.

Muslim matriliny in Sri Lanka

Sri Lanka's Muslims or 'Moors', 9% of the total population and overwhelmingly Sunni and Shafi'i in Islamic heritage, make up roughly 50% of the Tamil-speaking population in the Eastern Province of the island, a region comprising three coastal districts: Trincomalee, Batticaloa, and Amparai. In the latter district, where sea fishing and paddy farming are the foundations of the local economy, they outnumber the Tamil Hindus and Christians as well as the Sinhalese Buddhists. Throughout the island, the Sri Lankan Muslims or Moors have been historically and culturally linked with the coastal Marakkāyar Muslims of Tamil Nadu and the Māppiḷa Muslims of northern Kerala, a shared heritage from centuries of maritime trade between the Middle East and South Asia.[1] The term 'Moor' is an anglicized colonial usage derived from the Portuguese *mouro* (people of Morocco or the Mahgreb), the label applied to all Muslims in the Portuguese colonial lexicon. Today the more common term is simply 'Muslim', but the older term Moor, and its Tamil equivalent (*cōṉakar*), more accurately distinguishes the ethnicity of the community as Tamil-speaking Sri Lankan Sunni Muslims who follow the Shafi'i school of Islamic law. In the latter respect, they share their south Arabian Shafi'i legal heritage with coastal Muslim communities throughout southern India and Southeast Asia.[2] The ethnic designation of Moor or *cōṉakar* also serves to distinguish them from other, much smaller Sri Lankan communities that profess Islam: Malays, Bohras, Khojas, and Memons.

The medieval Hindu and Buddhist kingdoms of Kerala and Sri Lanka allowed Arab merchants – many of whom acquired local wives by whom they fathered Indo-Muslim progeny – to dominate pre-colonial trade in port settlements such as Calicut and Colombo.[3] Soon after Vasco da Gama's 1498 hostile naval encounter with the 'Moors' of Calicut, the Portuguese encountered Muslim traders in Ceylon who spoke Tamil and who had been given royal permission to collect customs duties and regulate shipping in the major southwestern port settlements under the suzerainty of the local Sinhalese Kings of Kotte.[4] Commercial, cultural, and even migrational links between Muslim towns in southern India and Sri Lankan Moorish settlements are confirmed in the historical traditions of Beruwala, Kalpitiya, Jaffna, and other coastal settlements where Sri Lankan Muslims have lived for centuries.[5] In a reciprocal gesture, many Sri Lankan Moorish families have longstanding devotional attachments to Sufi tomb-shrines located along the Tamil Nadu coastline, or are followers of contemporary saintly shaykhs and *tangal* sayyids from Kerala and the Lakshadweep Archipelago.

According to colonial eyewitness accounts between the sixteenth and eighteenth centuries,[6] Tamil-speaking Muslims were already well established as farmers, fishermen, and merchants living in enclaved villages on the east coast under the political domination of hereditary matrilineal Tamil Hindu chiefs and landlords of the Mukkuvar caste, a group who appear to have seized control of the region as mercenary soldiers and sailors from the invading south Indian army of Kalinga Magha in 1215 C.E.[7] Tamil Mukkuvar chiefs in Batticaloa and Amparai districts have long proclaimed their kingly warrior heritage in the oral traditions and ethno-historical chronicles of the east coast, but a maritime caste of the same name is also found today in coastal Kerala, a region anthropologically famed for its matrilineal family patterns.[8]

The (canonically) seven Mukkuvar chiefdoms encountered in the Batticaloa region by the Portuguese (1505–1658) and the Dutch (1658–1796) were strongly infused with a matrilineal ideology of political succession and landholding, and they supported a society-wide kinship structure in all castes based upon hierarchically ranked exogamous matrilineal descent groups (matriclans), referred to in Tamil as *kuṭi*. The presumptive origin of matrilineal politics, land tenure, and family organization among both the Tamils and the Moors is the historic 'Kerala connection' of the Mukkuvars, as well as the intermarriage of Muslim men with local matrilineal Tamil Hindu women. Circumstantial evidence for this can be seen in a number of Moorish matriclan names that are strikingly similar to those of their Tamil neighbours.[9] Under the British colonial administration that took control in 1796, and following Sri Lankan independence in 1948, the economic and political influence of the Mukkuvar chiefs and landlords (*pōṭiyār*) steadily weakened, giving the Moors an opening to acquire paddy land and free themselves from semi-feudal subordination to the Tamils.

Today, in the wake of the 2009 defeat of the LTTE – and despite the disproportionately devastating impact of the Indian Ocean tsunami of 2004 upon the Muslim community[10] – the Muslims today are visibly the most prosperous community on the east coast, and their educational achievements have caught up to those of the Tamils, who initially benefited from nineteenth-century Christian missionary schooling.

Today, in the coastal farming town of Akkaraipattu in Amparai District – with its population of about 65,000 – where I have based most of my ethnographic fieldwork, the matrilineal principle is still seen in the administrative structure of the oldest Hindu temples and Muslim mosques, which are run by committees composed of male trustees (Hindu *vaṇṇakkar*, Muslim *maraikkār*) of the leading matriclans in the congregation. On the Hindu side, these matriclans (and also lower-ranking service castes) continue to sponsor 'shares' of the annual week-long puja festivals for the temple deities, thus ceremonially exercising their hereditary rights and dramatizing their hierarchical status for all to see. On the Muslim side, I collected oral accounts of a now-defunct tradition of matriclan sponsorship of annual kandoori (*kantūri*, equivalent to north Indian *urs*) festivals on the death anniversaries of Sufi saints enshrined in tomb-shrines (*ziyāram*, equivalent to Indian *dargah*) at local mosques. There was a time, reportedly lasting up until the 1960s, when the matrilineal mosque trustees also meted out corporal punishment by caning Moorish miscreants and instructed Moorish voters on how to cast their ballots in local and national elections. Since then, however, the mosque trustees have been chastened by their unsuccessful efforts to dictate local politics, which are nowadays controlled by local 'big men' backed by national political parties.

The so-called Mukkuvar Law, an ancestral matrilineal property system in the Batticaloa region, was peremptorily invalidated by the British in 1876, and most of what we know of its prior application is contained in a short and frustratingly obtuse treatise on the subject by a Ceylon Burgher attorney, Christopher Brito, published in 1876.[11] Despite the temptation of some legal historians to view the Mukkuvar Law as based upon the strictly matrilineal Marumakkattayam Law historically followed by the Nayar caste of central Kerala,[12] the actual operation of the Mukkuvar Law seems to have featured a complex mixture of both matrilineal and bilateral inheritance. When the colonial government chose to discontinue the Mukkuvar Law in the civil courts after 1876, there appear to have been relatively few complaints from the Tamils in the Batticaloa region where it had been applied. The most plausible hypothesis is that, by then, most family property was already being passed to daughters in the form of dowry at marriage, rather than as post-mortem inheritance from parents. For both Tamils and Moors today the intergenerational transfer of real property – houses and paddy lands – is still overwhelmingly from parents to their daughters in the form of dowry (*cītaṉam*) at marriage, or as an outright gift (*naṉkoṭai*) to their daughters prior to marriage. The residence pattern itself is matrilocal at the outset, with the son-in-law moving into the house occupied by his wife and her parents and her unmarried siblings for the early years of marriage. When the time comes for a younger daughter to be married, her parents will – if possible – shift into a new dowry house they have built for her nearby, leaving the older married daughter and son-in-law in the older house as an independent nuclear family unit.[13]

For Hindu and Christian Tamil families, the preference is to sign a so-called 'dowry deed' (*cītaṉam uṟuti*) that legally gives joint undivided ownership of the house and land to the daughter and son-in-law. In contrast, Moorish parents are more likely nowadays to bestow outright ownership of family property as a gift to their daughters prior to marriage, sometimes even in childhood. This is said to avoid troublesome property litigation in the case of a divorce, and it responds to the complaints of Islamic reformists who object to recognizing the 'Hindu' practice of dowry as a part of modern Sri Lankan Muslim marriage. Surprisingly, in the context of global Islamic fundamentalism and purification of the faith, this ends up reinforcing, rather than weakening, Sri Lankan Muslim women's traditional property rights, since the preference for matrilocal dowry-house-based families remains unquestioned. The post-mortem inheritance of Moorish family property is always governed by Sri Lanka's version of sharia law, which is primarily Shafi'i in practice. In most cases, however, there is very little property left to inherit after all the daughters (and sometimes the mother's sororal nieces) have been provided for by 'pre-mortem' gifting.

This presumes, of course, that a bride's parents have the wealth necessary to offer a dowry house in the first place. Poor or dispossessed women have difficulty finding a husband, unless they are lucky enough to secure an independent love match. Such women, or their mothers, have been known to work as housemaids in the Middle East in order to construct the essential dowry houses needed for marriage in Sri Lanka.[14]

Because of this pervasive dowry-based system of property transfer to women – either as sole owners or as co-parceners with their husbands – the destruction caused by the 2004 tsunami posed a significant loss to the long-term household estates of many women, both Tamil and Moorish. Relief aid in the aftermath of the tsunami was often extended to men – husbands, fathers, brothers, sons – who were assumed to be the responsible 'heads of households,' rather than to the women who had been the legal proprietors. While this raised alarm bells among local women-centred NGOs, it has proven to be only a temporary problem, because most externally provided post-tsunami housing is destined to be passed again to women as dowry property when younger daughters reach marriageable age.[15]

Not surprisingly, however, the strength of matrilineal clan (*kuṭi*) identities appears to be gradually weakening in the twenty-first century along with the taboo on marriages within the clan, especially among younger Tamils and Moors for whom the old-fashioned ritual status (or stigma) of matriclan ranking affords less and less meaning or benefit. Still, because of the Dravidian-type kinship terminology shared by the Tamils and the Moors, it remains awkward to marry someone who is a member of your very own matriclan without at least a slight connotation of committing classificatory incest. Among Tamils and Moors of the senior generation, an awareness of matriclan identity, and of ancestral marriage alliances between specific matriclans, is still nostalgically preserved.

In sum therefore, the principal components of Muslim 'matrilineality' in eastern Sri Lanka are historically sanctioned administration of major temples and mosques by committees of matrilineal male clan elders; matrilocal post-marital residence, and transfer of family houses and paddy lands to daughters at, or sometimes prior to, marriage; and awareness, especially among older residents, of distinct matrilineal descent-group identities and rules of exogamy, including longstanding trans-generational marriage exchange alliances between specific matriclans, each with its own symbolic marks of social prestige.

Makkattar Vappa: a contemporary Sri Lankan Sufi shaykh

I have discussed elsewhere[16] the outbreak of violence directed against charismatic Sufi shaykhs in the densely populated Muslim town of Kattankudy in Batticaloa District, a problem attributed to the rise of staunchly reformist – some would say Salafist or Wahhabi or Towheed – groups who are hostile to all Sri Lankan Muslim traditions of saint veneration and Sufi mysticism. This is only one of the many global pan-Islamic influences that have been felt in Sri Lanka's Muslim community. Earnest, bearded, white-robed, door-to-door missionary teams from the Tablighi Jamaat are nowadays a familiar sight in Muslim neighbourhoods, urging lapsed worshippers to resume their daily prayers. Evening and weekend study-groups organized by the Jamaat-i-Islami are aimed at a more educated middle-class Muslim audience who desire a deeper and more detailed understanding of the Quran and Hadiths.[17] Increasingly, nowadays, one also finds independent mosques loosely labelled Towheed (*tawhid*, the unity and alterity of Allah) congregations that are widely alleged to receive funding from missionary 'Salafist' or

'Wahhabi' organizations abroad. Today Sri Lankan Muslims seeking to maintain their older, traditional religious practices feel obliged to identify themselves as *sunnattu jamaat*, members of the 'customary or standard' community of Muslims.

The primary targets of Sri Lankan Muslim reformist groups are the older traditions and institutions of Sri Lankan popular Islam, such as vow-making at the tombs of Sufi shaykhs and Maulana seyyids, and the celebration of the annual saints' festivals that women and children still so often attend and enjoy. These festivals may feature public exhibitions of ecstatic, self-mortifying Sufi devotional practice (*zikr*) by Bawa faqirs of the Rifai order, unchanged in over half a century.[18] When any of these events attracts an audience of non-Muslims, especially Hindus, it is taken as evidence that something 'non-Islamic' must be happening. For example, the popular Sufi pilgrimage shrine at Daftar Jailani in the Kandyan Hills has frequently generated complaints from Islamic reformist groups, although it lacks a tomb for saint Abdul Qadir Gilani (1077–1166 CE, buried in Baghdad) whose astral visit is celebrated there. Most recently, starting in 2013, the Daftar Jailani shrine has also been the target of militant anti-Muslim Sinhala Buddhist monks, such as the Bodu Bala Sena ('Buddhist Strength Force'), who seek to reassert control over it as an ancient Buddhist archaeological site.[19]

As the professionalization of the Islamic clergy has steadily increased through higher levels of seminary training, the regional and national councils of the Ulama have exerted greater theological control, including the issuance of *fatwas* (legal interpretations) to scold or to excommunicate particular heterodox Sufi shaykhs for their alleged pantheism or deviant interpretations of Islamic theology. In Kattankudy, a densely populated Muslim town near Batticaloa with historic commercial ties to South India, a controversial Sufi leader named Rauf Maulavi established his own mosque adjacent to the *ziyaram* (tomb-shrine) of his father several decades ago and developed a well-funded organization (All Ceylon Islamic Spiritual Movement) to disseminate his books and newsletters in Tamil. Because he espoused the allegedly 'pantheistic' doctrines of the twelfth-century Sufi philosopher Ibn Arabi (*wahdat-ul-wujūd*, or 'unity of creation'), his teachings were condemned by fundamentalist opponents as a violation of *tawhid*, the radical unity and alterity of Allah, and he was declared an apostate (*murtad*) in a fatwa issued by the All Ceylon Jamiyathul Ulama in 1979. Despite ostracism and periodic attacks on his property, Rauf successfully defied the fatwa for decades, backed up by his own muscular and well-financed group of local followers, and ultimately the decree was rescinded. He was driven from Kattankudy by mob violence in late 2006, and he is now based in Colombo. However, he retains a strong core of supporters and disciples, and he maintains an active website in the name of his saintly father, Al Haj Abdul Jawadh (http://www.ajawt.org).

The headquarters shrine of a second Sufi leader, the late Shaykh Abdullah Payilvan, was also attacked in December 2006 at the same time that Rauf was expelled, in a convulsion of mob violence sparked by the burial of Payilvan's body in a private tomb at his shrine near the seaside in Kattankudy. The followers of Payilvan belong to a new Sufi order he founded called Thareekatul Mufliheen, and they actively distribute a wide array of Payilvan's published books and recorded songs on their website (www.mufliheen.com). Payilvan, like Rauf, had been declared an apostate for his pantheistic theology, and his corpse was barred from burial within the boundaries of Kattankudy (a totally Muslim town) by conservative Muslims. Rumours also circulated that Payilvan's followers had filled his tomb with honey, an idolatrous gesture anathema to Islamic reformist sensibilities. As a result, mobs tore down the Mufliheen headquarters shrine and its imposing minaret, removed Payilvan's corpse from his tomb, and took it to a hidden location where it was reportedly burned. Even Sri Lankan Muslims with no sympathy for Payilvan's Sufi doctrines have found this desecration and cremation of his body to be appalling, with its symbolic implication that Payilvan was in fact a Hindu. The website maintained by the Thareekatul Mufliheen includes an archive of over 20 years of legal appeals and diligent civil rights injunctions lodged on behalf of Payilvan, along with photos of the 2006 violence. His followers have by now rebuilt most of his shrine and have also obtained a permanent Sri Lankan Police guardhouse for the premises.

For reasons that are not entirely clear, this sort of violent opposition to Sufi shaykhs and their devotional followers has not yet arisen in Akkaraipattu, located only 75 km south of volatile Kattankudy on the east coast road.[20] From the 1970s – and possibly earlier – several groups of Sufi-oriented Muslim laypeople have met for Thursday evening *zikr* (devotional practice) at private residences in Akkaraipattu, including a branch of the Tamil-speaking 'Sufi Manzil' organization originally founded in Kayalpattinam, Tamil Nadu, in 1975 with chapters in Tamil Nadu, Kerala, and Sri Lanka.[21] This organization also espouses the encompassing 'unity of creation' (*wahdat-ul-wujūd*) philosophy of Ibn Arabi, one of the theological issues that generated hostile anti-Sufi violence in Kattankudy. The Sufi shaykh described in this article, however, is locally rooted in Akkaraipattu, where he grew up and served for much of his life as an elementary school art instructor.

Born A.S.A. Abdul Majeed Makkattar, and popularly known for most of his life as 'Makkattar Majeed', he was a popular teacher known for his artistic creativity in the classroom and in staging dramatic productions with his students. Among his many grade school alumni and spiritual supporters is the local Member of Parliament, a cabinet minister (2001–present) in the government of President Mahinda Rajapakse,[22] who has provided ample patronage to his voter base in Akkaraipattu, including major road projects and a new municipal water supply. With such an influential ally on his side, Makkattar has enjoyed at least short-term insurance against any local anti-Sufi detractors. The only organization that might pose a formal threat in Akkaraipattu is a reformist *tawhid* mosque that calls itself the Centre for Call and Guidance (in Tamil, *vaḻikkāṭṭu nilaiyam*), headed by a sincere and resolute young Maulavi who told me he had become disillusioned with the Tablighi Jamaat after spending several years working with them in Pakistan and Bangladesh.[23] Although I did not learn the details, the clear implication was that his current theology was located to the right of the Tablighi Jamaat. His adherents are said to be growing among the poorer Moors who live on the periphery of the town.

In the mid-1970s, Makkattar encountered a visiting Sufi shaykh from Androth Island in the Lakshadweep archipelago, a Union Territory of India in the Arabian Sea to the west of Calicut, Kerala. Although it has not been noted in the scholarly literature, there has been a significant stream of Sufi shaykhs (often bearing the title of *tangal*, the Malayalam equivalent of *maulana*) travelling on circuit from Androth Island to Sri Lanka and back starting in the nineteenth century or possibly earlier. Today a *tangal* from Androth runs the Sri Lankan office of the Rifai Sufi order near the Grand Mosque in Colombo's Pettah district, and it is through the teaching of Androth and northern Kerala based shaykhs that the musical tradition of the *rifai ratib*, a devotional Sufi call and response performance genre, was spread to Sri Lanka.

The full title of the Androth shaykh to whom Makkattar became attached was Qutbul Aktab Hallajul Mansoor, but he was popularly called Maulana Vappa ('Father Maulana') in keeping with his *maulana* (sayyid) lineage and his role as a spiritual father to his disciples, whom he regarded as his 'children' (*piḷḷaikaḷ*). Over the course of several years and multiple visits to Akkaraipattu and to other places in Sri Lanka, he is said to have miraculously cured Makkattar of a life-threatening kidney disease. Makkattar eventually became Hallaj Mansoor's chief Sufi disciple (*murīd*) and his designated Sri Lankan

Figure 1. (Colour online) Hallaj Mosque, Akkaraipattu, Sri Lanka.

deputy when he was away in Androth. Leading a congregation of fellow Sufi initiates, Makkattar raised funds and built a private mosque to conduct *zikr* as taught by Hallaj Mansoor in Akkaraipattu, including a special room for the Androth shaykh to stay in when visiting and – it was hoped – to be buried in when he died (Figure 1). As it turned out, Hallaj Mansoor expired in 2005 and was entombed on his home island of Androth, but not before officially designating Makkattar as his successor kālifā to lead his entire *tāriqā* or spiritual lineage worldwide, which he identified as 'Qadiriyyi Chishti'.[24] During one of the Androth shaykh's tours of Sri Lanka in 2001, I was handed a cellphone by Makkattar who had dialed up Hallaj Mansoor in Puttalam on the opposite side of the island. It was not easy to have a spontaneous dialogue in Tamil over a crackly mobile connection with a mumbling holy man whom I had never met, but afterward I basked in the awe of Makkattar's Sufi acolytes. My conversation was regarded as verbal *darshan*, or *barakat* by cellphone!

Since assuming the black mantle, or *khirka*, of kālifā-hood, the Akkaraipattu shaykh has begun to refer to himself in print as al-Qutub as-Shaykh as-Sayyid Kalifatul Hallaj Abdul Majeed Makkattar, but in person he prefers people to address him as 'Father Makkattar' (*makkattār vāppā*) in the paternal fashion of his predecessor. With the intimacy of a parent at home, he transfers rice and curry directly from his own plate onto the plates of his 'children' and mixes their food with his own hand. Similarly, in official photographs he poses in ornate robes and rosary beads and a pleated turban bedecked with medallions like an Indian state guard of honour, but in his sandy yard at home he can usually be found wearing a worn short-sleeved shirt and a simple cotton handloom sarong, rocking on a child's plank swing hung from the low-hanging branch of a mango tree, smoking endless cigarettes, and constantly answering his cellphone in the company of a hovering cluster of younger male followers.

On every occasion I have met with Makkattar since 2002, he has displayed a newer model cellphone, each a gift from one of his disciples who is eager to receive the outdated model charged with the spiritual power (*barakat*) it has acquired through the constant traffic of Makkattar's healing words. Equipped with the latest mobile technology, Makkattar receives calls from followers in Dubai, Denmark, and New Zealand I was told, and he often uses his cellphone as a long-distance curing instrument. A remote patient is instructed to hold the receiver against the afflicted part of his or her body while Makkattar transmits curative blessings through his cellphone (Figure 2). He also counsels troubled women privately and draws pastel portraits of his deceased shaykh Hallaj Mansoor, practices that could readily attract the disapproval of fundamentalist critics (Figure 3). People often drop by without appointments, and Makkattar offers them a combination of pastoral advice,

Figure 2. (Colour online) Makkattar using cellphone to transmit curative blessings.

Figure 3. (Colour online) Makkattar holding personal portrait of his late Sufi master, Shaykh Hallaj Mansoor.

protective talismans, and erudite philosophical lectures, depending upon the situation. His gravely, tobacco-stressed voice never seems to wear out.

Saintly connections through women

My initial grasp of Makkattar's philosophy and personal background was derived from rambling conversations and meals with him while visiting Sri Lanka periodically over several decades.[25] However, in 2010 he gave me a 270-page compendium of his writings in Tamil entitled *Hallājin̲ Pōtan̲aikaḷ* ('Teachings of Hallaj') in which he explores topics ranging from the astronomical calculation of Islamic prayer times and the pros and cons of Ibn Arabi's doctrine of *Wahdat-ul-Wujūd*, to the alternative ways of tracing spiritual connections back to the Prophet Muhammad and the detailed history of his own spiritual and genealogical lineage or 'chain' (*silsila*). His initiation as a disciple of the Androth shaykh and his eventual designation as spiritual successor to lead the shaykh's Sufi order are documented in the book in multiple ways, both textually and photographically.[26] However, the book also seeks to validate Makkattar's sayyid family ancestry going back to the Prophet Muhammad, a connection that rests crucially upon his recent genealogical tree.

Practically speaking, the crucial test of Makkattar's identity as a hereditary member of the 'house of the Prophet' (*ahlul bayt*) is to be found not in the most distant links of his genealogy but in the preceding three generations of his family in Akkaraipattu who were descended from a well-known Yemeni (Zabidi) sayyid merchant, Shaykh Ismail, who migrated to Dutch Ceylon in the mid eighteenth century.[27] Shaykh Ismail is known to have fathered 11 sons by three different wives, and their tombs are to be found scattered in many parts of the island today, including the *ziyāram* of the youngest son of Ismail's third wife located on the premises of the second-oldest mosque in Akkaraipattu (*Sin̲n̲appaḷḷi*, also referred to as 'Town Mosque'). Oral tradition says that Shaykh Ismail originally stepped ashore near Akkaraipattu having floated in 'on a plank' from Yemen, so the return of his youngest son, Shaykh Abdussamat Maulana, to settle in the town was a source of local pride. Abdussamat's first wife was from Dikwela in the southern coastal region near Galle, but his children from that early marriage are seldom mentioned. When he moved to Akkaraipattu he took two additional wives, the first from the nearby town of Pottuvil and the second from Akkaraipattu itself. Makkattar is a grandson of Abdussamat Maulana by both of these marriages, and his late wife Ayisha was a great-great-granddaughter of the saint as well (Figure 4).

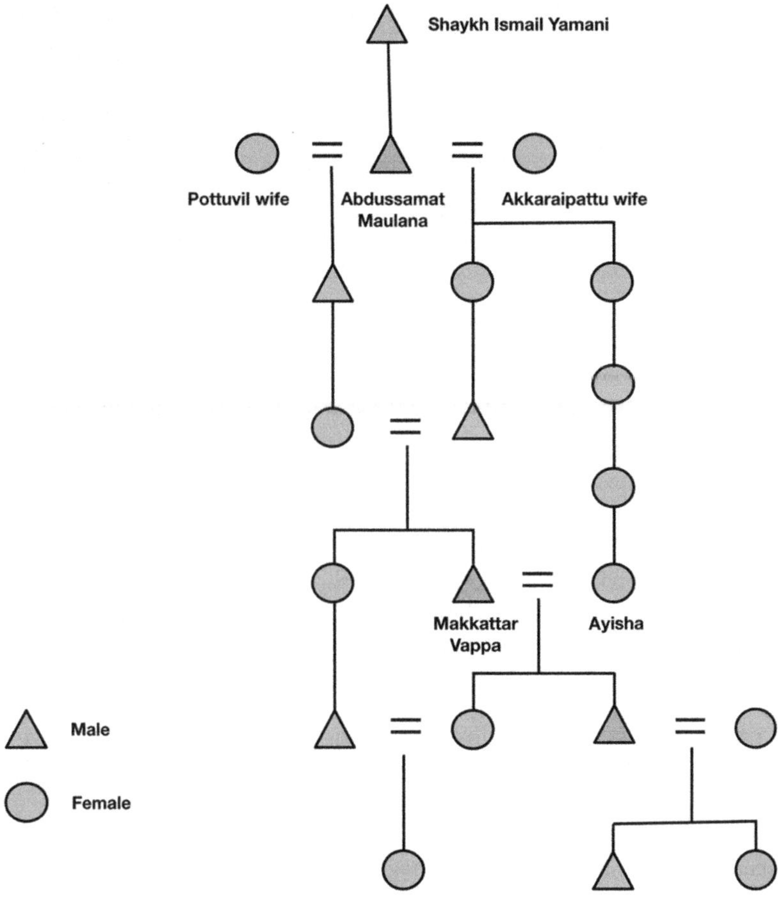

Figure 4. Kinship diagram.

However, none of Makkattar's ancestral connections with Abdussamat Maulana can be traced exclusively through males, as would be expected for sayyids throughout most of the Muslim world, and especially for the descendants of a Yemeni holy man. In each of these genealogical paths there is at least one female link. His late mother was Abdussamat's granddaughter by the Pottuvil wife. His father's mother was Abdussamat's daughter by the Akkaraipattu wife. Makkattar's own late spouse Ayisha – whom he explicitly honours as a female sayyid – traced her descent from Abdussamat and his Akkaraipattu wife entirely through three generations of women. Makkattar's son married a non-maulana bride, but their children can claim conventional patrilineal sayyid membership as long as Makkattar's own sayyid credentials are validated. Makkattar's daughter, on the other hand, married his sister's son. This is a perfectly correct Dravidian cross-cousin marriage, but one that will add two more female links to the future sayyid *silsila* of their children.

The logic of Makkattar's *silsila* is not strictly speaking matrilineal, which would require an exclusively unbroken line of descent through women. Rather, he recognizes the genealogical transmission of sayyid identity through both male and female ancestors, which in kinship jargon would qualify as a pattern of 'bilateral descent'. However, his openness to matrilineal possibilities is seen in the *silsila* of his late wife, Ayisha, whose sayyid qualifications were preserved entirely through three intermediate generations of women descended from Abdussamat Maulana.

The overlapping kinship connections between Makkattar and his saintly grandfather Abdussamat Maulana have been echoed in his close physical propinquity to the saint throughout his life (Figure 5). He was born in his mother's house located only two blocks away from the Town Mosque containing the saint's *ziyāram*. He married matrilocally into

Figure 5. (Colour online) Makkattar at tomb of Abdussamat Maulana.

Figure 6. (Colour online) Enshrined tombs of wife and mother, under construction.

his wife's home situated diagonally across the street from the tomb-shrine, and his current residence is located just around the corner from it.

In recent years, Makkattar has undertaken construction of a large new multi-storied seaside Sufi retreat centre in Akkaraipattu with accommodations for visiting devotees, madrasa instructional classrooms, space for prayer and performance of *zikr*, and a built-in *ziyāram* (tomb-shrine) containing the side-by-side graves of his mother and his wife, still under construction in 2012 (Figure 6). The *zikr* and prayer spaces (referred to as *Zāviyatul Hallājiya*) are named after Makkattar's own shaykh and predecessor, Hallaj Mansoor. The instructional quarters (referred to as *Matrasatul Āyishā*) are named after Makkattar's late wife Ayisha. A physical structure of comparable scale would be the headquarters shrine of the late Shaykh Abdullah Payilvan in Kattankudy, referred to earlier, which was attacked and desecrated by a fundamentalist mob in 2006.[28]

Questions and possibilities

The adjustment of Islamic property and inheritance rules, as well as Muslim marriage and domestic arrangements, to accommodate matrilineal social structures has been noted ethnographically in various parts of the world including south India and Malaysia.[29] The female dowry property, matrilocal marriage, and matrilineal mosque traditions I have documented among Moors in eastern Sri Lanka would belong in this category as well. However, I am now eager to determine if there are any historical precedents, ethnographic examples, or legal debates in the Islamic religious traditions of South Asia – or of any other parts of the Muslim world for that matter – concerning the transmission of sayyid status to women, and especially to the offspring of such women. Obviously, the historical and ethnographic literature on Kerala and Lakshadweep, as well as Sumatra (Minangkabau), deserves a second look with these questions in mind.[30]

Does this Sri Lankan Sufi shaykh have a credible case for tracing the genealogical charisma of the Prophet through both male and female sayyid descendants? He clearly has an interest in doing so, because without it he cannot trace a conventional patrilineal link to the local saint buried in the Town Mosque, despite the existence of a great many close family connections. In any case, it should be noted that social and political organization throughout eastern Sri Lanka is historically matrilineal, and that Makkattar's own family has played a leading role in the matrilineal clan administration of the Town Mosque. In a telling anthropological reversal, he pointed out to me in a 2012 interview that my own ethnographic research had shown matrilineal descent (*tāy vaḻi*, 'mother way') to be the foundational principle of kinship and descent in eastern Sri Lanka.

Quite possibly, too, he is inspired by a universalist belief in the spiritual equality of the sexes as exemplified by the Prophet's own daughter, and by the saintly virtues of his own wife and mother. In a conversation with Makkattar in November 2010, I remarked that all of the 'people of the house' of the Prophet Muhammad were uniquely connected through his only surviving child, his revered daughter Fatima Zahra.

He smiled and nodded approvingly.

Acknowledgements

This work was supported by research fellowships from the American Institute of Sri Lankan Studies (AISLS) and from the American Institute for Indian Studies (AIIS). For his essential role in this research, I wish to thank first of all Al-Qutub As-Shaykh As-Sayyid Kalifatul Hallaj Abdul Majeed Makkattar. I also gratefully acknowledge the research assistance provided by Nilam Hamead and family, as well as the support of M.A. Phakurdeen, K.M. Najumudeen, K. Kanthanathan, and many other Moorish and Tamil friends in Akkaraipattu.

Notes

1. See McGilvray, "Arabs, Moors, and Muslims."
2. See Fanselow, "Muslim Society in Tamil Nadu."
3. See Arasaratnam, *Ceylon*; Dale, *The Māppiḷas of Malabar*; and Kiribamune, "Muslims and the Trade of the Arabian Sea."
4. See Ameer Ali, "Some Aspects of Religio-Economic Precepts and Practices in Islam"; Indrapala, "Role of Peninsular Indian Muslim Trading Communities"; and Abeyasinghe, "Muslims in Sri Lanka in the Sixteenth and Seventeenth Centuries."
5. See Casie Chitty, *The Ceyon Gazeteer*; Denham, *Ceylon at the Census of 1911*; and Ameer Ali, "Genesis of the Muslim Community in Ceylon."
6. See Neville, "The Nâdu Kâdu Record"; de Graeuwe, *Memorie*; and Burnand, *Memorial.*
7. McGilvray, *Crucible of Conflict*, ch. 2.

8. Not all Mukkuvar caste communities in south India are matrilineal. See Ram, *Mukkuvar Women*, for an excellent account of the non-matrilineal Mukkuvar fishers of Kanya Kumari district, Tamil Nadu. Similarly, Mukkuvar fishermen in the Jaffna peninsula of Sri Lanka are not matrilineal.
9. See McGilvray, *Crucible of Conflict*, ch. 8.
10. See McGilvray and Rahim, *Muslim Perspectives on the Sri Lankan Conflict*; and McGilvray and Gamburd, *Tsunami Recovery in Sri Lanka*. The experience of the Eelam Wars (1983–2009) was highly traumatic for the Moors in the eastern and the northern parts of the island. In 1990 the Muslims of Jaffna and Mannar were expelled from their homes and lands at gunpoint by the LTTE, and the Muslims in the east were massacred in their mosques in Kattankudy and Akkaraipattu. Muslims also accounted for roughly a third of the victims of the Indian Ocean tsunami of December 26, 2004, with 13,000 Muslim fatalities in Ampara and Batticaloa Districts alone.
11. See Brito, *The Mukkuva Law*; and McGilvray, *Crucible of Conflict*, 118–33.
12. See Tambiah, *Laws and Customs of the Tamils of Ceylon*, 129–32.
13. See McGilvray, "Households in Akkaraipattu."
14. See McGilvray, "Matrilocal Marriage and Women's Property."
15. See McGilvray and Lawrence, "Dreaming of Dowry."
16. See McGilvray, "Sri Lankan Muslims between Ethno-Nationalism and the Global Ummah."
17. Unlike in Pakistan and Bangladesh where the Jamaat-i-Islami is an organized political party, in Sri Lanka it is only engaged in Islamic education and charitable works.
18. See Spittel, *Far Off Things*, 312–21; McGilvray, "Jailani"; and McGilvray, *Crucible of Conflict*, ch. 9.
19. See McGilvray, "Jailani."
20. See Klem, "Islam, Politics and Violence in Eastern Sri Lanka."
21. For details, see sufimanzil.org.
22. Mahinda Rajapaksa served as prime minister from 2004 until his election as president in 2005. He was re-elected to a 6-year term as president in 2010.
23. Interview August 8, 2010.
24. The mainstream Sufi orders in Sri Lanka include Qadiriya, Rifai, Shaduliya (Shadiliya), and more recently Naqsbandiya.
25. I have known Makkattar since 1978, when he was still a schoolteacher. The interviews upon which this article is based took place in 2002, 2005, 2010, 2011, and 2012.
26. See Makkattar and Juhais, *Hallājiṉ Pōtaṉaikaḷ*.
27. Some details of Shaykh Ismail and his descendants can be found on the web at http://www.rootsweb.ancestry.com/%7Elkawgw/gen108.html.
28. For details, see www.mufliheen.org
29. For examples, see Gough, "Mappila"; and Peletz, *A Share of the Harvest*.
30. Precedents of this sort of scholarship include Dube and Kutty, *Matriliny and Islam*; Kutty, *Marriage and Kinship in an Island Society*; and Hadler, *Muslims and Matriarchs*.

Bibliography

Abeyasinghe, T. B. H. "Muslims in Sri Lanka in the Sixteenth and Seventeenth Centuries." In *Muslims of Sri Lanka: Avenues to Antiquity*, edited by M. A. M. Shukri, 129–145. Beruwala, Sri Lanka: Jamiah Naleemia Institute, 1986.

Ameer Ali, A. C. L. "The Genesis of the Muslim Community in Ceylon (Sri Lanka): A Historical Summary." *Asian Studies* 19 (1981): 65–82.

Ameer Ali, A. C. L. "Some Aspects of Religio-Economic Precepts and Practices in Islam: A Case Study of the Muslim Community in Ceylon during the Period c. 1800–1915." Unpublished PhD thesis. Perth: University of Western Australia, 1980.

Arasaratnam, Sinnappah. *Ceylon*. Englewood, NJ: Prentice-Hall, 1964.

Brito, Christopher. *The Mukkuva Law, or the Rules of Succession among the Mukkuvars of Ceylon*. Colombo: H.D. Gabriel, 1876.

Burnand, Jacob. *Memorial Compiled by Mr. Jacob Burnand, Late Chief of Batticaloa, for his Successor, Mr. Johannes Philippus Wambeek*. Manuscript of an early nineteenth-century English translation in National Museum Library, Colombo, Sri Lanka. Dutch original in the Sri Lanka National Archives, dated, 1794.

Chitty, Casie. *The Ceylon Gazetteer*. Ceylon: Cotta Church Mission Press, 1834. Reprint edition New Delhi: Navrang, 1989.

Dale, Stephen F. *The Māppiḷas of Malabar, 1498–1922: Islamic Society on the South Asian Frontier*. Oxford: Clarendon Press, 1980.

Denham, E. B. *Ceylon at the Census of 1911*. Colombo: H.C. Cottle, Government Printer, 1912.

de Graeuwe, Pieter. *Memorie van de Heer Pieter Graeuwe aan des zelfs Vervanger de Heer Jan Blommert gedateered 8 April 1676* [Memorial of Pieter de Graeuwe to his successor Jan Blommert dated 8 April 1676]. V.O.C. 1.04.17, Hoge Regering Batavia. Algemene Rijksarchief, Den Haag, Netherlands.

Dube, Leela. and Kutty, A. R. *Matriliny and Islam: Religion and Society in the Laccadives*. Delhi: National Publishing House, 1969.

Fanselow, Frank S. "Muslim Society in Tamil Nadu (India): An Historical Perspective." *Journal of the Institute of Muslim Minority Affairs* 10, no. 1 (1989): 264–289.

Gough, Kathleen. "Mappila: North Kerala." In *Matrilineal Kinship*, edited by David Schneider and Kathleen Gough, 415–442. Berkeley: University of California Press, 1961.

Hadler, Jeffrey. *Muslims and Matriarchs: Cultural Resilience in Indonesia through Jihad and Colonialism*. Ithaca, NY: Cornell University Press, 2008.

Hasbullah, S. H. "Justice for the Dispossessed: The Case of a Forgotten Minority in Sri Lanka's Ethnic Conflict." In *Sri Lankan Society in an Era of Globalization: Struggling to Create a New Social Order*, edited by S. H. Hasbullah, and Barrie M. Morrison. New Delhi: Sage, 2004.

Indrapala, K. "The Role of Peninsular Indian Muslim Trading Communities in the Indian Ocean Trade." In *Muslims of Sri Lanka: Avenues to Antiquity*, edited by M. A. M. Shukri, 113–127. Beruwala, Sri Lanka: Jamiah Naleemia Institute, 1986.

Kiribamune, Sirima. "Muslims and the Trade of the Arabian Sea with Special Reference to Sri Lanka from the Birth of Islam to the Fifteenth Century." In *Muslims of Sri Lanka: Avenues to Antiquity*, edited by M. A. M. Shukri, 89–112. Beruwala, Sri Lanka: Jamiah Naleemia Institute, 1986.

Klem, Bart. "Islam, Politics and Violence in Eastern Sri Lanka." *Journal of Asian Studies* 70, no. 3 (2011): 730–753.

Kutty, A. R. *Marriage and Kinship in an Island Society*. Delhi: National Publishing House, 1972.

Makkattar, al-Qutub as-Shaykh as-Sayyid Kalifatul Hallaj Abdul Majeed Makkattar and M. A. C. M. Juhais. *Hallājiṉ Pōtaṉaikaḷ*. ISBN 978-955-53017-0-1. Akkaraipattu: Hallaj Wariyam, 2010.

McGilvray, Dennis B. "Arabs, Moors, and Muslims: Sri Lankan Muslim Ethnicity in Regional Perspective." *Contributions to Indian Sociology* 32, no. 2 (1998): 433–483. Reprinted in T. N. Madan, ed. *Muslim Communities of South Asia*, 3rd ed., 449–553. Delhi: Manohar, 2001.

McGilvray, D. B. *Crucible of Conflict: Tamil and Muslim Society on the East Coast of Sri Lanka*. Durham: Duke University Press, 2008. Reprint edition: Colombo: Social Scientists' Association, 2011.

McGilvray, Dennis B. "Households in Akkaraipattu: Dowry and Domestic Organization among the Matrilineal Tamils and Moors of Sri Lanka." In *Society from the Inside Out: Anthropological Perspectives on the South Asian Household*, edited by John N. Gray, and David J. Mearns, 192–235. New Delhi: Sage, 1989.

McGilvray, Dennis B. "Jailani: A Sufi Shrine in Sri Lanka." In *Lived Islam in South Asia: Adaptation, Accommodation and Conflict*, edited by Imtiaz Ahmad and Helmut Reifeld, 273–289. Delhi: Social Science Press. New York: Berghahn, 2004.

McGilvray, D. B. "Matrilocal Marriage and Women's Property among the Moors of Sri Lanka." In *Being Muslim in South Asia: Diversity and Daily Life*, edited by Robin Jeffrey, and Ronojoy Sen. Delhi: Oxford University Press, 2014.

McGilvray, Dennis B. "Sri Lankan Muslims between Ethno-Nationalism and the Global Ummah." *Nations and Nationalism* 17, no. 1 (2011): 45–64.

McGilvray, Dennis B. and Michel Ruth Gamburd, eds. *Tsunami Recovery in Sri Lanka: Ethnic and Regional Dimensions*. London: Routledge, 2010.

McGilvray, Dennis B. and Lawrence, Patricia. "Dreaming of Dowry: Post-tsunami Housing Strategies in Eastern Sri Lanka." In *Tsunami Recovery in Sri Lanka: Ethnic and Regional Dimensions*, edited by Dennis B. McGilvray, and Michele R. Gamburd, 106–124. London: Routledge, 2010.

McGilvray, Dennis B. and Mirak Raheem. *Muslim Perspectives on the Sri Lankan Conflict*. Policy Studies 41. Washington, DC: East-West Center, 2007.

Neville, Hugh. "The Nâdu Kâdu Record." *The Taprobanian* 127–128 (1887): 137–141.
Peletz, Michael G. *A Share of the Harvest: Kinship, Property, and Social History among the Malays of Rembau*. Berkeley: University of California Press, 1988.
Ram, Kalpana. *Mukkuvar Women: Gender, Hegemony, and Capitalist Transformation in a South Indian Fishing Community*. London: Zed Press, 1991.
Spittel, R. L. *Far Off Things*. Colombo: Colombo Apothecaries, 1933.
Tambiah, H. W. *The Laws and Customs of the Tamils of Ceylon*. Colombo: Tamil Cultural Society of Ceylon, 1954.
Thiranagama, Sharika. *In My Mother's House: Civil War in Sri Lanka*. Philadelphia: University of Pennsylvania Press, 2011.

EPILOGUE

Margins of anxiety and centres of confidence

A. Azfar Moin

Clements Department of History, Southern Methodist University, Dallas, TX, USA

Those who work on Islam in South Asia often come to face the realization that while Islam can be studied and taught without India, India cannot be studied and taught without Islam. This contradiction of an understated India in Islamic history and an overstated Islam in Indian history reminds one of Dipesh Chakrabarty's observation in *Provincializing Europe* about how historians of the non-West must keep Europe as a silent referent in their work, but not the other way around. Middle Eastern Islam, similarly, remains a silent referent in the scholarship on Islam in South Asia. The anxiety this generates is shared today, to a degree, between the scholars of South Asia and the peoples and cultures they study. Several among the articles included in this volume and the papers presented in the original conference grappled with this disquiet. Below, I present some thoughts on the issue, which were inspired by the work of three scholars, Mohammad Afsar, Torsten Tschacher and Dennis McGilvray, who spoke during the conference on peninsular Indian and Sri Lankan Islam.[1]

Afsar Mohammad presented a perceptive study of Islamic reform in the village of Gugudu in contemporary Andhra Pradesh, which focused on how Urdu-speaking and Telugu-reading Muslims struggle with what is and is not real (*asli*) Islam.[2] The reformers in this case, firm in their knowledge of 'real' Islam, were also local residents who had been inspired and trained by the Tablighi Jama'at, a twentieth century missionary organization of South Asian origin and worldwide reach. While these reformers were apprehensive about Hindu revivalists in their region, their central concern was not conversion to Islam of non-Muslims but the spread of proper religious behaviour among existing Muslims. In doing so, these Tablighi reformers followed a well-established pattern: they berated those who visited local Sufi shrines, those who venerated saints (*pirs*) and those who participated in the popular commemorative rituals of Karbala often alongside Hindus. They also guided their fellow Muslims to Islamic texts printed in local languages. Using such normative texts, the reformers emphasized universal rituals, such as fasting in Ramazan, and criticized locally adapted practices such as the collective – and sometimes festive – rituals associated with Muharram. Mohammad showed, however, that the effect of this reformist preaching was ambiguous. A significant number of Gugudu's 'unreformed' Muslims who when asked about the reformists' message agreed with it – that their Muharram rituals and shrine veneration are innovation (*bida'*) – but also ignored it and continued their 'deviant' customs. The reformers and the unreformed, it seems from Afsar's study, had learned to live with each other in Gugudu, perhaps not unlike the way many scholars of South Asian Islam have learned to live with those of their colleagues studying the supposedly 'real' version of the religion practiced in the Middle East.

But not everyone would be content with such an unhappy equilibrium. Torsten Tschacher certainly would not. In his conference paper, he cautioned against conflating the 'vernacular' and the 'local' with the 'popular' and the 'folk.'[3] He criticized the assumption that the purpose of all Islamic literature in local Indian languages – that is, languages other than Persian and Arabic – was to translate and explain Islam to new converts. According to him, this supposition certainly does not hold for the Islamic literary corpus in Tamil, a language that had a very complex and refined system of grammar and poetic conventions at the time Islamic literature was composed in it during early modern times. The authors of these Islamic texts were more concerned with following sophisticated Tamil literary conventions to win the appreciation of their highly literate patrons and less with translating, localizing or syncretizing Islam. By presenting the exceptional case of Tamil, Tschacher turned the usual approach to the study of Islamic literature in Indian languages on its head. While other Islamic literatures in languages such as Awadhi may have been *Islamicate*, he argued, the one in Tamil was very much *Islamic*. Thus, he left us to ponder the paradox that the rendering of the Quranic word *dallun* with the phrase 'those who miss your way without perceiving the lights inside the [syllable] om' is both authentically Islamic and authentically Tamil.

What is authentic and unauthentic Islam was also a question at the heart of Dennis McGilvray's conference paper.[4] He presented a fascinating ethnography of a chain-smoking, politically well-connected Sufi saint of contemporary Sri Lanka, Qutb Abdul Majeed Makkattar, a man who was as at home in explicating the finer points of Ibn 'Arabi's 'ontological monism' (*wahdat al-wujud*) as he was in distributing talismans and protective charms to his devotees. What was especially noteworthy about Makkattar was the way he traced his spiritual genealogy. He not only connected himself to another famous local saint – a veritable reincarnation of the divinely intoxicated mystic Hallaj Mansur (d. 922) – but also emphasized his physical descent from the Prophet Muhammad. In an unusual manner, however, Makkattar made his claim to being a Sayyid or Alid – that is, a descendant of the Prophet – not through patrilineal descent, but through his female kin, including his mother, patrilateral grandmother and even his wife. In doing so, he followed a kinship pattern that meshed well with Dravidian matrilineal and matrilocal practices prevalent in the region. At the end of the conference paper, McGilvray posed the question whether Makkattar's genealogical claim was a purely local one – with value only at the 'margins' – or one of broader significance that satisfied the norms of 'central' Islamic traditions.

This is a perfectly legitimate question. But it brings us back to the relational anxiety generated between margins and centres – a concern, if I may be permitted to point out, we scholars share with the Islamic reformers at Gugudu, of what is real or *asli* Islam. Is there, then, a way to historicize this anxiety? One approach, I suggest, would be to add another variable to our analysis – let us call it cultural confidence – and to trace its ebb and flow in the history of South Asian Islam.

Take for instance the case of the Mughal empire (1526–1857). At its height in the seventeenth century, the Mughal realm was greater in manpower and wealth than all other early modern Muslim ones including those of the Safavids, the Uzbeks and the Ottomans. The Mughals were supremely confident – perhaps, arrogant would be the right word – both politically and culturally. This confidence can be seen in the way they adopted Christian themes and symbols, in their vast collection of Catholic art, in their use of Christian paintings to adorn royal palaces and tombs, in how they titled their Rajput Hindu queens 'Mary,' while still calling themselves God's Caliph on Earth. Indeed the Mughals would have found it absurd if someone told them that in the early twentieth century the Muslims of India will launch a concerted effort to save the Ottoman Caliphate – the Khilafat Movement (1919–1924). The Mughal *padishahs* certainly did not consider the Ottoman sultan to be above themselves in sacred stature. After all, it was their ancestor, the world conqueror Lord of Conjunction Timur, who had defeated and subjugated the Ottomans.

Cultural confidence underwent a great and downward shift among the Muslims of South Asia between the Taj Mahal of the seventeenth century and the Khilafat Movement of the twentieth. After Mughal decline in the eighteenth century and British rise in the nineteenth, India could not be imagined as a centre of Islam or of anything else by its inhabitants. The Ottomans, as the last Muslim empire left standing, assumed central importance for Muslims worldwide. In India, as Islam became delinked with power and wealth, the rhetoric of reform and revival became dominant among its leaders. Muslim intellectuals preached a return to Islamic purity and piety, arguing it would lead to the revival of Muslim power. This story is known well and told often. But what gets lost in the telling is how, as Indian Muslim reformers conjured an Islam centred outside India and all things Indian outside Islam, an older set of Islamic ideals that had been universally Indian and Islamic were consigned to oblivion. In a paradigm shift, the centre became the margin. Nowhere better is this dynamic highlighted than in the case of Sufi sainthood.

Around the fourteenth century, Muslim Asia had seen the rise of a mass-based Sufism, centred on the cults of the saints, in which charisma could be transmitted bodily. This style of Sufism became not only 'local' and 'vernacular,' as the reformers in Afsar's study would have us believe today, but also universal and authentic, like the Tamil texts of Tschacher's essay. In other words, Sufi sainthood became hegemonic in early modern Islam. If we are to understand why spiritually ambitious Muslims such as McGilvray's Sri Lankan saint today give such importance to proving their Sayyid or Alid genealogy, we must do so in the backdrop of what can be called Islam's 'age of saints.'

The universalism and authenticity imparted to Sufi thought and practice in early modern times can be gauged by how sainthood supplied a model for the sovereignty of kings.[5] One question that drove courtly interest in Sufi cosmology was the answers it provided about the nature and power of the Perfect Man (*insan-i kamil*), a saintly being who maintained the cosmic balance of an entire age, the ideal sovereign. It was in the pursuit of such sacred power that the eponymous ancestor of the Mughal-Timurid dynasty, Timur (d. 1405) was proclaimed to have been descended from Ali, the first saint of Islam. Timur's descent was not through a physical connection, however. The inscription on his cenotaph in Samarkand, written in classical Arabic with references to the Quranic verses on Mary and the birth of Jesus, relates that Timur's female ancestor Alanquva was impregnated by a heavenly light which first took on the shape of a descendent of Ali. This miraculous impregnation of Alanquva was also mentioned in the chronicle-cum-hagiography of Timur's famous descendant in India, the Mughal emperor Akbar (d. 1605). This divine light, the *Akbarnama* states:

> which took shape, without human instrumentality or a father's loins, in the pure womb of her Majesty Alanqua, after having, in order to arrive at perfection, occupied during several ages the holy bodily wrappings of other holy manifestations, is manifesting itself at the present day, in the pure entity of this unique God-knower and God-worshipper (Akbar).[6]

So here we have Akbar, the most powerful Muslim sovereign of his time, and a very Indian king, publicly and loudly claiming to be a saintly being conceived Jesus-like by a divine light, which passed down through the ages in the bodies of both men and women. Is this Islam at the margins or at the centre?

Notes

1. Torsten Tschacher and Dennis McGilvray's articles included in this volume reflect their papers presented at the conference, though Afsar Mohammed's conference presentation is not published in this volume. See Mohammed, *Festival of Pirs*, particularly chapter 1, "Gugudu: The Emergence of a Shared Devotional Space," for elaboration of themes discussed at the conference. My references are to the conference presentations, which are cited here with permission from the authors.
2. Mohammad, "The Return of a Religious Text."
3. Tscacher, "Islamic Literature in Tamil."
4. McGilvray, "A Matrilineal Sufi sheykh in Sri Lanka."
5. Moin, *The Millennial Sovereign*.
6. I have slightly modified Beveridge's translation. Abu al-Fazl ibn Mubarak, *The Akbarnamah*, 1:12; Abu al-Fazl ibn Mubarak and Beveridge, *The Akbar Nama of Abu-l-Fazl*, 1–2:45.

Bibliography

Abu al-Fazl ibn Mubarak. *The Akbarnamah*. 3 vols. Edited by Maulawi ʿAbd-ur-Rahim. Calcutta: The Asiatic Society of Bengal, 1877–1886.

Abu al-Fazl ibn Mubarak, and Beveridge, Henry. *The Akbar Nama of Abu-l-Fazl: History of the Reign of Akbar Including an Account of His Predecessors*. 3 (1 and 2 bound in one) vols. Calcutta: 1897–1921. Reprint, Lahore: Sang-e-Meel Publications, 2005.

McGilvray, Denis. "A Matrilineal Sufi sheykh in Sri Lanka." Paper presented at the Margins and Centers in South Asian Islam: An Interdisciplinary Inquiry, University of North Texas, March 11, 2011.

Mohammed, Afsar. *The Festival of Pirs: Popular Islam and Shared Devotion in South India*. New York: Oxford University Press, 2013.

Mohammad, Afsar. "The Return of a Religious Text: The Politics of 'True Islam' in Andhra Pradesh." Paper presented at the Margins and Centers in South Asian Islam: An Interdisciplinary Inquiry, University of North Texas, March 11, 2011.

Moin, A. Azfar. *The Millennial Sovereign: Sacred Kingship and Sainthood in Islam*. South Asia Across the Disciplines. New York: Columbia University Press, 2012.

Tscacher, Torsten. "Islamic Literature in Tamil and the Study of Muslim Vernaculars in South Asia." Paper presented at the Margins and Centers in South Asian Islam: An Interdisciplinary Inquiry, University of North Texas, March 11, 2011.

Index

Lahore Resolution 14, 17
Laila Majnu 79
languages: names 59; overview 1, 2; religion and meaning 59, 60–3, 82; Sri Lankan Malays 49–53
Lebbe, M.C. Siddi 67
literary criticism 80–3
literary culture 3–4
Lived Islam in South Asia (Reifeld) 2–3
Love in a Palace (Penny) 101, 103

MacDonnell Hostel 14
Majaz, Asrar-ul-Haq 30, 31, 33
Makkattar Majeed 4–5, 118–25, 130
Malay culture 4, 43–5, 49–53
Mansur , Abul Ahmed 76
Mantō, Sā'adat Hasan 104
marginalization 1, 4, 15
'Margins and Centers in South Asian Islam› conference 3
marriage 115
matriliny 113–16, 125, 130
Maulana, Shayk Abdussamat 5
Maulana Vappa 118–21
Maulavi, Rauf 117
mawlid carnivals 105
McGilvray, Dennis B. 4–5, 130
meaning and religion *see* religion and meaning
Metcalf, Barbara 1
Minault, Gail 12–13
Minority and Nation 15
Mirza, Muhammad 30
Modern Medicine and Ancient Thought (Zaidi) 30
modernity 80–3
Mohammadan Anglo-Oriental College 11
Moin, A. Azfar 5
Moors 113–14
Mughal period 95–6, 130–1
Muharram festival 105
Muhsin-ul-Mulk 31
Mu'īnullāh Shāh 99
Mukkuvar chiefdoms 114
Mukkuvar Law 115
Muslim-Hindu encounter 62
Muslim/Islam 61
Muslim League 13, 14–15, 17–20
Muslim Literary Society 80, 82
Muslim Sahitya Samaj 77

Nadwi, Muinuddin Ahmad 30
names 59
Naoroji, Dadabhai 107
Narayanan, Vasudha 63
Nehru, Jawaharlal 14

opium 100, 102–3

Padmavati 78–9
Pakistan 1–2, 3, 9–10, 36
Pakistan Movement 9, 17, 19
Pakubuwana II 52
pan-Indian Islam 83–5
Pandey, Gyanendra 26
Parde ki Baat (Rudaulvi) 34–5
parganas 27–8, 29
partition 36
Payilvan, Abdullah 117–18
Penny, F.E. 101, 103
Perfect Man 131
Persian 31, 60, 62, 64, 69–71, 95–6
'Philosophical Iqbal' (Ahmed) 84
Phukan, Shantanu 70
Pirmuhammatu, Takkalai 65
Pirpur Report 14–15
Pollock, Sheldon 69
poverty 96
Poverty and Un-British Rule in India (Naroji) 107
Prachin Bangla Punthir Bibaran 78
Prain, David 103
Progressive Writers' Movement 25, 30–1, 33
property rights 115–16, 125
Provincializing Europe (Dipesh) 129
Punjab Muslim Students' Federation 16
punthis 78

Qadiriyya 48
qasbahs: definitions of 28; learned traditions 31–6; loss of 36; marketplace to intellectual hub 27–9; overview 3, 25–7; Rudauli 29–31
Quddus, Abdul 29
Quit India Resolution 14
Quran 62, 63–4, 65, 130

Raghunathji, K. 97
Rahman, M. Raisur 3
Ramanujan, A.K. 66
reformist Islam 4–5, 115, 116–18, 129–31 *see also faqirs*
Reifeld, Helmut 2–3
religion and meaning 59, 60–3, 82
religious festivals 104–6, 115, 117
Renan, Ernest 80–1
Revolt (1857) 11
Riazur Rahman Sherwani 13

For Product Safety Concerns and Information please contact our EU representative GPSR@taylorandfrancis.com Taylor & Francis Verlag GmbH, Kaufingerstraße 24, 80331 München, Germany

Batch number: 08153807

Printed by Printforce, the Netherlands